WYNN HANDMAN

Wynn Handman is both a distinguished acting teacher and Director of The American Place Theatre in New York City, which he co-founded in 1964. His role in the theatre since then has been to seek out, encourage, train and present new, exciting writing and acting talent. At The American Place Theatre, over two hundred productions of new plays by living American playwrights have advanced theatre culture and have been reproduced at other theatres and on television and film. Always devoted to development, The American Place Theatre has produced the early work of many important contemporary playwrights, covering a broad spectrum of styles and ethnic origins.

Since the time he taught at The Neighborhood Playhouse School of the Theatre in New York, Wynn Handman has made an important contribution to the training of actors. In more than thirty years of teaching, he has trained many outstanding actors including James Caan, Michael Douglas, Sandy Duncan, Mia Farrow, Richard Gere, Cliff Gorman, Joel Grey, Raul Julia, Margot Kidder, Frank Langella, Burt Reynolds, Tony Roberts and Christopher Walken, as well as hundreds of others appearing in all media. Mr. Handman has also taught at The Yale School of Drama.

Modern American Scenes for Student Actors

edited by **WYNN HANDMAN**
Director-Producer,
The American Place Theatre

BANTAM BOOKS
TORONTO • NEW YORK • LONDON • SYDNEY • AUCKLAND

RL8, IL 8+

MODERN AMERICAN SCENES FOR STUDENT ACTORS
A Bantam Book / September 1978
2nd printing .... April 1979
3rd printing .... September 1980

ISBN 0–553–14559–2

ACKNOWLEDGMENTS

CAUTION: *The use of the excerpts contained in this volume must be confined to study and reference. They are fully protected under the copyright laws of the United States of America, the British Empire, the Dominion of Canada, and all other countries of the Copyright Union. All rights, including professional, amateur, motion pictures, recitation, lecturing, public reading, radio broadcasting, television, and the rights of translation into foreign languages are strictly reserved. For information, contact the authors' representatives listed below or Bantam Books, Inc., the Permissions Editor. This and the following pages (iv-vi) constitute an extension of the copyright page.*

The Big Knife *by Clifford Odets; copyright 1948 as an unpublished work under the title, "A Winter Journey," copyright renewed © 1975 by Walt Whitman Odets and Nora Odets; copyright 1949, by Clifford Odets, copyright renewed © 1976 by Walt Whitman Odets and Nora Odets. By permission of Brandt & Brandt.*

Another Part of the Forest *by Lillian Hellman; copyright 1947 by Lillian Hellman, copyright renewed © 1974 by Lillian Hellman. By permission of Harold Matson Co., Inc.*

I Am a Camera *by John van Druten; copyright © 1955 by John van Druten. All rights reserved. By permission of Carter Lodge Productions, Inc.*

Look Homeward, Angel *by Thomas Wolfe, adaptation by Ketti Frings; copyright © 1958 by Edward C. Aswell, Administrator C.T.A. of the Estate of Thomas Wolfe, and/or Fred Wolfe and Ketti Frings. By permission of the Estate of Thomas Wolfe.*

A Social Event *by William Inge; copyright 1950, 1953, 1954, © 1955, 1958, 1960, 1962 by William Inge. By permission of International Creative Management.*

A Hatful of Rain *by Michael V. Gazzo; copyright © 1956 by Michael V. Gazzo. By permission of Random House, Inc.*

A Raisin in the Sun *by Lorraine Hansberry; copyright © 1958, 1959 by Robert Nemiroff as Executor of the Estate of Lorraine Hansberry. By permission of Random House, Inc.*

The Crucible *by Arthur Miller; copyright 1952, 1953 by Arthur Miller. By permission of The Viking Press.*

The Ballad of the Sad Cafe *by Carson McCullers, novella adapted for the stage by Edward Albee; copyright © 1963 by Edward Albee and Carson McCullers. By permission of Houghton Mifflin Company.*

The Beauty Part *by S.J. Perelman; copyright © 1963 by S.J. Perelman. By permission of the author and Samuel French, Inc.*

Published simultaneously in the United States and Canada

Bantam Books are published by Bantam Books, Inc. Its trademark, consisting of the words "Bantam Books" and the portrayal of a rooster, is Registered in U.S. Patent and Trademark Office and in other countries. Marca Registrada. Bantam Books, Inc., 666 Fifth Avenue, New York, New York 10103.

PRINTED IN THE UNITED STATES OF AMERICA

H   15 14 13 12 11 10 9

This book is dedicated to Sanford Meisner

Contents

Introductory Notes for the Actor

The Irish playwright John Millington Synge said, "On the stage one must have reality and one must have joy." It is my hope in putting this book together that it will add to the reality and the joy of the actors who use it. It is intended for all actors, from the young to the mature, the inexperienced to the experienced, the amateur to the professional.

All actors have one characteristic in common—they love to act, to perform for audiences. And just like musicians, dancers and athletes, they need training, they need exercising, they need to stay tuned up, they need to stretch. This is work done outside the actual performance of plays, with scenes and monologues providing the most useful tools.

In this book the selection of scenes is eclectic, but they do have certain common criteria. They work. That's always the operative word in the theatre and consequently in acting. I've seen them in performance and in acting classes over a period of three decades since the end of World War II. Scenes are events unto themselves, compressed segments of life that are parts of the imaginary world of the play. When well acted they can be revelatory or funny or moving or all of these and more. They also advance the play because the characters are actively striving to achieve objectives. Their interaction moves the scenes from beginning to middle to climax to end, and thus the progression within each scene brings about the progression of the play.

These scenes have another common aspect—they are all scenes from American plays produced since the late 1940s. I suppose that reflects my predilection, my own particular career in the theatre, which has focused on contemporary American playwrights and their work. As a student at the Neighborhood Playhouse School of the Theatre in 1946-48, I studied acting with a great teacher, Sanford Meisner, and in 1950, became his assistant. I was a teacher and a director all through the 1950s, and in the early 1960s I cofounded The American Place Theatre, a place for American writers who wish to write seriously for the theatre. My career since then has been devoted to directing The American Place Theatre while teaching professional acting classes.

It's instructive to take an overview of the main tendencies that came into drama in each of the three decades covered in this book. From it we can get a perspective on American lifestyle, dynamics and history, and better understand changing styles and emphasis in acting.

Serious plays in the postwar period of the late 1940s were concerned with moral issues and the heightened political awareness of a people emerging from years of war. Arthur Miller's *All My Sons* dramatically reveals individual responsibility to all mankind. Lillian Hellman's *Another Part of the Forest* deals with the greed and opportunism infecting a people at war and the postwar re-ordering of the class structure.

These are "well-made," clearly constructed plays in the realistic tradition of the preceding decades. Cause and effect are the basis of the plot and events within the play. Cause and effect also dictate the acting. What motivates the character (the cause) has to be discovered, identified, and used to initiate and justify the character's actions and attitudes. Realistic acting is required, so that the audience is convinced that they are seeing real people, characters that sound and behave like people in life. In these plays the emotional life of the actor should be truthful and internalized. The performance should have some realistic details but not be cluttered. Motives, behavior, gestures and rhythms should be explored and selected during rehearsals, so that the performance, while designed by the actor, flows naturally without calling attention to technique or deliberate theatricality.

The 1950s were essentially an apolitical period in the theatre, a reflection of the climate of fear created by Senator Joseph McCarthy and the forces of reaction. It was an era of introspection. Social protest was replaced by personal scrutiny. The theatre, reflecting this sociological change and the popularity of the small stories told on the television screen, developed naturalistic and realistic plays which dealt with deep personal problems within the family. Usually the characters lack love and the capacity for making and keeping relationships. This pattern of emotional incompleteness immobilizes their lives, leaving them prey to unscrupulous relatives and friends, and prompting unerring care from generous soul-mates.

The plays of this period also tend to focus on ordinary people in ordinary circumstances who yearn for more complete emotional fulfillment. William Inge's *Picnic* is about the dull and limited horizons of small town life, as is Horton Foote's *A Young Lady of Property,* a play written for live TV. These plays of detailed and key-hole intimacy generated a great emphasis on naturalism in the training of actors.

Naturalism is a style that strives for an exact representation of life. It makes for great emphasis on detail. The actors' ability to project sensory elements, like smells and temperature, physical states like fatigue or pregnancy, and to use props accurately are as important to the impact as the spoken text. Michael Gazzo's *Hatful of Rain* calls for this kind of acting. The physical manifestation of Johnny's dope addiction, of Celia's pregnancy, and the crowded, dreary apartment, including the dirty dishes and piles of laundry, provide the accumulation of details that give such naturalistic plays their distinctive texture.

Remember that naturalism is just one style of play and acting. I remind the reader of this because in the '50s it became the dominant style and began to be confused with acting itself. The training so emphasized naturalism and so closely (and inaccurately) identified it with the Stanislavsky "method," that many actors became inflexible; their acting was limited to being "natural."

A circumstance that compounded this tendency, and still does, is that good basic training of actors employs an organic approach, the inherent basis of Stanislavsky's work. This grounds the actor in his own inner truth. He learns to work from himself, becoming fully involved in the imaginary circumstances of the play, really using all his senses and emotional memories, really listening, really interacting with the other characters, learning to let each moment happen as if for the first time. These—and many other elements—help the actor live a full life on stage.

While such good basic acting has a similiarity to the naturalistic style, it is essential that actors go beyond the basics. An organic foundation is important, but it should not be so overemphasized as to be limiting. I myself advocate and teach thorough organic training. But it should be regarded as only preliminary: preparing the actor to move from self to character, to live in other styles, other kinds of language and reality, other imaginary worlds.

Something Victor Hugo said constantly informs my thinking on this: "Ballast yourself with reality, then throw yourself into the sea. The sea is inspiration."

As we moved into the '60s, alienation became a dominant theme—people in conflict with their society, their predecessors, the establishment and its values.

Edward Albee's *The Zoo Story* was an important early example of the estranged individual in a hostile society.

By the mid 1960s, and continuing through the early '70s, alienation no longer was the private battle of one individual, but rather of whole groups. Opposition to the Vietnam War, particularly among the young, led to angry rebellion against authority, active opposition to the "establishment," and confrontation on the campuses, in the streets and in the theatre. Indeed, there were Street Theatre, Assault Theatre, Living Theatre, Open Theatre, Participating Theatre, Ridiculous Theatre and many others with challenging and derisive names. Many plays with serious intent broke the rules of the conventional stage and employed new forms and styles reflecting chaos, fragmentation, ambiguity, terror, disorientation, discontent and the rapidity of social change. The private, internalized psychological and emotional state of individual characters was no longer the concern of the serious new playwrights. Their plot progressions were not based on cause and effect; they did not shape facts and events into clear resolutions. They were influenced by Europeans like Artaud, Beckett, Brecht, Genet and Grotowski. Their concern was with the ills and injustices of our civilization and society; myth and ritual became important tools for breaking the patterns of everyday reality to reveal deeper forces at work.

So actors had to use themselves in new ways and perform in a variety of styles, often switching styles within the play itself. This called for greater freedom and flexibility, throwing away rules like "always remain in character," or "observe the fourth wall."

Joseph Heller's *We Bombed in New Haven* embodies many of the new elements. The actors have to step in and out of character. They often speak and behave as themselves—the people who are the actors—and then quickly get back into character as if removing a mask and putting it on again. This mask analogy also relates to the nature of the roles in the play, which are prototypes rather than "real" individuals. At times, the actors step forward and speak to the audience, not narrating the action but rather confronting them or sharing feelings and thoughts. The audience members thus become involved not only in the life of the play but in the life of the real world; ambiguity and overlapping are desired results. The actors must also switch from a broad lampoon style to sections where the acting is serious, sober, deeply felt and realistic.

Sam Shepard's *La Turista* takes the actors and audiences on a trip that's all about the disappearing American, "the Great Society going downhill." The two main characters, Salem and Kent, are again not meant to be portrayals of real individuals but prototypes of the generation that grew up in the 1960s. They go on free associative, multi-level trips influenced by drugs, jazz, rock and roll, movies, TV and the awareness that their generation was born at the time of the atom bomb. The actors do not have to call upon cause and effect and ask "Why?" at each moment during the rehearsals of the play. The answers flow through them as they become filled with the core material. They become instruments through which the life of the play flows rather than characters in a realistic play.

This was also the period of the emergence of Black theatre, represented in this book with the writing of Ed Bullins, Phillip Hayes Dean and Ron Milner. Their plays were part of the effort of Black Americans to find a new awareness, a new definition of their lives, and to assert a racial identity. No surprise then that their plays are realistic portrayals of family and community life, with highly recognizable and identifiable characters. For the first time, many Black people came to the theatre and recognized themselves on the stage, identifying with the stage life and characters.

Although I have selected scenes from a sampling of plays of the '60s period, I could not include others written for an ensemble or those which are too fragmented in structure to lend themselves to scene selection. I recommend that the actor read the plays of the Open Theatre and important contemporary writers like Jack Gelber, Jean-Claude van Itallie, Rochelle Owens and Megan Terry, among others.

It is more difficult to characterize the late '70s. There is a lot of looking back to '50s kinds of plays and small middling effort in the commercial theatre. There are some plays about demythologizing our cultural heroes and cultural process, some about the dislocation in our contemporary thinking, but no distinct pattern in style or content has emerged.

There is great concern with relationships, especially between the sexes. Many of these plays, while seeming to be realistic, make subtle stylistic demands, but they are a long distance from the explosive, free-flowing plays of the '60s. Many serious plays of the '70s, like Sam Shepard's *Action* and William Hauptman's *Domino Courts,* continue to deal with characters who are not meant to be "real" people, but rather are archetypes. They are not plays in the conventional sense, but textured poetic events. There is also a trend towards naturalism, sometimes called "new naturalism." Plays like Maria Irene Fornes' *Fefu and Her Friends* don't have conventional linear plot structure but rather unfold with no external logic. However, the actor must create the inner life of the character while avoiding the detailed behavior associated with the old naturalism. The acting is distilled to its essence and does not attempt to be a slice of life.

This book is not intended to be a text on acting, but there are several basic elements I advise the actor to keep in mind while using it.

Naturally it is recommended that the actors read the entire play before performing a scene. However, the book has been organized with the cognizance that this is not always possible. Each introduction contains the information necessary to approach the task of acting the scene. The analysis of each scene's situation suggests the all-important given circumstances: What does my character want? Why does my character want it? When is the scene taking place and where? What is the relationship of my character to the other characters in the play? The actor's task is to make each of these elements exist so specifically and powerfully for himself that he can bring them to life on stage.

Acting comes from *wanting,* which is connected to the largest objective in the character's life, which is what the character needs for total fulfillment or happiness. What the character wants in a particular scene is thus related to what he or she wants in life, and this main objective and the objectives of all the other characters in the play are related to a super-objective—which in turn is related to the germinating force, idea or theme of the play. These structural and psychological connections unify the theme, plot and characters, producing the play's clarity and aesthetic harmony.

So Arthur Miller's *All My Sons* is about responsibility. Most of the characters are powerfully driven to fulfill their responsibilities to their families. Others like Chris are concerned with their larger responsibility to all mankind. Chris becomes conflicted between this responsibility and the responsibility he still feels for his family. It also causes conflict with his parents, and conflict, of course, is what creates drama on the stage—the conflict that comes from each character powerfully driven to achieve her or his objective in life.

Thus, drama comes out of urgent needs and invariably includes a "right now" element, which is the "when" of the given circumstances and gives the part its urgency and its active thrust. Also, the "why" or motivating factor must be specific and meaningful enough to personally trigger the want. The acting results from what happens as the characters carry out their intentions in each of the subdivisions of the play: act, scene, section of scene, moments within each section.

At the same time remember something Sanford Meisner says, "Acting is really doing; it's doing something to get what you want but remember it's also *what happens to you while you try to get what you want.*" The actor must keep in balance both elements: pursuing the objective by carrying out the actions taken by the character, and at the same time responding to the other characters, to the environment, and to the text itself. The transitions that unfold from this approach—and the changes of condition and attitude experienced by the character—will give variety, progression, and increase the possibility of revelation in the performance.

The rehearsal period, whether on a whole play or one of these scenes, should be an organic process, evolving from life. It should be enjoyable, creative, and a time of discovery. Discoveries are made about the play, about the part, about the other characters, and about what your character is striving for.

Picking up the significant clues in the text is a key part of the rehearsal process. For example, in the scene reprinted here from Tennessee Williams' *Streetcar Named Desire*, Stella says to Blanche, "But there are things that happen between a man and a woman in the dark—that sort of make everything else seem—unimportant." This is a large clue, a signpost to the actress, revealing what is essential to Stella. It's also directly related to the underlying theme of the play—desire.

The rehearsal is also the time to work on your own inner preparation. "Preparation" is a most important element too often overlooked. It means getting yourself into the state, or condition or character needed to begin the performance of the play or scene. This is largely a process of self-suggestion, which can generate feelings, behavior, attitudes and needs.

Take, for example, the preparation for Chris' monologue in *All My Sons*. Since Chris starts the scene feeling guilty and conflicted, the actor must be in this state at the opening moment; he must be prepared. His conflicted guilt feelings may just naturally evolve from work on the role and identification with the character. But often chance or intuition is not reliable enough. So the actor should pinpoint what he is "using" for his preparation. He may have personal analogies in his own life, current or past; or perhaps he can use an "as if," create an imaginary example, to personalize the guilt feeling and make it meaningful to him. The essence of this feeling can be a triggering phrase (for example, "I won't be able to live with myself if I marry her, and I won't be able to live with myself if I let her go.") The actor may then use it as an internal trigger each time he does the role.

Since each play makes its own stylistic demands, the actors and director should give themselves the opportunity to experiment and find and set the rhythms of the text as they work on the material. In the introductions to each of these scenes I have attempted to give insight into the nature of the play, to lead the actor to find a suitable style. The actor should be free to explore the material until the acting feels right. It's a sense of being in tune. (A comparison of the introductions to *A Hatful of Rain* and *Bad Habits* or *The Crucible* and *La Turista* can make one aware of how widely styles can vary.)

Here are a number of acting points and reminders I find myself constantly mentioning in class:

Nothing is happening because you haven't motivated yourself. The "why" must exist for you and be specific and meaningful enough to make you really want and really do.

*

Your opening moments are off and the acting that follows probably won't be good. Experiment with the first moment until you're secure, you feel right and alive, and you're in good contact with whatever or whomever is your object. Be sure to get a live impulse to start you off.

*

Do relaxation exercises before you prepare to go on stage; you need to be relaxed to act well.

*

Preparation is important, but remember—leave yourself open for what happens as the scene progresses.

*

You're rushing too much. This is a rehearsal. Take your time so you can explore and discover what you're doing, and make contact.

*

You're trying to give a performance too soon. Remember what Laurette Taylor said: "How can you give it, when it hasn't grown inside?"

*

Your relationship to the other character is not particularized enough. Who is this character to you, and what is the nature of your feelings about each other that make it a unique relationship?

*

You need better contact with the other actor. Really listen and react. Interplay is important.

*

You're playing face to face too much, so the acting gets very strained. Find things to do and ways of playing that make you less direct. There will be more revelation, interest and variety in the acting.

*

Your behavior is too general or hardly exists, so that it does not contribute to the acting. Acting from the neck down is important too. Acting should be a total use of yourself.

*

Stop illustrating what you are saying and doing. It's boring, redundant and detracts from the acting.

*

We can't focus on you—you're making a lot of unnecessary movements and you're bobbing your head all the time. It's distracting.

*

The acting doesn't find sufficient expression in your body. Take movement classes to tune up physically.

*

Your voice is inadequate for acting. You can't project sufficiently, it is too strained and lacks quality and color. Get instruction from a good voice teacher.

*

You need help with your speech. You cannot articulate clearly or rapidly enough and/or there are regionalisms in your speech that are too limiting.

*

There are rhythms in the language that must be part of your acting performance. Don't break up the lines and speeches too much and unnecessarily.

*

You're forcing. Don't push or put too much effort into the acting.

*

You can help your concentration by finding various characters, objects, actions or thoughts to focus your attention on as the scene progresses.

*

Don't anticipate—you're playing the end of the scene at the beginning. Find the progression.

*

Don't play the emotion—play the intentions and let the emotion happen by itself.

*

You're showing us that you're trying to be funny. Play the situation with conviction, so that we're convinced it's important to your character; then we'll find it funny.

*

Stop "indicating"—trying to show us feelings you don't really have.

*

You haven't found the style—there's no particular way of playing that makes your acting seem "right" for this role in this play.

*

Your acting is too conscientious, too deliberate, too calculated. Spontaneity and the "illusion of the first time" are important. Your acting should have a more improvisational feeling.

*

You're not really *doing* anything. *To act is to do!*

*

Remember what Isadora Duncan said to Stanislavsky: "Before I go on stage, I have to put a motor in my soul."

WYNN HANDMAN

The American Place Theatre
New York City
June, 1978

part 1

Scenes for One Man, One Woman

FROM **Another Part of the Forest** (1946)

by LILLIAN HELLMAN

Miss Hellman is the doyenne of American letters; herself the author of twelve plays and three books, she is also responsible for shepherding carefully chosen young writers toward successful careers. Her political and personal commitment to civil liberties has kept her in the forefront of socially conscious activity, and her plays reflect her battles with personal greed and public unscrupulousness. There is no subtlety to her characters; they move deliberately and judgmentally through the play Miss Hellman has created for them. Nothing is left to chance. This control is her writing skill.

Another Part of the Forest reflects the changing social structure of the South after the Civil War, as the old landed aristocracy gives way to the newly powerful middle class. It is a time of recognition, painful to the fading dignity and fortunes of the aristocrats, heady and corrupting to the emerging families. The Hubbards, Southern new rich of the 1880s, have just recovered from accusations of complying with the Northern enemy for their own profit during the war. Now we watch their internal family relations disintegrate under the burden of greed and power.

3

The scene chosen here is between Oscar, the younger Hubbard son, and Laurette Bagtry; both are in their 20s. Oscar genuinely loves Laurette; he wants to marry her and live in New Orleans, away from the family. Oscar will introduce her to the family tonight; he must win his domineering father's approval to get the money he needs to make the move. Laurette clearly doesn't "fit in." She has the reputation (deservedly) of the "town whore," dresses fashionably, and has a blank cuteness about her. She is in the rich Hubbard home for the first time and is totally impressed. (The actress can find valid business by using the furniture and objects in the room. This will help the actors avoid overly-direct face-to-face playing.) As silly as Laurette is, she has a great deal of pride in herself and her family, who come from the same background as the Hubbards. In the course of the scene, this feeling is made clear. Her anger is short-lived, however; she is good-natured and attracted enough to Oscar to accept him as her husband.

After a second, Oscar appears in the living room. With him is Laurette Sincee. Laurette is about twenty, pig-face cute, a little too fashionably dressed. She stands in the door, admiring the room.

LAURETTE: Squee!

OSCAR: Not bad, eh?

LAURETTE: This *is* nice. You born here, Oskie?

OSCAR: No. Like I told you. Right after the war Papa bought, or something, this house from old man Reed. Like it?

LAURETTE: Squee. Who wouldn't?

OSCAR: Well, maybe, someday——

LAURETTE: Ah, go on, Oskie. Go on.

OSCAR: You just wait and see.

LAURETTE: What's that?

OSCAR: What?

LAURETTE: The noise?

OSCAR: That's music, honey.

LAURETTE: Oh.

OSCAR: When you speak to Papa, tell him how much you like music. Tell him how fine he plays.

LAURETTE: What's he playing?

OSCAR: The violin.

LAURETTE: Ain't that a coincidence? I had a beau who said he played the violin. A Frenchman, much older than me.

OSCAR: I don't like to hear about him, Laurette, him or any other men. I am deeply and sincerely in love with you.

LAURETTE: Are you really, Oskie?

OSCAR: Laurette, I'm going to ask Papa for a loan. Then we'll go on down to New Orleans. Would you, Laurette——

LAURETTE: You've asked me the same question for the last year, twenty times. But you never yet asked your Papa for the loan.

OSCAR: I've been waiting for the right opportunity, I want you to be my *wife*, honey, I am deeply and——

LAURETTE: We can't eat on deeply and sincerely.

OSCAR: No, I know. But this is the big night, don't you

see? I never thought he'd let you come here. I mean—I mean a chance like this. And he's in a good humor about something. Now, darling, be very very —well, er. I tell you: you speak with him about what *he* likes. Tell him how much you think of music, not new music, mind you, but he's fond of Mozart. Talk about Mozart.

LAURETTE: I can't do that.

OSCAR: Well, just try to please him. So much depends on it. We could have our own little place in New Orleans . . .

LAURETTE: What kind of place?

OSCAR: I'd find a job. You bet I would, and with you behind me to encourage and love me, with you to fight for, I'd forge ahead.

LAURETTE: Oh. Well, I'd certainly like to go to New Orleans. I know a girl there. She has an embroidery shop on Royal Street. I'm good at embroidery. That's what I always wanted to do. Did I ever tell you that? Always wanted to do embroidery.

OSCAR: Did you?

LAURETTE: Yep. Instead of whoring. I just wanted to do fancy embroidery.

OSCAR: Don't, Laurette, don't talk that way. We better go out now.

LAURETTE: Why did your Papa let me come tonight?

OSCAR: Don't let him worry you, honey. Just take it nice and easy. Pretend nobody knows anything about you, pretend you're just as good as them—

LAURETTE: *Pretend?* Pretend I'm as good as anybody called Hubbard? Why, my Pa died at Vicksburg. He didn't stay home bleeding the whole State of Alabama with money tricks, and suspected of worse. You think I been worried for that reason?

OSCAR: No, no. I—For God's sake don't talk like that—

LAURETTE: You may be the rich of this County, but everybody knows how. Why, the Frenchman I used to eat dinner with and his sister, the Countess. What you mean, boy, your folks—?

OSCAR: I didn't mean anything bad. Haven't I just said I wanted to *marry* you? I think you're better than anybody.

LAURETTE: I'm not better than anybody, but I'm as good as piney-wood crooks.

OSCAR: *Stop, please.* We've got to go outside. *Please*—

LAURETTE: Sometimes you bring out the worst in my nature, Oskie, and make me talk foolish. Squee, it's the truth: I am a little twitchy about coming here and meeting your folks. That's why I'm talking so brave. I ain't been in a place like this before . . . All right, I'll be very good and nice. I would like to go to New Orleans.

OSCAR: Course you would, with me. You love me, honey? (*Takes her in his arms, tries to kiss her. She draws back a little*) Tell me you love me.

LAURETTE: Now, Oskie, you know this ain't the place or the time for mush—

The Big Knife (1949)

by CLIFFORD ODETS

Clifford Odets is the playwright of emotional territory, well traveled by him from the depths of the Depression to the heights of Hollywood and filthy lucre. "Success and fame or just a lousy living," he says in *Golden Boy*, one of his earlier plays, and neither he nor his characters were ever able to release themselves from the tantalizing pull of those red-white-and-blue come-ons. Actors love to play Odets because the passions are ripe and accessible, the language charged and fully flavored. Directors are excited by the brilliant characterizations and energized scenes that seem to play themselves.

The Big Knife, set in Hollywood in the 1940s, illuminates the pitfalls of the pursuit of money and fame. Charlie Cass, gifted former theatre actor, has become the property of a typical movie mogul, Hoff, and his studio empire. Charlie is being blackmailed into renewing his lucrative contract with the studio by their concealed intelligence that he is a hit-and-run driver.

In this scene between Charlie and his estranged wife, Marion, the conflict revolves around the contract. Marion has separated from Charlie because she can't stand what he has become. The difficulties of their marriage have reached the acute stage as this

scene begins. Marion has just verified her
pregnancy. As she arrives, she tells an important gossip columnist, dubbed "Lady
Pry," to mind her own business. Now, Marion
must solve the main issue between them:
Charlie must not sign the contract, he must
return to the theatre in New York, and try to
become the whole man she married. Charlie
loves Marion, trusts her with his soul, but
is terrified by the threat of disgrace which
the studio holds over him.

CHARLIE: Tell me, Angel, what the hell did you think
you were doing?

MARION: I'll tell her lots more if she plays Lady Pry
again!

CHARLIE: I'm in the movie business, darling. I can't
afford these acute attacks of integrity.

MARION: Why don't you talk to me the way you talk
to her?

CHARLIE: How do I talk to her?

MARION: Your mouth is liquid honey.

CHARLIE: I'm insincere with her.

MARION: Husband, dear, be insincere with me. . . .

CHARLIE: Would you use your brain, darling? Free
speech is the highest-priced luxury in this country
today. Patty's got eighteen million readers. Why an-
tagonize her? Where's the sense?

MARION: From time to time I believe in being completely senseless. I'm a human being, a woman, not
a diplomat. Doesn't it make you blench to say "God
bless" to Patty Benedict? But, of course, you're not
sincere.

CHARLIE: Don't you think you're exaggerating a teenie-weenie bit?

MARION: I'll stop . . . (*She opens her purse and takes a pill from a little box*)

CHARLIE: What's that pill? Don't you feel well?

MARION: Half grain codeine. That's what I went upstairs for. (*Charlie puts his glass on the bar and looks in her purse*)

CHARLIE: What's in that other box?

MARION: A pill that runs a little faster . . .

CHARLIE: What do you do, Angel, eat these pills like candy? They're dangerous drugs!

MARION: Don't you take drugs, Handsome, to put yourself to sleep and pep you up?

CHARLIE: Sure, if I'm low or tired, but not in ten assorted flavors!

MARION: Migraines and sinus never bother solid Charlie. Don't you know the fancy world you live in yet? What can a doctor do if the women come to his office looking for life? Can he give them life? So they settle for easy solutions, fifty in a bottle—pills and twenty-dollar injections.

CHARLIE: For what?

MARION: For a substitute for a normal, happy life. I know all about it—I saw it in a movie. . . . (*Lapsing again, Marion walks to the Rouault painting. Charlie, a little sheepish, says of the picture*)

CHARLIE: I'm beginning to like that picture. You're right—it broods. This Rouault guy may make the Olympics Team. I had no idea, all those pills . . .

MARION: You're supposed to have Billy this week.

CHARLIE: I was about to ask—how is my son, Mommy?

MARION: Billy's fine, but I can't send him in without the nurse, and she won't work with Negroes.

CHARLIE: Fire her! The hell with *that!*

MARION: Except I'm too tired just now to break in another nurse. I'm in the mood to sleep the clock around—as if I were pregnant. (*Charlie goes to the bar and makes a drink*)

CHARLIE: I haven't seen you for two weeks, Angel. . . .

MARION: Three, Handsome.

CHARLIE: Three? Really?

MARION: Really, three.

CHARLIE (*Pausing*): Are you lonely out at the beach?

MARION: Yes. . . .

CHARLIE: Very lonely?

MARION: Medium rare.

CHARLIE: Marion, in the whole world I care about only three-and-a-half people: You, little Billy, Hank Teagle . . . and the half a man that's me. Marion, be as brutally frank as you like. Why don't you come back? Does that hurt? (*Seated, Marion is rubbing her forehead. Without waiting, Charlie steps behind her and begins massaging her forehead with his fingertips; she yields*)

MARION: I'm going for a treatment in twenty minutes.

CHARLIE: Marion, I can change. I know I can make you happy.

MARION: How, darling, how can you change in the

twelfth year of this fantastic career? Why did I leave you once before? Why don't I come back *this* time? Because a man, darling, can live only two ways— either married or like a bachelor. But all you want, Charlie, is the best features of both.

CHARLIE: Marion, you don't think that those occasional girls—

MARION: Oh, yes, I *do* think those occasional girls! Surprised? (*Marion smiles at this herself. Charlie massages in slow silence*) Charlie Cass was a wonder and I was Mrs. Cass. Now you're Hoff's Mr. Castle.

CHARLIE: Sorry, sweet, I don't buy that—I don't belong to Marcus Hoff.

MARION: What about the new contract?

CHARLIE: I'm far from perfect, but you're making a big mistake if you think you can face the wide world alone. Don't tell me you have little Billy—he still eats a grape in four bites! You don't have a family— you don't even have a confidant, unless it's Hank Teagle, and he's *my* friend as much as yours.

MARION: Hank asked me to marry him last night. (*Charlie slowly stops massaging*)

CHARLIE: And . . . what did you say?

MARION: Nothing.

CHARLIE: He's got his goddam nerve!

MARION: All he said was *if*.

CHARLIE: Repeat that—there was so much traffic going by!

MARION: I tried to avoid this conversation.

CHARLIE: Okay, you win! Famous husband remarks— you win! (*Charlie is gloomily prowling the room by now; he takes a strap watch from his pocket. Tired,*

Marion crosses and takes some soiled glasses to the bar) Don't be such a housewife all the time—leave the glasses where they are. Damn strap's broke on my watch, too. . . .

MARION: I'll need a check for Monday. Bills are coming in.

CHARLIE: I'll have Harold send it from his office.

MARION: Are you renewing with Hoff or not?

CHARLIE: Where the hell does Hank Teagle come off to propose to you?

MARION: Put Hank aside—he's leaving for New York in two weeks.

CHARLIE: What, to find a forty-cent gin?

MARION: To write a new book. He's been on the wagon for months. Charlie, I want you to believe me: I won't come back if you sign the new contract.

CHARLIE: I never expected to see the day when a three-and-a-half-million-dollar deal would give you chills and fever. . . .

MARION: Neither did I. I'm as human as the next one. It's a fabulous deal. But it's for fourteen years and I don't believe in the life that goes with it. Charlie, you're half asleep right now! I haven't seen you sparkle since the day Billy was born! You used to take sides. Golly, the zest with which you fought. You used to grab your theater parts and eat 'em like a tiger. Now you act with droopy eyes—they have to call you away from a card game. Charlie, I don't want you to sign that contract—you've given the studio their pound of flesh—you don't owe them anything. We arrived here in a pumpkin coach and we can damn well leave the same way!

CHARLIE: Pulled by a flock of mice? Please! I'm Hoff-Federated's biggest star. I'm worth millions a year to them in ice-cold profits! Hoff's got me by the tail and he won't let go and you know why!

MARION: Tell him you're leaving Hollywood for good. Promise him never to make pictures for anyone else.

CHARLIE: Just what do you expect me to do? Pick up, without a backward glance—and what? Go back and act in shows?

MARION: What's wrong with shows? You started in the theater. We'd go back to New York, yes—the theater still can give you a reasonable living. And away from this atmosphere of flattery and deceit we might make our marriage work.

CHARLIE: The theater's a stunted bleeding stump. Even stars have to wait years for one decent play.

MARION: But here, of course, they plan your future, don't they? They buy books out here, idiot's tales! From dividend to dividend, they don't waste your talents for a minute: In your last ten pictures you were electrocuted four times!

CHARLIE: Listen, monkey, I know I'm a mechanical, capering mouse. But Charlie Cass is still around in dribs and drabs—don't you think he'd like to do a fine play every other year? Don't you think I want our marriage to work? (*Pausing*) But I have to face one horny fact: I'm Hoff's prisoner now, and signing the contract is the ransom fee! (*Pausing*) I didn't have the nerve that night, in this room . . . I made the wrong decision . . . (*They have both dropped their voices by now. Marion speaks gently, as if to a child*)

MARION: Come here, Charlie. Hold my hands . . . (*He looks across at her, slowly puts down his glass and comes to her, taking her hands in his. Gently*) God help me, I often wished you'd lost your nose and ears in the war. (*Smiling*) Then the other women wouldn't want you and I'd have you to myself. I know you, deeply, darling . . . I've had you with my morning coffee. (*Pausing*) I know the sleepless nights you've had since Christmas Eve. Look at me, darling. We *both* made a mistake that night in this room.

CHARLIE: You could have pushed me the other way that night.

MARION: You needed sympathy. . . . I wasn't strong enough. It was a difficult choice that night. We failed together, but now we have a second chance. It's a gamble—I know what Hoff can do if you refuse to sign.

CHARLIE: You're *sure* you know what he can do?

MARION: Yes, but that's the chance we have to take. We may lose everything we own. This time we have to make the right decision together. (*Charlie turns away, thinking, hesitant and confused*)

CHARLIE: Marion, is that what you want me to do? . . .

MARION: Yes. I know I'm talking about our lives and your fabulous career. But if you sign, you sink in even deeper than before. Refuse to sign, Charlie. (*She is watching Charlie keenly, hopefully. Now, abruptly, he turns back to her, a decision almost made*)

CHARLIE: All right, I'll try. I haven't agreed to sign. I've been stalling them for months. Nat'll be here any minute. He may come up with some big idea. (*Both are sad and unsteady, deeply moved*)

MARION: I like Nat—he's very fatherly—but Hollywood agents aren't worth their weight in feathers.

CHARLIE: Just what you suggested. It may not work with Hoff, but I'll try. I don't want to lose you, Marion.

MARION: Everything is in your hands, Handsome . . .

CHARLIE: We love each other . . . you've been faithful to me all these years.

MARION: Don't be too sure of that. . . .

CHARLIE (*Turning away*): Who could blame you? I don't deserve it.

MARION: From now on I want a man who has the right to blame me. Nowadays, to be faithful . . . it gives you that loony, old-fashioned moral grandeur of an equestrian statue in the park. (*Half smiling*) Poor horse . . . (*Then, starting out*) I'll call you later, from the doctor's office. . . .

CHARLIE: Tell the cook again, will ya, to stop sprinkling parsley on everything she cooks. (*Smiling musingly, Marion takes up her purse and drifts out of the room*)

I Am a Camera (1952)

by JOHN VAN DRUTEN

The play, based on Christopher Isherwood's "Berlin Diaries," takes place in Berlin in the 1930s just as the Nazi Party is emerging.

In the foreground are Christopher and Sally, both winning, clever Britishers, living in the same rooming house and sharing many free hours. Their relationship is symbiotic, mutually beneficial, but not romantic. Christopher describes himself as a "camera, shutter open, quite passive." An observer by nature and occupation, he writes. Sally, a cabaret singer, is bouyant, impulsive, and provocative. She gives him much to observe. She thinks of herself as a "strange, extraordinary person," delights in whimsy and shocking behavior which often leads to trouble. She uses whatever is around for her own purposes and pleasure without so much as a thought of the consequences. Christopher is one of her useful personal belongings, like a toothbrush or a comfortable chair.

They have had a serious quarrel. He challenges her lack of concentration and commitment; she claims her right to be a free spirit. In this scene she is returning from a marvelous drunk but needs his comfort and his home. She's still angry at him for his admonition, but grateful that he's there. She is conflicted with guilt about her lapse in the agreement they had reached prior to her binge, and so attacks him for "suffocating" her. He is impatient to hear her opinion of an article he has written at her request. With her typical capriciousness, she demeans his effort and boasts of a superior replacement. The argument ends with their separation, though it is short-lived.

The actress in this scene has a complicated task because the motivation is not stated in the text. Although she cannot conceive of life as having the limits Christopher suggests, she also questions her life-style; her wings are clipped by guilt.

Sally enters. She is wearing a robe, and looks hung over. She is smoking.

SALLY: Oh, hello, Chris.

CHRISTOPHER: Hello, Sally. I haven't seen you for a day and a half.

SALLY: I know. I've missed you, Chris.

CHRISTOPHER: I've missed you, too. I say, you don't look too well this morning.

SALLY: I've got a terrible hangover.

CHRISTOPHER: What have you been up to?

SALLY: Oh, not *that*.

CHRISTOPHER: I wasn't thinking of that!

SALLY: But we never stopped going around. And then I got drunk and sentimental the first night, and I telephoned Mummy in London.

CHRISTOPHER: Good God, what for?

SALLY: I suddenly felt like it. But we had the most awful connection, and I couldn't hear a word. And last night was worse. We went to the most boring places. Oh, Chris, I need someone to stop me. I really do. I wish I'd stayed home with you.

CHRISTOPHER: Well, thank you, Sally.

SALLY: But you're awfully nice to come back to.

CHRISTOPHER: You're awfully nice to have back. I say, that sounds like a popular song.

SALLY: Oh, it does. Maybe we could write it together and make a fortune. (*Improvises a tune*) "You're awfully nice to come back to."

CHRISTOPHER (*Doing the same*): "You're awfully nice to have back."

SALLY:
CHRISTOPHER: } (*Singing together*) { "You're awfully nice to come back to . . ." (*They laugh*)

SALLY (*Her arms around Christopher*): I do think we belong together. Much more than if we'd ever had an affair. That little quarrel we had didn't mean anything, did it? (*Goes to screen for stockings and shoes*)

CHRISTOPHER: I don't think two people can live as close as we do, and not have them.

SALLY: But it was that that sent me out on that idiotic binge.

CHRISTOPHER (*Pause*): Did you read the article I left you?

SALLY: The what, dear?

CHRISTOPHER: My article.

SALLY: Oh, yes, I—looked at it.

CHRISTOPHER: Well?

SALLY: I'm terribly sorry, Chris. But it won't do.

CHRISTOPHER: Why, what's wrong with it?

SALLY: It's not nearly snappy enough.

CHRISTOPHER: Snappy?

SALLY: But it's all right, Christopher. I've got someone else to do it.

CHRISTOPHER: Oh? Who?

SALLY: Kurt Rosenthal. I called him this morning.

CHRISTOPHER: Who's he?

SALLY: Really, Chris, I thought you took an interest in the cinema. He's miles the best young scenario writer. He earns pots of money.

CHRISTOPHER: Then why's he doing this?

SALLY: As a favor to me. He said he'd dictate it while he's shaving, and send it round to the editor's flat.

CHRISTOPHER: Well, journalism isn't really in my line. But I think you might have let me know.

SALLY: I didn't think you'd want to be bothered.

CHRISTOPHER: And *he* would? (*Sally takes off and drops dressing gown on couch. Goes to chair for skirt*)

SALLY (*Starting to dress*): He doesn't make such a fuss about writing as you do. He's writing a novel in his spare time. He's so terribly busy, he can only dictate it while he's having a bath. (*Does skirt up*)

CHRISTOPHER: I bet that makes it wonderful. Of course it depends how many baths he takes.

SALLY: He read me the first few chapters. Honestly, I think it's the best novel I've ever read.

CHRISTOPHER (*Drops article on couch*): But that doesn't add up to very many, does it? (*Sally comes to table for cigarette, then goes to washstand and brushes hair*)

SALLY: He's the kind of author I really admire. And he's not stuck up, either. Not like one of these young men who, because they've written one book, start talking about art, and imagining they're the most wonderful authors in the world.

CHRISTOPHER: Just who are you talking about, Sally?

SALLY (*Brushing her hair*): Well, you do, Chris. You know you do. And it's silly to get jealous.

CHRISTOPHER: Jealous? Who's jealous?

SALLY: There's no need to get upset, either. (*Puts hat on*)

CHRISTOPHER: I am not upset. You don't like my article. All right, you needn't go on about it. I can't think why I expected you to; or your rich, successful friends either, from whom you seem to have got all this stuff about me.

SALLY: Would you like to know what my friends said about you?

CHRISTOPHER: No, I wouldn't.

SALLY: Well, I'll tell you. They said you were ruining me. That I'd lost all my sparkle and my effervescence. And that it was all due to you. I've let you eat me up, just sitting here, pouring myself into you.

CHRISTOPHER: Oh, is that what you've been doing?

SALLY: It's all you want. You're like a vampire. If you don't have someone around you, you sit about in bars waiting to devour someone.

CHRISTOPHER: Your friends said that?

SALLY: My friends are a lot better than the tatty people you run around with. (*Spits into mascara and does her eyelashes*) All your friends seem to be interested in, is just flopping into bed.

CHRISTOPHER: And since when have you had anything against bed?

SALLY: I haven't anything. So long as it leads somewhere.

CHRISTOPHER: You mean not just for the fun of it.

SALLY: That's disgusting. That's like animals. (*Puts jacket on*) But, you know, Chris. I'll tell you something. I've outgrown you.

CHRISTOPHER: You've *what*?

SALLY: I've gone beyond you. I'd better move away from here.

CHRISTOPHER: All right. When?

SALLY: The sooner the better, I should think.

CHRISTOPHER: That's fine with me.

SALLY: Good.

CHRISTOPHER: So, this is the end for us?

SALLY (*Picks up handbag*): Yes. If you want it that way. We'll probably bump into each other somewhere, sometime, I expect.

CHRISTOPHER: Well, call me sometime, and ask me around for a cocktail.

SALLY: I never know whether you're being serious, or not.

CHRISTOPHER: Try it and find out, if your friends will spare you the time.

SALLY: You know, you make me sick. Goodbye, Chris. (*Goes out, slamming door*)

The Crucible (1953)

by *ARTHUR MILLER*

The Crucible was written as a response to a particular political moment, the cold-war hysteria of the early 1950s, but it remains Miller's most riveting, contemporaneous work. It is set in a parallel time, the Salem witch hunt of 1692, and it is based on historic fact. Miller reveals to us a citizenry suffering from fear of the unknown, fear of loss of order, fear of individualism: "There is a prodigious guilt in the country."

The play concerns itself with interior terror as well as with political treachery and compliance. Sexual repression dominates the drives and actions of the characters. From this emotional deprivation come betrayal, the killing of conscience, the killing of personality, the killing of goodness.

The informant for the witch hunt is a crazed, ecstatic 17-year-old servant girl, Abigail Williams, who inspires herself with demons and wild visions. The object of her desire and the ultimate hero of conscience in the play is John Proctor; the object of her vengeance is his wife Elizabeth, whom she has accused of witchery.

Proctor, a Puritan farmer in his mid-30s, has a "troubled soul," for he has sinned against the moral code and against his own sense of decency. All that follows, he believes, is an agony he deserves because he committed fornication with Abigal, and because he senses in himself a passion he cannot control. He feels responsible for the fate of his wife and their neighbors, and he abhors the policy of witch-hunting.

In this scene between Abigal and John, John's action is clear and urgent. He must get Abigal to admit that she has falsely accused Elizabeth. He must control his rage and passion for her because he doesn't want to generate more wildness in her. He must repress his guilt and appear reasonable to try to get her to be reasonable. Abigal, on the other hand, is thrilled with the night, the place, the closeness with her lover. With an animal wit and tenacity, she toys with him and lures him. But when he is unmoved by her bait, she flies into a hysteria of anger and resolve.

The actors must avoid the trap of letting the somewhat stilted and archaic-sounding dialogue lead them into playing bloodless people. On the contrary, they are very full-blooded, and when their repressed passion comes to the surface, it must burst out.

A wood. Night.

Proctor enters with lantern, glowing behind him, then halts, holding lantern raised. Abigail appears with a wrap over her nightgown, her hair down. A moment of questioning silence.

PROCTOR: I must speak with you, Abigail. (*She does not more, staring at him*) Will you sit?

ABIGAIL: How do you come?

PROCTOR: Friendly.

ABIGAIL (*Glancing about*): I don't like the woods at
night. Pray you, stand closer. I knew it must be you.
When I heard the pebbles on the window, before
I opened up my eyes I knew. (*Sits on log*) I thought
you would come a good time sooner.

PROCTOR: I had thought to come many times.

ABIGAIL: Why didn't you? I am so alone in the world
now.

PROCTOR: Are you! I've heard that people ride a hundred mile to see your face these days.

ABIGAIL: Aye, my face. Can you see my face?

PROCTOR (*Holds lantern to her face*): Then you're
troubled?

ABIGAIL: Have you come to mock me?

PROCTOR (*Sets lantern on ground. Sits next to her*):
No, no, but I hear only that you go to the tavern
every night, and play shovelboard with the Deputy
Governor, and they give you cider.

ABIGAIL: I have once or twice played the shovelboard.
But I have no joy in it.

PROCTOR: This is a surprise, Abby. I'd thought to find
you gayer than this. I'm told a troop of boys go step
for step with you wherever you walk these days.

ABIGAIL: Aye, they do. But I have only lewd looks from
the boys.

PROCTOR: And you like that not?

ABIGAIL: I cannot bear lewd looks no more, John. My
spirit's changed entirely. I ought be given Godly
looks when I suffer for them as I do.

PROCTOR: Oh? How do you suffer, Abby?

ABIGAIL (*Pulls up dress*): Why, look at my leg. I'm

holes all over from their damned needles and pins. (*Touching her stomach*) The jab your wife gave me's not healed yet, y'know.

PROCTOR (*Seeing her madness now*): Oh, it isn't?

ABIGAIL: I think sometimes she pricks it open again while I sleep.

PROCTOR: Ah?

ABIGAIL: And George Jacobs (*Sliding up her sleeve*) he comes again and again and raps me with his stick —the same spot every night all this week. Look at the lump I have.

PROCTOR: Abby—George Jacobs is in the jail all this month.

ABIGAIL: Thank God he is, and bless the day he hangs and lets me sleep in peace again! Oh, John, the world's so full of hypocrites! They pray in jail! I'm told they all pray in jail!

PROCTOR: They may not pray?

ABIGAIL: And torture me in my bed while sacred words are comin' from their mouths? Oh, it will need God Himself to cleanse this town properly!

PROCTOR: Abby—you mean to cry out still others?

ABIGAIL: If I live, if I am not murdered, I surely will, until the last hypocrite is dead.

PROCTOR: Then there is no good?

ABIGAIL: Aye, there is one. *You* are good.

PROCTOR: Am I! How am I good?

ABIGAIL: Why, you taught me goodness, therefore you are good. It were a fire you walked me through, and all my ignorance was burned away. It were a fire, John, we lay in fire. And from that night no woman dare call me wicked anymore but I knew my answer. I used to weep for my sins when the wind lifted up my skirts; and blushed for shame because some old Rebecca called me loose. And then you burned my ignorance away. As bare as some December tree I saw them all—walking like saints to church, running to feed the sick, and hypocrites in their hearts! And God gave me strength to call them liars, and God made men to listen to me, and by God I will scrub the world clean for the love of Him! Oh, John, I will make you such a wife when the world is white again! (*She kisses his hand*) You will be amazed to see me every day, a light of heaven in your house, a— (*He rises, backs away amazed*) Why are you cold?

PROCTOR: My wife goes to trial in the morning, Abigail.

ABIGAIL: Your wife?

PROCTOR: Surely you knew of it?

ABIGAIL: I do remember it now. How—how— Is she well?

PROCTOR: As well as she may be, thirty-six days in that place.

ABIGAIL: You said you came friendly.

PROCTOR: She will not be condemned, Abby.

ABIGAIL: You brought me from my bed to speak of her?

PROCTOR: I come to tell you, Abby, what I will do tomorrow in the court. I would not take you by surprise, but give you all good time to think on what to do to save yourself.

ABIGAIL: Save myself!

PROCTOR: If you do not free my wife tomorrow, I am set and bound to ruin you, Abby.

ABIGAIL (*Her voice small—astonished*): How—ruin me?

PROCTOR: I have rocky proof in documents that you knew that poppet were none of my wife's; and that you yourself bade Mary Warren stab that needle into it.

ABIGAIL (*A wildness stirs in her, a child is standing here who is unutterably frustrated, denied her wish, but she is still grasping for her wits*): I bade Mary Warren—?

PROCTOR: You know what you do, you are not so mad!

ABIGAIL: Oh, hypocrites! Have you won him, too? John, why do you let them send you?

PROCTOR: I warn you, Abby!

ABIGAIL: They send you! They steal your honesty and—

PROCTOR: I have found my honesty!

ABIGAIL: No, this is your wife pleading, your sniveling, envious wife! This is Rebecca's voice, Martha Corey's voice. You were no hypocrite!

PROCTOR: I will prove you for the fraud you are!

ABIGAIL: And if they ask you why Abigail would ever do so murderous a deed, what will you tell them?

PROCTOR: I will tell them why.

ABIGAIL: What will you tell? You will confess to fornication? In the court?

PROCTOR: If you will have it so, so I will tell it! (*She utters a disbelieving laugh*) I say I will! (*She laughs louder, now with more assurance he will never do it. He shakes her roughly*) If you can still hear, hear this! Can you hear! (*She is trembling, staring up at him as though he were out of his mind*) You will tell the court you are blind to spirits; you cannot see them anymore, and you will never cry witchery again, or I will make you famous for the whore you are!

ABIGAIL (*Grabs him*): Never in this world! I know you, John—you are this moment singing secret hallelujahs that your wife will hang!

PROCTOR (*Throws her down*): You mad, you murderous bitch!

ABIGAIL: Oh, how hard it is when pretense falls! But it falls, it falls! (*She wraps herself up as though to go*) You have done your duty by her. I hope it is your last hypocrisy. I pray you will come again with sweeter news for me. I know you will—now that your duty's done. Good night, John. (*She is backing away, raising her hand in farewell*) Fear naught. I will save you tomorrow. (*As she turns and goes*) From yourself I will save you. (*She is gone. Proctor is left alone, amazed, in terror. Takes up his lantern and slowly exits*)

FROM # A Hatful of Rain (1955)

by *MICHAEL V. GAZZO*

The text of this play was developed from
improvisations by actors at the Actors' Studio
in New York. It is a good example of this
genre of theatre material: highly charged
situations, clearly motivated characters in
very immediate trouble, intricate relationships, all of which are about to explode.

Celia is the long-suffering pregnant wife.
Her husband Johnny is an undisclosed dope
addict. Johnny's secret is known only to his
brother, Polo; he has helped Johnny with
money in the past but is filled with sibling
ambivalence. Celia interprets Johnny's night-
ly absences as infidelity. She is exhausted
from anxiety about their marriage and about
his inability to hold a job, particularly with the
baby on the way. Johnny, loving and needing
Celia, will not let her in on his addiction because of his shame and because his life is in
danger. He owes large sums of money to the
merciless gangsters of drug addiction.

In the scene which follows, the suppressed inner tensions form a powerful sub-
text. Each yearns for a reconciliation, even
though they seem so far apart. Johnny's
action is to bring about this harmony. The
acting is "moment-to-moment," enriched
by their emotional ambiguities. Their current
physical state also colors their behavior.

Celia is exhausted, hyperanxious. Johnny is feeling good (at the moment, he doesn't need a fix), with a gaiety and charm which he lacks when he is in physical distress.

Johnny, wearing a neatly pressed shirt, is in the kitchen, spreading a tablecloth. He moves to the sink, and, as he turns around, we see that he has a bouquet of flowers; he sets them on the table. As he hears Celia approach, he moves hurriedly into Polo's room, leaving the door ajar. Celia enters.

CELIA: Polo.

JOHNNY: Yeh.

CELIA: Did Johnny go to the game?

JOHNNY: Yeh.

CELIA: The flowers are beautiful. What smells so good? What are you doing in there? The kids are riding the carousel. The old horse looks like he wants to go home and sleep. (*Johnny sneaks up behind her and puts his hands over her eyes*) What are you doing? A surprise ... what's the surprise?

JOHNNY: Me.

CELIA: I thought you were going to the game with your father.

JOHNNY: Let's go down and ride the carousel.

CELIA: I've got to get things ready. Did Polo go to the game?

JOHNNY: Yeh. Come on, let's go down and take one ride on it.

CELIA: We'd break the horses.

JOHNNY: How was your day?

CELIA: What?

JOHNNY: I said, how was your day?

CELIA: Like any other day. Why?

JOHNNY: Why? I thought you said that a day wasn't just a day.

CELIA: Oh. I'll have to make a salad.

JOHNNY: It's in the icebox.

CELIA: I'll have to make the dressing.

JOHNNY: It's in the blue cup. I've looked for the shoe polish all day and I can't find it. Where do you hide it?

CELIA: The cabinet . . . under the sink. You did the floors.

JOHNNY: I swished a mop around. I took all my clothes to the cleaners, and I fixed that clock.

CELIA: You didn't look for a job today, did you?

JOHNNY: No, I didn't have time.

CELIA: I didn't mean anything. I was just curious . . . that's all.

JOHNNY: Yeh. You want to sit in a tub of hot water? . . . I'll rub your back with alcohol.

CELIA: What is this? Flowers, the floors mopped, meat in the oven, shining your shoes—what's the occasion? I mean, what's all this for?

JOHNNY: Don't you like the flowers?

CELIA: Of course, I like the flowers, I didn't expect to find you home, flowers and the floor mopped.

JOHNNY: You just said that.

CELIA: Said what?

JOHNNY: Flowers and the floor mopped, you said that twice.

CELIA: All right, supposing I did say that twice, what difference does it make!

JOHNNY: No difference, I wasn't criticizing you, I was just—

CELIA: Can we forget it, Johnny, please?

JOHNNY: Forget what?

CELIA: That I said something twice!

JOHNNY: What is it? I was out last night again, is that it?

CELIA: No.

JOHNNY: How many more guesses do I get?

CELIA: It's over.

JOHNNY: What's over? What are you talking about?

CELIA: We've tried.

JOHNNY: I'm behind the times. I thought it was just going to begin. What you said yesterday, that I never came home . . . all the things you said, I've been thinking about them.

CELIA: I'll leave tonight.

JOHNNY: Is it because I lost my job?

CELIA: It's not the job, Johnny.

JOHNNY: What is it?

CELIA: I don't love you.

JOHNNY: And we snap our fingers and that's that?

CELIA: That's the way it is.

JOHNNY: I don't like this talk. Everything's so cold. What is this, a formal dance or something?

CELIA: Johnny, I refuse to get emotional. . . . I just refuse to. My mind is made up. It's not easy, but it's something that has to be done. Now I refuse to get emotional. I'm not going to blame you for anything and I don't want to be blamed for anything. We have to concede that the marriage has failed, not you, not I . . . but we have. I refuse to get emotional. Nothing will be settled by emotion.

JOHNNY: A day isn't just a day, that's what you said. It's not my day or your day. It's not just you and I now.

CELIA: If I understand you correctly, you are talking about the baby?

JOHNNY: Yeh, you understand me correctly.

CELIA: It's amazing, honestly.

JOHNNY: What's amazing? What?

CELIA: For four months I've been waiting for you to say something, one word, one syllable about the baby.

JOHNNY: Today isn't yesterday . . . things can change, you know.

CELIA: Johnny. I don't want to talk anymore because I don't want to get emotional.

JOHNNY: I'm home! Do you understand that? I'm home now! I haven't been but I am now. Here! I bought this today.

CELIA: What is it?

JOHNNY: You said it was going to be a girl, didn't you? Five dresses, one for every day of the week . . . that's another thing I did today.

CELIA: Where did you get the money?

JOHNNY: We don't need electric orange-juice squeezers. I can squeeze oranges with my hands.

CELIA: Well, thank you, Johnny. Thank you very much.

JOHNNY: Look, it's my turn to cry, to beg . . . you reached out your hand and I turned my back, you've looked at me and I've closed my eyes. You're not listening to me. Please listen to me. . . . Please.

CELIA: I'm listening.

JOHNNY: All right, you don't love me anymore. There was something in me worthwhile loving. You must have loved me for some reason! What was the reason? Celia? Celia? I haven't even used your name. I say baby . . . and I say honey . . . but now I'm saying Celia. Celia. I love you.

CELIA: Oh, Johnny, please. Please stop . . . please.

JOHNNY: I know I've been deaf, dumb and blind but please don't do to me what I did to you. Something happened to me. It's something that's hard to understand. Honey, I don't know whether I'm laughing or crying, but, Celia, you don't have to love me . . . not for a long time. You just don't even have to bother . . .

CELIA: Oh . . . oh . . . oh . . . Do you want to feel something? Johnny, give me your hand . . . Lightly, do you feel it? . . . You see?

JOHNNY: Oh—Wow! Holy cats . . . I felt it move. I swear I felt it move. Let me feel that again. I don't feel anything. What happened?

CELIA: Nothing happened. It doesn't move all day long. Just every once in a while.

JOHNNY: Well, let me know the next time you think it's going to move.

CELIA: I will.

JOHNNY: That's a real miracle, you know. Heh . . .

CELIA: Hold me, Johnny. Please . . . hold me.

JOHNNY: Oh, you're going to see some changes . . . I've been making plans all day. I've been like a kid waiting for you to come home. I kept looking at the clock.

CELIA: I don't have a handkerchief.

JOHNNY: You're not going to leave me? Are you? Tell me?

CELIA: No, Johnny, I'm gonna get an apron.

Look Homeward, Angel (1958)

by KETTI FRINGS

Winner of both the Pulitzer Prize and the
New York Critics Award, this play was
adapted from the autobiographical novel by
Thomas Wolfe. Set in North Carolina in 1916,
it concerns a family of complicated people
struggling among themselves for survival.

Eugene is seventeen, the youngest of
the six Gant children, tall, awkward, with a
craving for romance and learning. He adores
his mother, although he is repelled by her
acquisitiveness and possessiveness. He is
determined to leave home, to marry, or to go
to college.

Eliza Gant is both the strength of the
family and its most destructive force. Her
husband, close to alcoholism, settles for
dreams and bouts of frenzied frustration.
Eliza feels that she is the family's beast of
burden. Her children are deeply ambivalent
about her. They need her strength, but they
need "the freedom of the world" as well.
She possesses them with dauntless energy
and greed, beyond love, but when she is
threatened by their gestures of independence,
she can show a more motherly countenance.

The scene chosen here is that timeless
moment when the child tries to break the
stranglehold of his mother and prepare her
and himself for his departure. The mother

starts the scene by an act of cruelty. Eugene has been left by his girlfriend Laura; his mother makes the loss more painful. She is mercurial, instinctive, full of wounds and scars herself, unprepared for this threat, but she doesn't lose easily. She tries cruelty, bribery, fear of God, and finally love. The son unleashes feelings and resentments for the first time. The actor should let it gush out. Avoid being deliberate and conscious; it is not the head being released but the emotions, and they are furious and profound. He must break free!

ELIZA (*Sits beside Eugene, his back still turned to her*): Gene. You know what I'd do if I were you? I'd just show her I was a good sport, that's what! I wouldn't let on to her that it affected me one bit. I'd write her just as big as you please and laugh about the whole thing.

EUGENE: Oh, God, Mama, please, leave me alone, leave me alone!

ELIZA: Why, I'd be ashamed to let any girl get my goat like that. When you get older, you'll just look back on this and laugh. You'll see. You'll be going to college next year, and you won't remember a thing about it. I told you I'd sold that Stumptown property, and I have. This year's term has started already but next year—

EUGENE: Mama, *now! Now!* I've wasted enough time!

ELIZA: What are you talking about? Why you're a child yet, there's plenty of time yet—

EUGENE: Mama, Mama, what is it? What more do you want from me? Do you want to strangle and drown me completely? Do you want more string? Do you want me to collect more bottles? Tell me what you want! Do you want more property? Do you want the town? Is that it?

ELIZA: Why, I don't know what you're talking about, boy. If I hadn't tried to accumulate a little something, none of you would have had a roof to call your own.

EUGENE: A roof to call our own? Good God, I never had a bed to call my own! I never had a room to call my own! I never had a quilt to call my own that wasn't taken from me to warm the mob that rocks on that porch and grumbles.

ELIZA: Now you may sneer at the boarders if you like—

EUGENE: No, I can't. There's not breath or strength enough in me to sneer at them all I like. Ever since I was this high, and you sent me to the store for the groceries, I used to think, "This food is not for us—it's for them!" Mama, making us wait until they've eaten, all these years—feeding us on *their* leftovers—do you know what it does to us?—when it's you we wanted for us, *you* we needed for us. Why? Why?

ELIZA: They don't hurt me like the rest of you do—they wouldn't talk to me like you are, for one thing.

EUGENE: Because they don't care—they're strangers. They don't give a damn about you! They'll talk like this about you behind your back—I've heard them do that plenty!

ELIZA: What? What? What kind of things do they say about me?

EUGENE: What does it matter what they say—*they* say! Doesn't it matter to you what I say?

ELIZA (*Beginning to weep*): I don't understand.

EUGENE: Oh, it's easy to cry now, Mama, but it won't do you any good! I've done as much work for my wages as you deserve. I've given you fair value for your money, I thank you for nothing.

ELIZA: What's that? What are you saying?

EUGENE: I said I thank you for nothing, but I take that back. Yes, I have a great deal to be thankful for. I give thanks for every hour of loneliness I've had here, for every dirty cell you ever gave me to sleep in, for the ten million hours of indifference, and for these two minutes of cheap advice.

ELIZA: You will be punished if there's a just God in Heaven.

EUGENE: Oh, there is! I'm sure there is! Because I have been punished. By God, I shall spend the rest of my life getting my heart back, healing and forgetting every scar you put upon me when I was a child. The first move I ever made after the cradle was to crawl for the door. And every move I ever made since has been an effort to escape. And now, at last I am free from all of you. And I shall get me some order out of this chaos. I shall find my way out of it yet, though it takes me twenty years more—alone.

ELIZA: Gene! Gene, you're not leaving?

EUGENE: Ah, you were not looking, were you? I've already gone.

FROM **A Raisin in the Sun** (1959)

by LORRAINE HANSBERRY

This play by the late Lorraine Hansberry
made a tremendous impact when it was first
produced and was the forerunner of the
strong, realistic plays about urban life and
Black aspirations that emerged in the 1960s.

The Youngers, a Black family, have been
living in a run-down, over-crowded apartment in Chicago's Southside. They have
been suffering from "acute ghetto-itis," and
with money acquired through an insurance
policy have planned to move to a house in a
better neighborhood. However, Walter, the
only man of the family, has invested the
money and lost it.

This scene immediately follows the report of the loss. It is a time for recouping, for
finding new strength, for rebuilding family
harmony and struggle. Beneatha, Walter's
younger sister, is a medical student. Asagai
is a young Black man from Nigeria. He has
been studying in the United States and has
met Beneatha on campus. The scene between them shows both their separateness
and their togetherness. He is very open and
direct; she is moody, discouraged and preoccupied—the new world of Africa versus
the old new world of America. Play the scene
realistically; the conflict and ideas will
emerge.

In the living room Beneatha sits at the table, still sur-
rounded by the now almost ominous packing crates.
She sits looking off. We feel that this is a mood struck
perhaps an hour before, and it lingers now, full of the
empty sound of profound disappointment. We see on
a line from her brother's bedroom the sameness of their
attitudes. Presently the bell rings and Beneatha rises
without ambition or interest in answering. It is Asagai,
smiling broadly, striding into the room with energy and
happy expectation and conversation.

ASAGAI: I came over . . . I had some free time. I thought
I might help with the packing. Ah, I like the look of
packing crates! A household in preparation for a
journey! It depresses some people . . . but for me . . .
it is another feeling. Something full of the flow of life,
do you understand? Movement, progress . . . It makes
me think of Africa.

BENEATHA: Africa!

ASAGAI: What kind of a mood is this? Have I told you
how deeply you move me?

BENEATHA: He gave away the money, Asagai . . .

ASAGAI: Who gave away what money?

BENEATHA: The insurance money. My brother gave it
away.

ASAGAI: Gave it away?

BENEATHA: He made an investment! With a man even
Travis wouldn't have trusted.

ASAGAI: And it's gone?

BENEATHA: Gone!

ASAGAI: I'm very sorry . . . And you, now?

BENEATHA: Me? . . . Me? . . . Me I'm nothing . . .
Me. When I was very small . . . we used to take

our sleds out in the wintertime and the only hills we
had were the ice-covered stone steps of some houses
down the street. And we used to fill them in with
snow and make them smooth and slide down them
all day . . . and it was very dangerous you know . . .
far too steep . . . and sure enough one day a kid
named Rufus came down too fast and hit the sidewalk . . . and we saw his face just split open right
there in front of us . . . And I remember standing
there looking at his bloody open face thinking that
was the end of Rufus. But the ambulance came and
they took him to the hospital and they fixed the
broken bones and they sewed it all up . . . and the
next time I saw Rufus he just had a little line down
the middle of his face . . . I never got over that . . .

ASAGAI: What?

BENEATHA: That that was what one person could do
for another, fix him up—sew up the problem, make
him all right again. That was the most marvelous
thing in the world . . . I wanted to do that. I always
thought it was the one concrete thing in the world
that a human being could do. Fix up the sick, you
know—and make them whole again. This was truly
being God. . . .

ASAGAI: You wanted to be God?

BENEATHA: No—I wanted to cure. It used to be so important to me. I wanted to cure. It used to matter.
I used to care. I mean about people and how their
bodies hurt . . .

ASAGAI: And you've stopped caring?

BENEATHA: Yes—I think so.

ASAGAI: Why?

BENEATHA: Because it doesn't seem deep enough, close
enough to what ails mankind—I mean this thing of
sewing up bodies or administering drugs. Don't you

understand? It was a child's reaction to the world.
I thought that doctors had the secret to all the hurts.
. . . That's the way a child sees things—or an ideal-
ist.

ASAGAI: Children see things very well sometimes—and
idealists even better.

BENEATHA: I know that's what you think. Because you
are still where I left off—you still care. This is what
you see for the world, for Africa. You with the
dreams of the future will patch up all Africa—you
are going to cure the Great Sore of colonialism with
Independence——

ASAGAI: Yes!

BENEATHA: Yes—and you think that one word is the
penicillin of the human spirit: "Independence!" But
then what?

ASAGAI: That will be the problem for another time.
First we must get there.

BENEATHA: And where does it end?

ASAGAI: End? Who even spoke of an end? To life? To
living?

BENEATHA: An end to misery!

ASAGAI: You sound like a French intellectual.

BENEATHA: No! I sound like a human being who just
had her future taken right out of her hands! While
I was sleeping in my bed in there, things were happening in this world that directly concerned me—and
nobody asked me, consulted me—they just went out
and did things—and changed my life. Don't you see
there isn't any real progress, Asagai, there is only
one large circle that we march in, around and
around, each of us with our own little picture—in
front of us—our own little mirage that we think is
the future.

ASAGAI: That is the mistake.

BENEATHA: What?

ASAGAI: What you just said—about the circle. It isn't a circle—it is simply a long line—as in geometry, you know, one that reaches into infinity. And because we cannot see the end—we also cannot see how it changes. And it is very odd but those who see the changes are called "idealists"—and those who cannot, or refuse to think, they are the "realists." It is very strange, and amusing too, I think.

BENEATHA: You—you are almost religious.

ASAGAI: Yes . . . I think I have the religion of doing what is necessary in the world—and of worshipping man—because he is so marvelous, you see.

BENEATHA: Man is foul! And the human race deserves its misery!

ASAGAI: You see: *you* have become the religious one in the old sense. Already, and after such a small defeat, you are worshipping despair.

BENEATHA: From now on, I worship the truth—and the truth is that people are puny, small and selfish. . . .

ASAGAI: Truth? Why is it that you despairing ones always think that only you have the truth? I never thought to see *you* like that. Your brother made a stupid, childish mistake—and you are grateful to him. So that now you can give up the ailing human race on account of it. You talk about what good is struggle; what good is anything? Where are we all going? And why are we bothering?

BENEATHA: *And you cannot answer it!* All your talk and dreams about Africa and Independence. Independence and then what? What about all the crooks and petty thieves and just plain idiots who will come into power to steal and plunder the same as before —only now they will be black and do it in the name of the new Independence— You cannot answer that.

ASAGAI (*Shouting over her*): *I live the answer!* (*Pause*) In my village at home it is the exceptional man who can even read a newspaper . . . or who ever *sees* a book at all. I will go home and much of what I will have to say will seem strange to the people of my village . . . But I will teach and work and things will happen, slowly and swiftly. At times it will seem that nothing changes at all . . . and then again . . . the sudden dramatic events which make history leap into the future. And then quiet again. Retrogression even. Guns, murder, revolution. And I even will have moments when I wonder if the quiet was not better than all that death and hatred. But I will look about my village at the illiteracy and disease and ignorance and I will not wonder long. And perhaps . . . perhaps I will be a great man . . . I mean perhaps I will hold on to the substance of truth and find my way always with the right course . . . and perhaps for it I will be butchered in my bed some night by the servants of empire . . .

BENEATHA: *The martyr!*

ASAGAI: . . . or perhaps I shall live to be a very old man respected and esteemed in my new nation . . . And perhaps I shall hold office and this is what I'm trying to tell you, Alaiyo; perhaps the things I believe now for my country will be wrong and outmoded, and I will not understand and do terrible things to have things my way or merely to keep my power. Don't you see that there will be young men and women, not British soldiers then, but my own black countrymen . . . to step out of the shadows some evening and slit my then useless throat? Don't you see they have always been there . . . that they always will be? And that such a thing as my own

death will be an advance? They who might kill me
even . . . actually replenish me!

BENEATHA: Oh, Asagai, I know all that.

ASAGAI: Good! Then stop moaning and groaning and
tell me what you plan to do.

BENEATHA: Do?

ASAGAI: I have a bit of a suggestion.

BENEATHA: What?

ASAGAI: That when it is all over—that you come home
with me—

BENEATHA (*Slapping herself on the forehead with exasperation born of misunderstanding*): Oh—Asagai
—at this moment you decide to be romantic!

ASAGAI: My dear, young creature of the New World—I
do not mean across the city—I mean across the
ocean; home—to Africa.

BENEATHA: To—to Nigeria?

ASAGAI: Yes! . . . (*Smiling and lifting his arms playfully*) Three hundred years later the African Prince
rose up out of the seas and swept the maiden back
across the middle passage over which her ancestors
had come—

BENEATHA (*Unable to play*): Nigeria?

ASAGAI: Nigeria. Home. (*Coming to her with genuine
romantic flippancy*) I will show you our mountains
and our stars; and give you cool drinks from gourds
and teach you the old songs and the ways of our
people—and, in time, we will pretend that—(*Very
softly*)—you have only been away for a day—
(*She turns her back to him, thinking. He swings her
around and takes her full in his arms in a long embrace which proceeds to passion*)

BENEATHA (*Pulling away*): You're getting me all mixed up—

ASAGAI: Why?

BENEATHA: Too many things—too many things have happened today. I must sit down and think. I don't know what I feel about anything right this minute.
(*She promptly sits down and props her chin on her fist*)

ASAGAI: All right, I shall leave you. No—don't get up. (*Touching her gently, sweetly*) Just sit awhile and think . . . Never be afraid to sit awhile and think. (*He goes to door and looks at her*) How often I have looked at you and said, "Ah—so this is what the New World hath finally wrought . . ."
(*He exits. Beneatha sits on alone*)

FROM The Beauty Part (1961)

by S. J. PERELMAN

S. J. Perelman is one of our foremost humorists, and *The Beauty Part* is considered a major American satire on materialism and the manners and mores of the urban rich. Perelman's weapon is words, barrels and buckets of them—out of whack, out of sync, complicated nonsequiturs and inversions, and random craziness.

In this scene we meet the two young protagonists of the play, Lance and April. Lance's family is powerfully rich, vulgar, and disharmonious. Lance, recently graduated from Yale, represents the antithesis. He is our Candide, innocent, willing, uncomplicated, without guile or deviousness. His purity makes him easy prey for April, the prototypical city girl, fake, fashionable, pitilessly rapacious, desensitized by her limited horizons and unlimited ambitions.

The actors must play their roles in a broad, clear manner. These characters are representative rather than deeply individual. Lance is total innocence; April, the pure exploiter without an editor on her deeds or words. There is no sub-text, no feelings are hidden; loud, fast, hard-edged playing will reveal the characters and their life-styles.

LANCE (*Off*): April! April!

APRIL: Lance Weatherwax! Whatever in the world are you doing here?

LANCE: April—I've got to talk to you. Right away.

APRIL: Of course, dear. Come in—You look so distrait. Has something happened?

LANCE: Well, yes—kind of. I bet I've walked fifty miles the past couple of days, trying to think things through.

APRIL: You must have been in real travail.

LANCE: I was.

APRIL: You poor boy.

LANCE (*Reacts to decor for the first time*): What—what's going on here?

APRIL: I've had it done over. Isn't it delectable?

LANCE: Oh, it's great. I mean, it like hits you right in the eye.

APRIL: Does it say anything to you? You don't feel it's overdone?

LANCE: *Over*done? It's underdone! You couldn't omit a single detail without damaging the—the entire concept.

APRIL (*Hugs him*): You old sorcerer. You know just the words to thaw a woman's heart. Let's have a drink to celebrate. Set ye doon—and I'll open a bottle of Old Rabbinical. (*The phone rings; she answers hurriedly*) Yes? . . . Who? . . . Oh, hi! . . . No, I can't. I have people here. . . . What? No, I have to wash my hair. . . . Yes, silly. . . . Why don't you do that? I'm always here. . . . 'Bye. Honestly, some men are just impossible. They think all they have to do is whistle.

LANCE: Who was that?

APRIL: My ex-fiancé, of all people.

LANCE: Hanh? You never told me you'd been engaged.

APRIL: Oh, Sensualdo and I haven't seen each other in ages. He's a monster—an absolute fiend.

LANCE: Sensualdo? His name sounds Mexican.

APRIL: Uh-uh—Peruvian. One of those insanely jealous types. Tried to stab a man I was having a Coke with. That's what broke up our engagement.

LANCE: Is he—er—back there now?

APRIL: In Peruvia? Well, he shuttles between there and Staten Island. Something to do with vicunas or emeralds, I believe—I really don't know. . . . I haven't been in touch with him in ages!

LANCE: April, there is something very important I—

APRIL: As a matter of fact, he was a prince compared to my first fiancé. Did you ever hear of Benno Vontz, the sculptor?

LANCE: No, I can't say that I have, but—

APRIL: Benno designed that abstract saddle on top of Neiman-Marcus's in Dallas. A brilliant boy, but terribly neurotic. He used to wake me up in the middle of the day, claiming I'd had affairs with all kinds of people—osteopaths, carhops, bakers. It was a nightmare, my dear—an absolute *cauchemar*. I was practically on the verge of a neurasthenia when I met Ricky.

LANCE: Ricky?

APRIL: He was an auctioneer that I met in Atlantic City. Naturally, one thing led to another.

LANCE: And you got engaged.

APRIL: No! Benno found out! One night Ricky and I

were driving home in a downpour and his brakes overheated near Asbury Park and we had to take refuge in a motel. Next thing we knew, Benno was all over us with flashbulbs. My *dear,* it was too sordid.

LANCE: You poor kid. It's a wonder to me you could live through so much and still remain gay and joie de vivre.

APRIL: That's because I sublimate myself in my work, Lance. Whenever life gets frantic, why I rush to my bench and fashion a brooch or earrings that crystallize a dewdrop of ecstasy. Your great craftsmen have always done that, right back to Cellini.

LANCE: April, if you only knew how your eyes light up when you talk about art.

APRIL: Do they?

LANCE: There's a kind of a glow in them. They're like mysterious violet pools, full of wisdom and understanding . . . and—oh, terrific tolerance. Not like those empty-headed little debs I used to date before I met you.

APRIL: Why, Lance, I've never heard you so articulate before. It's as if you'd been freed, somehow.

LANCE: I have. I've come to a very important decision about my future, April. I have to know right away how you feel.

APRIL: Please, Lance, for both our sakes—don't say anything you might regret.

LANCE: No, no—I've got to. You see, this door suddenly opened in my mind and I realized what truly matters to me.

APRIL: Oh, Lance, do you know what you're saying?

LANCE: Yes, yes, I do. April, I've decided to become a writer.

APRIL: You *what?*

LANCE: Or maybe a painter.

APRIL: Oh, Lance, don't be an Airedale.

LANCE: What's the matter? Don't you think I have the ability?

APRIL: Er—of course, but—well, I was just a little overwhelmed. I mean, it's such a tremendous challenge.

LANCE: I want to accept that challenge—I want to unleash whatever creative powers there are inside me. But my problem is—how do I become a writer?

APRIL: Buy a magazine—or maybe a chain of them. I understand the *Saturday Evening Post* is up for grabs—

LANCE: No, siree, I won't be a lousy dilettante. I'm going to start humbly, get the smell of printer's ink . . .

APRIL: Wait—wait! Eureka!

LANCE: I beg your pardon?

APRIL: What a blind little fool I've been! The perfect way to express yourself—it's right in front of you!

LANCE: I don't follow.

APRIL: Let's plunge into the depths together. Scale the heights together.

LANCE: How?

APRIL: Well, you know what a disorganized scatter-brain I am away from my workbench—I haven't a clue to facts or figures. I need someone with divine good taste to counsel me—someone whose judgment I respect.

LANCE: But where would I contribute my creative talent?

APRIL: Why, in a hundred ways. . . . Right here, for example— (*Extracts crumpled paper from under phone*) this came in the morning mail. What does it mean?

LANCE: It's from the bank. It says they're returning your check for $471 due to insufficient funds.

APRIL: It must be that consignment of turquoise nutpicks I ordered from Santa Fe. Those Navajos are so grasping. What should I do about it?

LANCE: You must put the money in the bank to cover the overdraft.

APRIL: There—you see how much more practical you are than I? Very well—you handle it, love.

LANCE: How do you mean?

APRIL: Why, when you leave here, just drop by the Centerboard National and deposit that amount—until I get straightened out.

LANCE: But I haven't any money.

APRIL: Of course—how dense of me. Nobody carries that much around. Well, here's a thought—ring up your father's accountant and tell him to deposit it.

LANCE: I don't think you understand, April—I've cut myself off. I've broken with my family.

APRIL: But you haven't broken with your accountant, surely.

LANCE: With everybody.

APRIL: You're teasing.

LANCE (*Exhibiting a few coins*): This is all the money I have.

APRIL: Lance, I don't think we're quite ready to work together. Obey your original impulse—go and get the smell of printer's ink. Go see Hyacinth Beddoes Laffoon, right away.

LANCE: Who is she?

APRIL: The woman who publishes all those magazines—"Gory Story"—"Sanguinary Love"—"Spicy Mortician."

LANCE: But they're just pulp fiction, full of blood and thunder....

APRIL: My dear Lance, wake *up*. Some of our most enduring American authors come out of that milieu.

LANCE: Maybe you're right, April. Maybe I ought to contact her.

APRIL: Without further ado! Now you buzz right over to Laffoon House and storm the redoubts. I'd help you storm except I have to rush out to an appointment.

LANCE: When am I going to see you again?

APRIL: *Quien sabe corazon?* I'll tell you what—why don't you drop in at my housewarming next Tuesday? And dig up an itty-bitty case of Scotch on the way, will you? There's a dear.

FROM The Red Eye of Love (1961)

by ARNOLD WEINSTEIN

With *The Red Eye of Love,* the theatre showed signs of emerging from its years of natural-ism by giving birth to a fresh-faced fantasy, a spoof of our mores and seriousness. This gentle lampoon laced with sugar-candy romance set the tone, style, and content for much of the theatre material of the 1960s and freed many young playwrights to pursue their own special voices.

Underneath the soft breeze that moves the play is a serious theme for America: the idealist confused by life in a materialist so-ciety, the contradiction between what one wants to do and what one is required to do.

The actors should not over-analyze the characters or try to root them in psychologi-cal backgrounds. See them as figures in an urban landscape, representative rather than individual. Just flow with the dialogue as you would respond to music. You might even play romantic music in the background dur-ing rehearsals so that the lyricism and the free-spirited interplay between Wilmer and Selma are incorporated in the acting.

Wilmer goes to Selma, gives her half a sandwich, sits beside her, and they eat in silence on the bench.

57

SELMA: Let's not tell each other our names. It's more romantic.

WILMER: I believe in no names. Makes forgetting much more beautiful. (*They eat in silence*) I'm on vacation, spending it in the city.

SELMA: Where do you live?

WILMER: In the city. Up there in my bookkeeping office. You live in the city year in, year out, and forget what sights there are. I have two weeks off, each day to a place I haven't seen in years. Old Cohn and I always went to a museum of natural art or someplace. Now, I like my job, but getting up in the morning, going to work, coming home, the result is you don't go anywhere else because you're just nervous. You're tangled, you're twisted, and the result is you think that going anywhere is going to work. Morning becomes night, week becomes weekend, yesterday becomes today. Whatever's happened has not had time to matter. The result is I spend my vacation in the city going places, trying to catch up. The result is I've seen twelve movies in three days.

SELMA: When you look through leaves, the universe looks green.

WILMER: The key!?

SELMA: The key to the green universe?

WILMER: What is it? I know you know. Bookkeeping, right?

SELMA: Movies.

WILMER: I knew she knew.

SELMA: It's the only way out.

WILMER: The only?

SELMA: In the movies, no world falls on you.

WILMER: Yes, no world!
(*They look at each other and kiss*)

SELMA (*Breaks from the embrace suddenly*): What movies?

WILMER (*Still reacting to the kiss*): "Alexander the Great."

SELMA: Saw it.

WILMER: "The Good Earth."

SELMA: Saw it.

WILMER: "The Ten Commandments."

SELMA: Saw them.

WILMER: The key!

SELMA: I *think* I saw it.

WILMER: No. Movies as key to the universe. Along with bookkeeping. Not that I want to take any glory and responsibility away from movies.

SELMA: Are you a bookkeeper?

WILMER: Yes.

SELMA: Exactly. Bookkeeping is the other key to the universe.

WILMER: Say that again!

SELMA: Bookkeeping: other key to universe.
(*Wilmer stares, moved to tears. He forces himself to speak*)

WILMER: Why are *you* so lonely?

SELMA: Did I say I was lonely?

WILMER: Yes.

SELMA: That's a lie, but I *am* lonely.

(*She is staring in the direction of Martinas build-ing*)

WILMER: I was staring at that building before, but you were in front of it. Why are you staring at it? Is it yours too?

SELMA: No, but it will be. I'm engaged to the owner, O. O. Martinas. We're to be married soon. A week or two or three years.

WILMER (*Screams at the top of his voice*): Lonely!! (*Pause*) Old Cohn, crazy fool, last night married some girl who had eyes that went all the way *in*, dark. *Dark* dark. I was invited to the wedding. I don't drink: just last night a few; I kept eating not to get sick from the booze. (*Pause*) I got sick from the eating. (*Pause*) This morning I got sick from the booze. I bit his bride when I was drunk. Old Cohn laughed. (*He laughs*) I fail to see what's funny.

SELMA: Who is Old Cohn?

WILMER: Old Cohn. My best friend till the eighth grade. We used to go everywhere together and he used to make faces and sing on top of the open-air bus. We lost touch.

SELMA: Lost touch. *You* talk about lost touch! I've lost such touch! I never go to sleep without thinking of Geraldine, the greatest friend you'd ever want to find in the fourth grade. We used to walk through the streets for hours identifying automobiles. We saw them all; we could guess the year from two blocks away. And you talk about losing touch! I can't bear it.

WILMER: Did she die?

SELMA: She moved out of the neighborhood. At the very wrongest time. We had seen all the cars, except one: the Lincoln Zephyr. It was our dream to see in person the Lincoln Zephyr zooming down the street. I saw it two days after she moved away. I didn't know where she lived: her father must have got poorer or richer; they didn't let anyone know where they went. And here I was, completely unable to let Geraldine know I had seen the Lincoln Zephyr. I'm haunted with that. I think her name was Geraldine.

WILMER: Today I tried singing on top of the open-air bus like Old Cohn, there in the open, the wind and noise all around. I always turned red, *red* red, made believe I didn't know him. "Stop making fools of the two of us," I'd yell, yell because of the wind and noise all around. Embarrassed me to death, making funny faces to all the city, singing at the top of his voice on top of the open-air bus.

SELMA: Today *you* wanted to sing. I once wanted to dance to all the city. And I did. Look what it got me. Money and wealth.

WILMER: I couldn't sing today.

SELMA: Why?

WILMER: No more open-air buses.

SELMA: Why?

WILMER: I don't remember any songs.

SELMA: Everywhere you turn—a wall.

WILMER: I can hum. (*He hums two notes, then stops*) No, I can't. There were boys—Cohn was one—could memorize anything. "The Declaration of Independence," "Friends, Romans, Countrymen—," "Stardust," anything. Where did it get them? I took up bookkeeping, guess what I became. A bookkeeper. Those boys memorizing, what do they become? Memorizers? Heasly, seventh grade, won the elocution prize; sells lawn furniture in the A & P. My motto is let people do what they want. Only, take up something that can be the key. Bookkeeping's no drudgery either, it's interesting, responsible too. Think of the chaos the world would be in today if we had no bookkeeping. (*Pause*) Why is bookkeeping not the key?

SELMA: Soft people interest me. I like you.

WILMER: Do you love me? That's important too!

SELMA: As a matter of fact, I do.

WILMER: What about Mr. Martinas?

SELMA: Was he here? O. O. was here?

WILMER: Yes.

SELMA: O. O. and I, we don't get along.

WILMER: Why are you going to marry him?

SELMA: Was I going to marry him? I *was* going to marry him, I guess. But O.O. and I don't get along and I love you.

WILMER: This is the thing, I don't go around breaking up love affairs.

SELMA: Shake. I'm the same way. (*Kisses him passionately as they shake hands*) I don't like O. O. Him forever talking about his accomplishments, owner of thirteen stories of store. So what, I ask you, so what?

WILMER: Yes, so what!

SELMA: So it's my duty to marry money. He can be very kind.

WILMER: I suppose.

SELMA: He can be very cruel.
(*Shows Wilmer her arm*)

WILMER: I don't see anything.

SELMA: Yes, well, anyway, O. O. and I, we just don't hit it off, in any manner or form, if you know what I mean.

WILMER: You mean—

SELMA: In any manner or form. I mean—

WILMER: In any manner or form. We mean—

BOTH: In any manner or form.

SELMA: The result is, I pick you. You're nice, soft: you know I like that. I'm blunt.

WILMER: Yes!

SELMA: You be blunt.

WILMER: Yes! Yes!

SELMA: If you don't like the idea, get up and walk away.

WILMER: No! No!

SELMA: Fast get up and walk away. I see you hate me, you think I'm a terrible person. Go, I don't blame you, you're nice, you're soft.

WILMER: I cry in the movies.
(*Romantic music is heard*)

SELMA: You cry in the movies? (*She kisses him*) What movies?

WILMER: "Autumn Leaves."

SELMA: Saw it.

WILMER: "Rhapsody," starring Elizabeth Taylor.

SELMA: Saw it.

WILMER: Cowboy films.

SELMA: You cry in cowboy films?

WILMER: Yes.

SELMA: Which cowboy films?

WILMER: All cowboy films.

SELMA: Saw them.
  (*They kiss long. Music stops*)

WILMER: You feel soft to *me*.

SELMA: My name is Selma Chargesse.

WILMER: My name is Wilmer Flange. But you said no names.

SELMA: Names, now that we're in love . . . names.

WILMER (*Embracing her*): Not only in love, good friends.

SELMA: You're quite a guy, Wilmer.

WILMER: My name isn't Wilmer Flange, it's William Flinge. I lied about my name. I wasn't sure then; now that I've made a sacrifice I know you must be worth it.

SELMA: I am, William, I am!

A Social Event (1962)

by WILLIAM INGE

In this short play, Inge is making fun of the ludicrous display of egocentricity shown by hungry young Hollywood starlets in their grasp for fame and the flashbulb. Randy and Carole are consumed by their desire to be invited to the "right" funeral, where they feel they must be seen to establish their social and professional standing. Given their immature priorities, no machination is beneath or beyond them. The characters are totally self-centered and preoccupied with their careers.

The actors should take their plight seriously and really struggle to cope with what they consider a most urgent situation. It is a good exercise to experiment in rehearsal with a variety of character interpretations and ways of playing the scene. A good deal of humor comes from the physical life, and the behavior can be filled out in every section: the waking-up ritual, the mutual signalling during the telephone call, and their narcissistic preoccupation with their looks.

The scene is the bedroom in the home of a young Hollywood couple, Randy Brooks and Carole Mason, who have been married only a short time and whose careers are still in the promising stage. There is abundant luxury in the room but a minimum of taste. It

*is late morning and both Randy and Carole are asleep,
but Randy soon comes awake, reaches for a cigarette,
lights it, and rubs his forehead discouragedly. Something profound is troubling him. He gets out of bed,
slips a robe on and paces the floor discouragedly. Finally, he presses the buzzer on the house phone and speaks
to the cook.*

RANDY (*Into house phone*): Muriel? We're getting up
now. Bring up the usual breakfast. (*He hangs up
and goes into the bathroom to wash. Now Carole
wakes up. She too lights a cigarette and looks troubled. Then she calls to Randy*)

CAROLE: I hardly slept a wink all night, just thinking
about it.

RANDY: There's nothing to do but face the fact that
we're not invited.

CAROLE: Oh, there's *got* to be a way. There's *got* to
be.

RANDY (*Entering*): But, honey, the services start at
noon. It's now ten-thirty.

CAROLE: Everyone in the business will be there.

RANDY: After all, honey, there's no reason to feel
slighted. We're both pretty new in pictures. It's not
as though we were old-timers who had worked with
Scotty.

CAROLE: Sandra and Don never worked with Scotty,
either. Neither did Debby and Chris, or Anne and
Mark.

RANDY: I know, honey. We've been through all this before.

CAROLE: And I may never have worked with Scotty,
but I did meet him once, and he danced with me
at a party. He was very nice to me, too, and said

some very complimentary things. I met his wife, too. I didn't much like her.

RANDY: Maybe I better call Mike again. (*He picks up the telephone and dials*)

CAROLE: What good can an agent do? We're not looking for jobs.

RANDY: He may have found some way of getting us invited.

CAROLE: I bet.

RANDY: Mike Foster, please. Randy Brooks calling.

CAROL: All the invitations are coming from Scotty's wife. Tell Mike you think there's been an oversight. Maybe he could call her and remind her that you've been referred to in all the columns as "the young Scotty Woodrow," and that Scotty's always been your idol and ...

RANDY: Mike? Randy. Look, Mike, Carole and I still haven't been invited, and I can't help wondering if there's been an oversight of some kind. After all, Carole was a great friend of Scotty's and she feels pretty hurt that she's been overlooked ... I never knew him but everyone knows how much I've always admired him. In an interview just last week, I said "Scotty Woodrow is still the greatest." Now, I didn't *have* to say that ... if you ask me, it showed a lot of humility on my part to say a thing like that when, after all, I've got a career of my own to consider ... well look, try to do *some*thing, Mike. Carole and I both should be seen there ... O.K., Mike, call us as soon as you find out.

CAROLE: He couldn't get us an invitation to Disneyland.

RANDY: He said just Scotty's closest friends are being invited.

CAROLE: Oh yes! Half the people going, I bet, have never met him.

RANDY: Well! What are we going to do?

CAROLE: Sandra had an entire new outfit made. Perfectly stunning. And she had the dress made so that she can have the sleeves taken out later and wear it to cocktails and supper parties. After all, black is a very smart color now.

RANDY: Did you tell Sandra and Don we weren't invited?

CAROLE: Of course not. I lied and said we were going. Now, if we don't get an invitation, I'll have to lie again and say we came down with food poisoning, or something.

RANDY: How did Anne and Mark get invited?

CAROLE: Mark played Scotty's son in a picture once.

RANDY: When? I don't remember.

CAROLE: A long time ago, before either of us came on the scene.

RANDY: That means Mark's a little older than he admits.

CAROLE: I don't know. The part was very young, practically an infant.

RANDY: Just the same, I'll bet Mark's thirty.

CAROLE: Damn! what am I going to tell Sandra? She invited us to come to her house afterwards and I accepted.

RANDY: She's not giving a party!

CAROLE: No. She just invited some friends to come in afterwards to have a few drinks and talk about what a great guy Scotty was, and everything. She said she thought we'd all feel terribly depressed. After all, Scotty Woodrow was practically a landmark, or something. Think of it. He's been a star for forty years.

RANDY: Yes. He was really great. It makes me very humble to think of a guy like Scotty.

CAROLE: They say flowers came from the President, and from Queen Elizabeth, and . . .

RANDY: The guest list is going to be published in every paper in the country.

CAROLE: You know, we *could* crash.

RANDY: No, honey.

CAROLE: Who'd know the difference?

RANDY: How would we feel afterwards, when we had to shake hands with Mrs. Woodrow?

CAROLE: She's probably forgotten whether she invited us or not.

RANDY: Honey, I'm *not* going to crash. That's all. I'm *not*.

CAROLE: Everyone would just take it for granted we'd been invited. I mean, we're both just as prominent as Sandra and Don, or any of the others. If you ask me, it'd be a lot better to crash than not to be seen at . . . well, you can't call it a social *affair* exactly, but it's a social *event*. Anyway, *every*one will be there. *Every*one.

RANDY: It could be some of the others are lying about their invitations, too. You realize that, don't you?

CAROLE: I wonder . . . well, anyway, they're all going. I *think* they got invitations.

RANDY: I don't know why the studio couldn't have managed it for us with a little pull. They should realize it's in the best interests of my career to be seen there, and my career means as much to them as it does to me.

CAROLE: Same here. Oh, I just don't know how I can face Sandra and Anne and all the others, and make them believe that we really did have food poisoning.

RANDY: You know, we could give ourselves food poisoning. Just a light case. A little rotten meat would do it. Then we'd call the doctor and . . .

CAROLE: No! I'm not going to make myself sick.

The Ballad of the Sad Cafe (1963)

by EDWARD ALBEE

This play, adapted from the novella by Carson McCullers, is the story of three people—the strong, vibrant, Junoesque Miss Amelia; her dwarfed-runt cousin Lyman; and her incorrigible, hero-like, jail-bird husband Marvin Macy—living out their bizarre, fierce, competitive love relationships in a small town in the deep South.

This scene flashes back to an earlier time in Miss Amelia's life when she was a mature nineteen and being proposed to by the romantic, wild, and "handsomest man in the region," Marvin Macy. Marvin has screwed up his courage to approach her after two years of reform. His days as a reckless swain are over. He is now a church-going, devoted, and responsible young man. Amelia pragmatically and unsentimentally accepts. They love each other but their relationship is dominated by forces beyond love; she is interested in his newly-acquired timberland. Amelia is a survivor—even at great cost.

The acting cannot be separated from the rhythms in the writing. The author indicates that there are "varying pauses between speeches in this scene," and those silences should have substance. Much of the acting is in the behavior: a look, a pause, a gesture.

MARVIN MACY (*Still not looking at her*): Evenin' Miss Amelia. (*No response*) Sure is hot.

MISS AMELIA (*After a pause*): It so hot, what you all dressed up for a funeral for?

MARVIN MACY (*With a blushing laugh*): Oh, I . . . I am come callin'.
(*Let it be understood here that there are, unless otherwise stated, varying pauses between speeches in this scene*)

MISS AMELIA: Yeah? On who?

MARVIN MACY: Oh . . . on you . . . Miss Amelia.

MISS AMELIA (*Restating a fact*): On me.

MARVIN MACY (*Laughs briefly*): Yep . . . on you.

MISS AMELIA (*Considers it; then*): Somethin' wrong?

MARVIN MACY: I . . . (*He makes a sudden decision, hurriedly brings the bag of chitterlins and the flowers over to where Miss Amelia is, puts them on the ground below where she is sitting, the flowers on top of the bag, and returns to his position*) . . . I brought you these.

MISS AMELIA (*Stares at them*): What be these?

MARVIN MACY (*Terribly shy*): Flowers.

MISS AMELIA: I can see that. What be in the bag?

MARVIN MACY (*As before*): They be . . . chitterlins.

MISS AMELIA (*Mild surprise*): Chitterlins.

MARVIN MACY: Yep.

(*Miss Amelia descends the stairs, picks up the flowers as though they were a duster*)

MISS AMELIA (*Reseating herself*): What for?

MARVIN MACY: Miss Amelia?

MISS AMELIA: I say: what for? Why you bring me chitterlins and flowers?

MARVIN MACY (*Bravely taking one or two steps forward*): Miss Amelia, I am . . . I am a reformed person. I have mended my ways, and . . .

MISS AMELIA: If you are come to call, sit down. Don't stand there in the road.

MARVIN MACY: Thank . . . Thank you, Miss Amelia. *He comes onto the porch and seats himself, but four or five feet from Miss Amelia*) I have mended my ways; I am, like I said, a reformed person, Miss Amelia . . .

MISS AMELIA (*Looking at the flowers*): What are these called?

MARVIN MACY: Hunh? . . . Oh, they . . . they be swamp flowers.

MISS AMELIA: But what are they *called?*

MARVIN MACY (*Shrugs, helplessly*): Swamp flowers.

MISS AMELIA: They got a name.

MARVIN MACY: I . . . I don't know.

MISS AMELIA: I don't neither. (*Pause*) They got a name in some *language;* all flowers do.

MARVIN MACY: I don't know, Miss Amelia.

MISS AMELIA: I don't neither. (*Smells them*) They don't smell none.

MARVIN MACY: I'm . . . sorry.

MISS AMELIA: Don't have to smell; they pretty.

MARVIN MACY (*Blurting*): Miss Amelia, I have mended my ways; I go to church regular, an' I have . . .

MISS AMELIA: I see it. You go to church now, services an' meetings . . .

MARVIN MACY: . . . yes, an' I have learned to put money aside . . .

MISS AMELIA: . . . you have learned thrift; that good . . .

MARVIN MACY: . . . an' I have bought me some land, I have bought me ten acres of timber over by . . .

MISS AMELIA: . . . I hear so; timber is good land . . .

MARVIN MACY: . . . an', an' I don't drink none no more . . .

MISS AMELIA: . . . don't drink? . . .

MARVIN MACY (*Blushes*): . . . well, you know what I mean . . .

MISS AMELIA: Man don't drink none ain't natural.

MARVIN MACY: Well, I don't squander my wages away on drink an' all that I used to . . .

MISS AMELIA: Uh-huuh.

MARVIN MACY: . . . an' . . . Miss Amelia? . . . an' I am less sportin' with the girls now . . . I have reformed my character in that way, too . . .

MISS AMELIA (*Nods slowly*): I know; I hear.

MARVIN MACY: . . . an', an' I have stopped pickin' fights with folks . . .

MISS AMELIA: You still got that ear? You still got that ear you cut off that man in Cheehaw you fight? . . .

MARVIN MACY (*Embarrassed*): Oh, Miss Amelia, I never done that.

MISS AMELIA (*Disbelieving*): I *hear*.

MARVIN MACY: Oh, no, Miss Amelia, I never done that. I . . . I let that story pass 'round . . . but I never done that.

MISS AMELIA (*The slightest tinge of disappointment*): Oh. That so.

MARVIN MACY: So, you see, I have reformed my character.

MISS AMELIA (*Nods*): Would seem.
(*A long pause between them*)

MARVIN MACY: Yes.

MISS AMELIA: Land is good to have. I been dickerin' over near Society City to pick up thirty-five acres . . . timber, too . . . man there near broke, an' he wanna sell to me.

MARVIN MACY: Miss . . . Miss Amelia . . . (*Brings the ring from his pocket*) I brought somethin' else with me, too . . .

MISS AMELIA (*Curious*): Yeah?

MARVIN MACY: I . . . (*Shows it to her*) . . . I brought this silver ring.

MISS AMELIA (*Looks at it; hands it back*): It silver?

MARVIN MACY: Yep, it silver, Miss Amelia, will you . . .

MISS AMELIA: Bet it cost some.

MARVIN MACY (*Determined to get it out*): Miss Amelia, will you marry me?

MISS AMELIA (*After an interminable pause, during which she scratches her head, then her arm, then very off-hand*): Sure.

MARVIN MACY (*Almost not having heard*): You . . . Yes?! . . . You will?

MISS AMELIA (*Narrowing her eyes, almost unfriendly*): I said sure.

MARVIN MACY (*Not rising, begins sliding himself across the step to her*): Oh, Amelia . . .

MISS AMELIA (*Sharply*): What?

MARVIN MACY (*In a split second studies what he has said wrong, realizes it, keeps sliding*): Oh, *Miss* Amelia . . .
(*He reaches her, begins the gesture of putting one arm behind her back, the other in front, preparatory to kissing her. Miss Amelia reacts swiftly, leans back a bit, swings her right arm back, with a fist, ready to hit him*)

MISS AMELIA: Whoa there, you!

MARVIN MACY (*Retreats some, slides back a few feet*): Wait 'til I tell Henry; wait 'til I tell *everybody*. (*Very happy*) Oh, Miss Amelia.

MISS AMELIA (*Rises, stretches*): Well . . . g'night.
(*Marvin Macy, momentarily confused, but too happy to worry about it, rises also, backs down the porch steps, begins backing off*)

MARVIN MACY: G' . . . G' . . . G'night, Miss Amelia. (*Reaches the far side of the stage, then just before turning to run off, shouts*) G'night, Miss Amelia. (*Exits*)

MISS AMELIA (*Standing on the porch, alone; long pause*): G'night . . . (*Pause*) Marvin Macy.
(*Miss Amelia goes indoors*)

Enter Laughing (1963)

by JOSEPH STEIN

A lot of very funny people went into making this hilarious farce. Carl Reiner wrote the somewhat autobiographical novel, set in New York City in the mid 1930s. Joseph Stein adapted it, and Reiner returned to direct the Broadway production, which featured the warm and riotous Alan Arkin as David.

Enter Laughing is the story of a young man's journey beyond his parents' aspirations. They want him to be a druggist; he seeks the glamour of the theatre and joins a semi-professional band of hammy actors. In this scene, the impressionable David is swelled with romantic expectation as he enters into a flirtation with a young woman about his age. She is the daughter of the manager, an equally unschooled actress-seductress. They both feel they have the license to behave extravagantly because they are part of the sophisticated "theatre world." She plays the torturer and French charmer. He emerges from this timeless dressing room seduction scene closer to the Bronx druggist he scorns than the leading romantic actor he yearns to be.

Scene: Dressing room. Angela is seated at dressing ta-

ble taking off her makeup. She examines self in mirror. There is a knock on the door.

ANGELA: Entrez!
   (*David enters, with script in hip pocket*)

DAVID: Oh, I'm sorry. (*Closes door*)

ANGELA: How did you like the play, Don?

DAVID: Miss Marlowe, I thought it was great. I mean, very good acting and everything. You were great, your father was great, everybody was great.

ANGELA: You can turn around. I'm sure this isn't the first time you've been in a room where a girl was dressing, *n'est ce pas?*

DAVID: No, ma'am.

ANGELA: I thought not.

DAVID: I have a kid sister.

ANGELA: You are sweet. (*She rises, gets a stocking from light bracket and sits beside him. He rises*) What you're like, where you live, what you've done, everything. (*Pause*) Go! (*Rises, fastens stocking to garter*)

DAVID: Well— (*Pauses, watching her*) I was born in the Bronx, and I went to school there and I still live there. My mother and father want me to be a druggist, but—

ANGELA: But you don't want to be a druggist. Will you hand me that stocking? You want to be an actor. Why do you want to be an actor? (*She changes other shoe then rises and fastens other stocking to garter*)

DAVID (*Staring at what she's doing*): It's exciting. It's —everybody watches you. You're doing something, and everyone knows it and watches you. Nobody watches druggists, but no one *wants* to be one. But an actor—well, that's something to *want* to be!

ANGELA: Are you in love?

DAVID: You mean right now?

ANGELA: Yes.

DAVID: You mean, with you?

ANGELA: No, of course not. Unless you are. Are you?

DAVID: Well, I don't know. I mean, how can I tell? But I think you're very—glamorous and you know, beautiful.

ANGELA (*Gets dressing gown, puts it on and looks in mirror*) Good. Have you had a chance to study your lines? (*Sits on bench*)

DAVID: A little. . . . Your father told me I'll need a tuxedo suit for tomorrow night.

ANGELA: You could get a secondhand one for about ten dollars—

DAVID: Ten dollars?

ANGELA: Well, now, can I help you in any way?

DAVID: What do you mean?

ANGELA: With your part.

DAVID: Oh, the play. I only know a little of it so far. Just the front part of where he comes in and laughs.

ANGELA: Oh. Well, try to get it all by tomorrow. You just have two scenes, that one and the love scene with me . . . it shouldn't be too difficult.

DAVID: No, ma'am.

ANGELA: Besides, that second scene has very little dialogue.

DAVID: I know. It's mainly kissing.

ANGELA: I'm sure that won't be too hard.

DAVID: Oh, no, I'm a very good kisser.

ANGELA: I'm sure you are—I imagine you have a good many girl friends, *n'est-ce pas?*

DAVID: Oh, I'd say so. You want to rehearse something now?

ANGELA: If you like.

DAVID: You want to rehearse that kissing part?

ANGELA: Well, you are quite mature. And I was just thinking what a shy young thing you are. (*Looks in mirror, fixing hair*)

DAVID: Gee, Angela, I think you're a wonderful actress, and the most exciting person I ever met.

ANGELA: Well! *Merci beaucoup.* For that, you may kiss me.

DAVID: On the cheek?

ANGELA: Oui.
(*David kisses her right cheek*)

DAVID: Gee, Angela, you smell great. I don't think I ever smelled anybody who smelled so great.

ANGELA: Perfume and kisses, the language of love!

DAVID: You said it.

ANGELA: Though there is only one real way to express love.

DAVID: I know.

ANGELA: Everything else is superficial, shallow—

DAVID: That's what I think.

ANGELA (*Softly, takes David's hands in hers*): Poetry.

DAVID: What?

ANGELA: The language of the stars.

DAVID: You mean poems? Like Rudyard Kipling?

ANGELA (*Recites from memory, holding David's hands*):

> "If I were queen of pleasure,
> And you were king of pain,
> We'd hunt down love together,
> Pluck out his flying-feather,
> And teach his feet a measure,
> And find his mouth a rein;
> If I were queen of pleasure,
> And you were king of pain."

DAVID: You can say that again.

ANGELA: You do feel it, don't you? (*Seats him on stool at dressing table*)

DAVID: I certainly do.

ANGELA: But that's not the only way to show love.

DAVID: Of course not!

ANGELA: I know what you're thinking. Something more turbulent, more violent, more exciting.

DAVID: That's right. It's just what I was thinking.

ANGELA (*Yelling*):

> "I cried for madder music and for stronger wine,
> But when the feast is finished and the lamps expire,
> Then falls thy shadow, Cynara,
> The night is thine,
> And I am desolate and sick of an old passion,

Yea, hungry for the lips of my desire,
I have been faithful to thee, Cynara, in my fash-
    ion . . ."

DAVID: Who's Cynara?

ANGELA (*Taking off dressing gown*): I don't know, but
somehow I felt that you would love poetry as I do.
(*Hangs up gown, puts on dress*) The true emotion
caught in a web of song. *Le mot juste, le mot grand.*
. . . You are a dear, dear boy. (*Kisses him on cheek
and mouth*) Now I simply must be getting home.
(*Gets bag from floor and crosses to door*)

DAVID: Home? Now?

ANGELA: Yes, I'm frightfully tired. And you must be
too, it's quite late.

DAVID: No. I'm not tired. You sure you want me to
go home? Can't we rehearse?

ANGELA: I'll see you tomorrow. Till then, *bon soir*,
"good night, good night, parting is such sweet sor-
row."

DAVID (*Takes her hand*):
    "Though I've beaten you and flayed you,
      By the living God that made you,
      You're a better man than I am, Gunga Din!"

Hogan's Goat (1965)

by WILLIAM ALFRED

A verse play by an American author is very
infrequently come by, and the language of
this play is so evocative and beautiful that it
makes you joyous to read it—and, when
acted well, to hear it. William Alfred, playwright, poet, and Harvard professor, had
hesitated over this material for several years
until his good friend, Robert Lowell, urged it
out of his typewriter and onto my desk at the
American Place Theatre. It was clear from
the first scene that it was a moving drama of
American realities: the power and corruption
of our politics, the humiliation forced on our
immigrants, and their need for revenge. It is
also about the universal anguishes: love and
loneliness, religion and the pain of withdraw-
ing from it.

This scene opens the play and introduces us to the Stantons, the principal characters. Matt Stanton is the young Irish American politician, filled with charisma, wiles, and
political instinct. Like many immigrants, he
has suffered during his early years in this
country when he was forced to take any job
offered. He becomes the paramour of aging
Agnes Hogan and the lacky for the political
boss of Brooklyn. These violations of pride
give him the strength, the anger, and the determination to reshape his lot. He takes the

beautiful Kathleen as his wife. Her gentler
background, her finer ways, and the shame
that she expresses in this scene cause her
pain and despair that have become unbearable.

While the language is poetic, it requires
a fully-experienced reality in the playing. The
actors must find the rhythm, sound, and emotion inherent in each line and fuse them.
Kathleen's action in the scene is to give
Matt a deeper insight into the torment she's
been going through since they've been married. He is trying to placate her and make her
stay with him while he seizes his opportunity
to be Mayor.

Note that this scene contains two superb
monologues that can be used separately.

---

*Ten o'clock, the evening of Thursday, April 28, 1890.
The parlor of Matthew Stanton's flat on the second
floor of his house on Fifth Place, Brooklyn. The set
is on two levels, the lower level containing the kitchen
of the Haggertys, which is blacked out. To stage right
there is a steep, narrow staircase. Enter Matthew Stanton, carrying a bottle of champagne. He is a handsome,
auburn-haired man in his late thirties, dressed carefully
in a four-buttoned suit of good serge, and a soft black
hat. He bounds up the stairs and into his flat, and
throws his hat on a chair and hides the bottle of champagne behind the sofa. The furnishings of the room are
in period: the chairs are tufted and fringed, the mantel-
piece covered with a lambrequin, the window heavily
draped.*

STANTON: Katie? Katie! Where the devil are you?
 Come on out in the parlor.
 (*Enter Kathleen Stanton, closing the door behind
 her. She is tall and slim and dressed in a black*

broadcloth suit which brings out the redness of her
hair and the whiteness of her skin)

KATHLEEN: I wish you wouldn't take those stairs so
    fast;
    They're wicked: you could catch your foot and
    fall—
    I had a bit of headache and lay down.
    Why, Mattie darling, what's the matter with you?
    You're gray as wasps' nests.

STANTON: I'm to be the mayor!
    No more that plug who runs the Court Café
    And owes his ear to every deadbeat sport
    With a favor in mind and ten cents for a ball,
    But mayor of Brooklyn, and you the mayor's lady.
    They caught Ned Quinn with his red fist in the till,
    The Party of Reform, I mean, and we
    "Are going to beat their game with restitution
    And self-reform." Say something, can't you, Kate!
    (Kathleen sits down heavily, and puts her hand to
    her temple)

KATHLEEN: Oh, Mattie, Mattie.

STANTON: Jesus! Are you crying?
    I've what I wanted since I landed here
    Twelve years ago, and she breaks into tears.

KATHLEEN: It's that I'm—

STANTON: What? You're what?

KATHLEEN: Afraid.

STANTON: Kathleen, now please don't let's go into that
    again.

KATHLEEN: Would you have me tell you lies?

STANTON: I'd have you brave.
    (Kathleen rises angrily, and strides towards the bed-
    room)

Where are you going, Kate? To have a sulk?
Wait now, I'll fix a sugar teat for you,
Unless, of course, you'd rather suck your thumb,
Brooding in your room—

KATHLEEN: I have the name!
As well to have the game!

STANTON: It's riddles, is it?

KATHLEEN: Riddles be damned! You think me idiotic;
I might as well fulfill your good opinion—
(*Stanton walks towards her*)
Come near me, and I'll smash your face for you.
(*Stanton embraces her*)

STANTON: You're terrible fierce you are. I wet me
pants.

KATHLEEN: You clown, you'll spring my hairpins.
Mattie, stop.

STANTON: Are these the hands are going to smash my
face?
They're weak as white silk fans . . . I'm sorry, Kate:
You made me mad. And you know why?

KATHLEEN: I do. You're as afraid as I.

STANTON: I am. I am.
You know me like the lashes of your eye—

KATHLEEN: That's more than you know me, for if you
did,
You'd see what these three years have done to me—
(*Stanton breaks away from her*)
Now it's my turn to ask you where you're going.

STANTON: I begged you not to bring that up again.
What can I do?

KATHLEEN: You can tell Father Coyne,
And ask him to apply for dispensation,
And we can be remarried secretly.

STANTON: Now?

KATHLEEN: Yes, Matt, now. Before it is too late. We
aren't married.

STANTON: What was that in London,
The drunkard's pledge I took?

KATHLEEN: We're Catholics, Matt.
Since when can Catholics make a valid marriage
In a City Hall? You have to tell the priest—

STANTON: Shall I tell him now? Do you take me for
a fool.
To throw away the mayor's chair for that?

KATHLEEN: I slink to Sunday Mass like a pavement
nymph.
It's three years now since I made my Easter Duty,
Three years of telling Father Coyne that we
Receive at Easter Mass in the Cathedral,
Mortal Sin on Mortal Sin, Matt. If I died,
I'd go to Hell—

STANTON: I think the woman's crazy!

KATHLEEN: Don't you believe in God?

STANTON: Of course, I do.
And more, my dear, than you who think that He
Would crush you as a man would crush a fly
Because of some mere technical mistake—

KATHLEEN: Mere technical mistake? It's that now, is
it?
A blasphemous marriage, three years' fornication,
And now presumption— Technical mistake!
(*Kathleen takes a cigarette out of a box on the table
and lights it*)

STANTON: I wish you wouldn't smoke them cigarettes.
High-toned though it may be in France and En-
gland,
It's a whore's habit here. (*Pause*)

KATHLEEN: "Those cigarettes."
    Don't try to hurt me, Matt. You know you can,
    As I know I can you.

STANTON: What do you want!

KATHLEEN: I want to be your wife without disgrace.
    I want my honor back. I want to live
    Without the need to lie. I want you to keep faith.

STANTON: Not now! Not now!

KATHLEEN: You've said that for three years.
    What is it you're afraid of?

STANTON: Losing out.
    You do not know these people as I do.
    They turn upon the ones they make most of.
    They would on me, if given half a chance.
    And if it got around that we were married
    In an English City Hall, lose out we would.

KATHLEEN: Matt, losing out? What profit for a man
    To gain the world, and lose his soul?

STANTON: His soul!
    That's Sunday school! That's convent folderol,
    Like making half-grown girls bathe in their drawers
    To put the shame of their own beauty in them,
    And break their lives to bear the Church's bit.
    We are not priests and nuns, but men and women.
    The world religious give up is our world,
    The only world we have. We have to win it
    To do the bit of good we all must do;
    And how are we to win the world unless
    We keep the tricky rules its games are run by?
    Our faith is no mere monastery faith.
    It runs as fast as feeling to embrace
    Whatever good it sees. And if the good
    Is overgrown with bad, it still believes
    God sets no traps, the bad will be cut down,
    And the good push through its flowering to fruit.

Forget your convent school. Remember, Katie,
What the old women in the drowned boreens
Would say when cloudbursts beat their fields to
    slime,
And the potatoes blackened on their stalks
Like flesh gone proud. "Bad times is right," they'd
    say,
"But God is good: apples will grow again."
What sin have we committed? Marriage, Kate?
Is that a sin?

KATHLEEN: It is with us.

STANTON: Because
You feel it so. It isn't. It's but prudence.
What if they should make a scandal of us?

KATHLEEN: Could we be worse off than we are?

STANTON: Kathleen!

KATHLEEN: Could we be worse off than we are, I said?

STANTON: Could we! We could. You don't know pov-
    erty.
You don't know what it is to do without,
Not fine clothes only, or a handsome house,
But men's respect. I do. I have been poor.
"Mattie, will you run down to the corner,
And buy me some cigars" or "Mattie, get
This gentleman a cab." Nine years, I served
Ned Quinn and Agnes Hogan, day by day,
Buying my freedom like a Roman slave.
Will you ask me to put liberty at stake
To ease your scrupulous conscience? If you do,
You're not the woman that I took you for
When I married you. Have you no courage, Kate?

KATHLEEN: Will you lecture me on courage? Do you
    dare?
When every time I walk those stairs to the street
I walk to what I know is an enemy camp.

I was not raised like you. And no offense,
Please, Mattie, no offense. I miss my home.
Whore's habit it may be to smoke, as you say,
But it brings back the talk we used to have
About old friends, new books, the Lord knows
   what,
On our first floor in Baggot Street in Dublin.
This following you think so much about,
We live in Mortal Sin for fear you'll lose it,
I never knew the likes of them to talk to,
Person to person. They were cooks and maids,
Or peasants at the country houses, Matt.
All they can find to talk of, servants' talk,
Serfs' talk, eternal tearing down.
I'm like a woman banished and cut off.
I've you and May in the flat downstairs. That's all.
Don't tell me I don't know what poverty is.
What bankruptcy is worse than loneliness.
They say the sense of exile is the worst
Of all the pains that torture poor damned souls.
It is that sense I live with every day.

STANTON: Are you the only exile of us all?
You slept your crossing through in a rosewood berth
With the swells a hundred feet below your port-
   holes,
And ate off china on a linen cloth,
With the air around you fresh as the first of May.
I slept six deep in a bunk short as a coffin
Between a poisoned pup of a seasick boy
And a slaughtered pig of a snorer from Kildare,
Who wrestled elephants the wild nights through,
And sweated sour milk. I wolfed my meals,
Green water and salt beef, and wooden biscuits,
On my hunkers like an ape, in a four-foot aisle
As choked as the one door of a burning school.
I crossed in mid-December: seven weeks
Of driving rain that kept the hatches battened
In a hold so low of beam a man my height
Could never lift his head. And I couldn't wash.

Water was low; the place was like an icehouse;
And girls were thick as field mice in a haystack
In the bunk across. I would have died of shame,
When I stood in the landing shed of this "promised
   land,"
As naked as the day I first saw light,
Defiled with my own waste like a dying cat,
And a lousy red beard on me like a tinker's,
While a bitch of a doctor, with his nails too long,
Dared tell me: "In Amurrica, we bathe!"
I'd have died with shame, had I sailed here to die.
I swallowed pride and rage, and made a vow
The time would come when I could spit both out
In the face of the likes of him. I made a vow
I'd fight my way to power if it killed me,
Not only for myself, but for our kind,
For the men behind me, laughing out of fear,
At their own shame as well as mine, for the women,
Behind the board partition, frightened dumb
With worry they'd be sent back home to starve
Because they'd dirty feet. I was born again.
It came to me as brutal as the cold
That makes us flinch the day the midwife takes
Our wet heels in her fist, and punches breath
Into our dangling carcasses: Get power!
Without it, there can be no decency,
No virtue and no grace. I have kept my vow.
The mayor's chair is mine but for the running.
Will you have me lose it for your convent scruples?
(*Pause*)

KATHLEEN: You never told me that about your landing.

STANTON: There's many things I never told you, Kate.
   I was afraid you'd hold me cheap.

KATHLEEN: Oh, Mattie,
   Don't you know me yet?

STANTON: Stand by me.

Stand by me, Kate. The next four days count hard.
By Sunday next, I'll have won all or lost.

KATHLEEN: What's Sunday next?

STANTON: The Clambake for Quinn's birthday:
We're to make things up between us and make the
   announcement
On the steamer voyage to Seagate Sunday evening.
Stand by me, Kate. As sure as God's my judge
The minute I get into City Hall
The first thing I will do is call the priest,
And ask him to make peace with God for us.
Stand by me, Kate.

KATHLEEN: I will though it costs my life.

The Journey of the Fifth Horse (1965)

by RONALD RIBMAN

The Journey of the Fifth Horse is set in mid-nineteenth-century Russia and is based, in part, on the "Diary of a Superfluous Man" by Ivan Turgenev. It is a play to read for its haunting personal revelations, for its remarkable architecture, and for its exquisite language. Read it aloud and savour it.

Chulkaturin is the "superfluous man," the unnecessary "fifth horse." Friendless and deeply lonesome, he becomes bored during a stay in a rural town and decides to call on Illya, an acquaintance from college. Illya is abroad, and he has clearly never mentioned Chulkaturin to his sister Liza. But Chulkaturin falls in love with Liza at first glance. She too has been living an isolated and confined life and is prey to any contact.

The scene that follows is in the wooded area of a large park. While on a walk with her parents, Liza runs off with Chulkaturin in pursuit. She is exhilarated and filled with romantic fantasies. She wants Chulkaturin to be her "King of the May" or some other fairytale figure. He cannot fulfill the role, his feelings remain locked within him, and he can only make absurd attempts at prosaic conversation. Liza's reverie ends; her only

> release is to reprimand him ironically and pour out her frustrations. The encounter has come to nothing.

Sound of Liza's laughter is heard. Liza bursts out into the open and whirls herself around. Chulkaturin appears and watches her as she is lost in her reveries. She spirals to the ground. For a long moment she remains on the floor of the forest as Chulkaturin stares at her.

Liza, resting on her extended arm, slowly opens her eyes and stares at Chulkaturin. The moment is poignant and Chulkaturin breaks the mood abruptly by striding forward in cheerful embarrassment.

CHULKATURIN (*A bit too loud*): Well, you see you have fallen. That's what you get for running so fast. Come. Let me help you up.
(*Extends his hand to her. She looks at him for a moment and then turns away. He drops his hand*)

LIZA: I'm all right. Please, just a moment.

CHULKATURIN (*Stands by her, uneasily feeling that something should be said but not knowing, or rather not daring, to say what is in his heart. Instead, he makes conversation*): I suppose they will be wondering what happened to us. I cannot imagine how we came to be separated from your parents. (*Pause in which there is no answer*) Well, we've certainly taken our exercise for the day. If the summer continues at such a pace we shall all be in fine health. I haven't run this far since my father raced me in the meadows of Lambswater. (*Pause. Change of tone. Serious*) You grow older you run less.

LIZA (*Suddenly turning to him*): You think it was childish of me to run?

CHULKATURIN: No. No, I didn't mean to imply that.

LIZA: Well, it was. Perhaps it will be a long time before I run again. (*Her mood changes from seriousness to fresh exuberance*) Come. Sit down beside me. (*Extending her hand to him as he had before to her*)

CHULKATURIN: We ought to sit on the bench. Your dress is going to be covered with grass stains.

LIZA (*She drops her hand as he, before, had dropped his. She becomes thoughtful for a second and then that passes and she smiles again, playfully*): If you make me sit on the bench, I shall fold my hands in my lap and not allow you to become what you should become.

CHULKATURIN: And what is that?

LIZA: What do you think that is?

CHULKATURIN: I don't know.

LIZA: Guess.

CHULKATURIN: I can't.

LIZA: Then you shan't become it. (*She plays with the wildflowers*)

CHULKATURIN: Tell me.

LIZA: What would you like to become?

CHULKATURIN: I don't know.

LIZA: Poor Nikolai Alexeevich Chulkaturin doesn't know what he would like to become. Shall I be kind and tell you, then? (*Pause, and she breaks into a smile*) King of the May! The king of all the hearts of young ladies. Here and now I shall give you your new identity. But you must kneel properly and lower your head. Come. On your knees, or else I shall be forced to find another to be King of the May and you shall have lost your identity for good. Don't dally. Shall you be crowned or not? (*There is a mo-*

*ment in which they look at each other directly in the
eyes, and then Chulkaturin goes on his knees and
lowers his head. She begins putting the wildflowers in
his hair*) What fine silky hair you have, Nikolai
Alexeevich. Have there been many young ladies who
have loved you for your fine brown hair?

CHULKATURIN: There has been no one.

LIZA: Perhaps you have forgotten them. The woods are
full of the sighs of young girls. I think there must
be many girls you have loved and forgotten.

CHULKATURIN: Do not think that there have been others.

LIZA: You must hold still. If you raise your head the
flowers will fall.

CHULKATURIN: There has been no one who has loved
me. Do not think that of me.

LIZA: I think men must be very cruel creatures to play
with the heart of a girl and then not even remember
her name. Men are like that according to my brother.
(*She laughs*)

CHULKATURIN: Why do you laugh?

LIZA: Illya says that the hearts of young girls are strewn
about the world like grains of sand upon the shore
and that there are not as many stars in the night
sky as unremembered girls. Do you think that is true?

CHULKATURIN: I think that is poetic.

LIZA: And is that the same as true? What is your answer
to that, Nikolai Alexeevich who has fine silky hair?

CHULKATURIN: You are making fun of me.

LIZA (*Stops as if suddenly wearied*): Yes.
(*She stands up and turns to face the sun*)

CHULKATURIN: Have I offended you?

LIZA: No.

CHULKATURIN: Then what is the matter? Why are you staring into the sun?

LIZA: Must I have reasons for everything? Is it not enough reason to stare at the sun because it is up there, because it is flaming across the sky, because we may never see the light again, because, because, because, because. (*The mood becomes a trifle lighter as if she attempted to recover*) Have I found enough "becauses" to satisfy you? (*He is hurt. She reaches out to him, sincerely*) Poor Nikolai, it is I who have offended you. Am I completely intolerable to be with?

CHULKATURIN (*As he stands up, the flowers fall off his head*): No. You cannot offend me. How could you ever think that you . . .

LIZA: See how soon every flower must fall. (*Brushing her hand through his hair to dislodge the other flowers*) Every flower. Don't be angry with me, ever, Nikolai. (*She takes his hands in hers and kisses them. Chulkaturin bends down to kiss her, but she almost flippantly turns away*) Papa thinks young girls should be placed in hibernation along with Siberian Mastodons until we become eighteen years old, then we are to be melted from the ice and returned to our homes in time for marriage. Isn't that terribly clever of papa?
(*She begins to cry*)

CHULKATURIN: Liza, why are you crying?

LIZA: Isn't that terribly clever. I suppose I should take my dear bullfinch to sing to me in the ice and . . .

CHULKATURIN: What is wrong? Please don't cry. Please, Liza, Liza. Please! (*She turns her back to Chulkaturin and, bowing her head, runs off. Chulkaturin picks up the fallen flowers*)

FROM **The Loveliest Afternoon of the Year** (1966)

by JOHN GUARE

Like many playwrights today, John Guare
takes his audience on a free-wheeling trip,
a merry-go-round of associative writing
whose sudden and unexpected turns reveal
the absurdity of contemporary living. His wild
sense of humor has terror at its base, and although his characters are capable of loving,
they are always dominated by violence.

This early short play is presented here
in its entirety. In it, the character He says,
"Everything I say is true." John Guare means
that. The actors should have such faith in the
truth of everything they say that it involves
the audience, pulls them in not just as
witnesses but as part of the world of the
play. Audience involvement is aided by pass-
ages that address them directly.

Play the scene as if you're on a condemned roller coaster—unaware of the peril
but speeding toward it. Underneath is the
desperation that comes from living in the
contemporary world. And yet the actors
mustn't let the loneliness that motivates them
sap the bouyancy of the playing. Move along
rapidly with the dialogue without pauses for
introspection.

Calliope music plays and fades as the curtain rises. A shy young girl sits feeding pigeons in the park for want of anything better to do. Autumn day. Crisp air: the kind called invigorating. A young man enters in a panic, sees her, gasps.

HE: I wish you wouldn't feed the pigeons! (*She freezes*) Please. I wish you wouldn't feed the pigeons . . .

SHE: Huh?

HE: I wouldn't mind you feeding—

SHE (*Stands up, clutching her purse*): Are you a mugger?

HE: —the pigeons —No! I'm not a mugger. I'm just trying to tell you—

SHE: Because if you are a mugger, I'll scream. I'll have those cops after you so quick—

HE: I am trying to tell you—

SHE (*A warning whisper*): I love to scream. I have a very loud voice.

HE: I don't believe that.

SHE (*Rummaging in her purse*): Where is my tear gas gun?

HE: I don't want you feeding pigeons because I just saw pigeons at the Seventy-ninth Street entrance and the covey of them—the whole bunch of them—whatever you call a bunch of pigeons—a gaggle—all those pigeons had *foam*— (*She stops rummaging through her purse*) Were foaming at the mouths.

SHE: I'll scream.

HE: At the *beaks?* Pigeons were foaming at the beaks —all of them.

SHE: Who the hell are you?

HE: I'm very hungry and hate to see you feeding pigeons when I'm hungry. A Crackerjack at this point would be a feast.

SHE: I don't believe you.

HE (*Sits on bench*): You're very perceptive. I—actually, it's the birthday of this child and I promised this child a present and I know at the bottom of that box *is* a present and I was wondering if you'd let me have it. (*She's shocked. She swings her bag at him. He ducks to protect himself*) The present! The little plastic present . . .

SHE: Buddy, I bet you got more money in the silk change pocket of that fancy sport coat of yours than I got in my whole imitation alligator bag.

HE (*Stands up*): That's not true! My wife takes all my money and she bends it in her teeth so I can't use it. I have to walk everywhere because she bends all my subway tokens. And she has a blue rifle with a silencer on it and shoots my feet so I have to dance this crazy darting dance whenever I come in late. (*A moment of silence. She bursts out laughing and hands him the Crackerjack*) Please? Believe me? Everything I say is true. Please don't laugh. (*She is so happy. He eats Crackerjacks nervously. He finds a plastic ring in the box.*)

SHE: I have been in this city eleven months now and you are the first person I've spoken to. That's spoken to me. Eleven months of silence—till now. I feel like I've just been released from a convent—a goddam convent. No, I'm not laughing at you. I'm a young girl and I'm pretty and nobody ever speaks to me —not even to ask directions—and you're the funniest man I've ever met and I thank you in all the languages there are. Thank you for speaking to me.

HE: Everything I've said is true! (*He turns to go. She touches his arm*)

SHE: Oh god—please? Don't leave. (*He turns to her. They look at each other. He puts the Crackerjack under the bench and slips the plastic ring on her finger. She looks at it. Then at him. A shy kiss that turns into a long kiss. Then they both turn joyously out front to us in the audience*)

HE: And that's how we met two Sundays ago. And we walk in the park. This is the third Sunday we've met now. We talk about the future . . . (*They walk in place, their arms locked. They are lovers. They talk to us in the audience*)

SHE: It's autumn and orange and green and blue and yellow leaves are all over the ground and our feet make a scuffing noise like this . . . chh chh chh . . .

HE: And when we get home, our socks have orange and green and blue and yellow leaf shreds in them stuck in the wool.

SHE: Now wait—his socks and his home. I wear nylons and I have my apartment and he doesn't know where I live and I don't know where he lives. He has his life and I have mine.

HE: Except for Sunday. Today. We walk along and talk about the future. We never mention the past. And our feet make a scuffing noise like this . . . chh chh chh . . .

SHE: Now wait, just because we don't talk about the past, don't get the idea I'm any slut or something. I'm just an Ohio girl. O-H-Ten. You only talk about the past when you have a past. (*Embarrassed smile*) I must remember not to wear this sweater any more Sundays.

HE: I think she still thinks I'm a mugger.

SHE: I spent all last Monday picking these long shreds of dead grass out of the back of my sweater with a silver tweezer. Oh, I don't care if he's a mugger or not!!! I'm not going to take any chances, no siree, like meeting him at night or during the week when there's nobody around. But Sundays are okay—and, mugger or not—I like him very much. He's really an odd person—an odd duck. But he does tell me awfully funny stories. Hey, tell me a funny story.

HE: They're not funny stories. They're true!

SHE (*To audience*): True! Listen to this one, please. We're in the Zoo near the polar bear cage. Now I have never seen a polar bear. Hey, look at the polar bear! (*She reaches out to touch it through the bars*)

HE (*Violently pulling her back*): Don't do that!!!!

SHE: I never saw a polar bear, for God's sake. It won't kill me.

HE: Won't kill you! Listen, ten years ago, my sister Lucy was a top debutante—

SHE: Really?

HE: And after her coming-out party at the Hotel Plaza back there, Lucy and her two escorts broke into this part of the Zoo and Lucy stuck her arm into this cage—this very cage—just as you did now before I stopped you. And this polar bear— (*He follows the polar bear with an accusing finger. Three count beat*) No, I don't think it was *this* polar bear—this one doesn't look familiar—But the polar bear—the one ten years ago—bit my sister Lucy's arm right off at the *breast!* (*He turns away covering his face*)

SHE: OMIGOD!

HE: And we heard her screams clear over to the Plaza and the doctors came and we all had to leave the coming-out party. I was very young—well, eighteen—

SHE: What did they do?

HE: My parents shrieked, "Do something, do something," and the doctors and all the ambulances which came (*Pantomimes dramatically*) pulled Lucy's arm out of the polar bear's mouth and quickly sewed it back on. Modern surgery can do things like that.

SHE: What happened?—Omigod!!!!

HE: The arm grew back—thank God—but Lucy never went to another coming-out party again.

SHE: Boy, I can see why not.

HE: Because enormous amounts of—she developed all over her body—enormous amounts of white polar bear hair and for her comfort we had to ship her to Alaska in a cage.

SHE: You're putting me on.

HE: You're from Ohio. You come from a nice little family. You don't understand the weirdness, the grief that people can spring from—

SHE: You're the oddest duck I have ever met.

HE: Ducks! You stay away from ducks. I can tell you a story about my aunt—

SHE (*Hands over her ears*): Please. I don't want to hear anymore stories. We said we'd just talk about the future.

HE: The future! If you came from a past like I have— such as mine—the idea of riding—galloping into a future which would ultimately turn into past would make you break out in hives and your hair would fall out.

SHE (*Backs away from him*): Well, it won't fall out and if you keep on talking like that, I'll go home and wash it and massage it and make sure—damn good and sure—that it doesn't fall out. So let's just walk in silence and— (*She extends her hand. He takes it. They walk in place. They smile at each other, remembering they are lovers*) Listen, do you hear that merry-go-round? I always like calliope music. Isn't that what they call it?

HE: Yes. They run on steam. My father fell in one and was scalded to death.

SHE (*Stops walking*): Please . . . let's just walk and sing. (*They stroll arm in arm. The tune is "Over the Waves." They both hum as they stroll*) Do you really have a wife?

HE: Shhhhh . . .

SHE (*Over his humming*): That's one story you told me I wonder if it's true. You told me your wife had a blue rifle with a silencer on it and shot you in the feet if you came in late. You told me that three weeks ago. I hope you don't have a wife. I'd hate it if you had a wife.

HE: Since I met you, I don't have a wife.

SHE: Are you divorced?

HE: No.

SHE: But you do have a wife?

HE: No.

SHE (*Laughing, snuggling up to him*): At least not a wife who carries a blue rifle and shoots you if you come in late.

HE (*Stops their walking and turns to her*): I have no wife. Listen, since I met you—these last three Sundays—the last three weeks have had music. I don't mean all violins and trombones. I mean I've been conscious of the rhythm in people's walking, the music in the turning of the turnstiles in the subway at rush hour.

SHE (*Pulling his hands away*): I thought you said your wife bent your subway tokens so you couldn't go anywhere.

HE: I don't have a wife and I sneak under the turnstiles. You've saved my life. I've never picked anybody else up before but something about you—the way you fed those pigeons—I wanted to know you, and now . . . now it looks like I'd better thank you. (*She smiles, puzzled. He sits her on the bench and kneels in front of her. Both are in profile to the audience. He begins to sing loudly and sweetly to her to the tune of "Over the Waves"*)

> You knelt and you fed
> Little pigeons sweet pieces of bread

(*She takes a long embarrassed look out to audience. He continues singing*)

> Those pigeons could kill
> Or at least make you feel very ill

SHE (*Over his singing*): What do you mean—thanking me? Is this the last time? Aren't I going to see you anymore? Don't *sing* so loud!

HE (*Lost in the romance of his song*):
> We saved both our lives
> Which should lead to husbands and wives

SHE: People are staring at you! Please, tell me—why are you thanking me? (*He's lost in his song. She beats him on the chest to get his attention*)

> But since we must part
> Feed the pigeon that cries in my heart

SHE: Are you leaving me?

HE:
Pigeons that (*Changes key three tones higher*) cry in my heart!

(*He stops singing suddenly. He stands up. Pause. Quietly*) I can't marry you. I can't see you during the week. I owe you something at least for all the music. Maybe we could meet a few times during the year. Bump into each other? Do you like that song?

SHE: I don't give a damn about that song.

HE: Do you know who sang that song?

SHE: I don't care who sang that song.

HE: Mario Lanza . . . and right after he sang it, he grew very fat and died. And then a few months later, his wife took drugs and she died too. Now that's true. You can read that in the newspapers.

SHE: So it's all off . . .

HE: Do you know what my job is? I've never told you.

SHE: So I'll spend the rest of my life feeding pigeons in the park. Maybe I'll meet somebody else . . .

HE: I'm a seeing-eye person for blind dogs. And that's very ironic. Because you've made me see so many things—to hear music in those subway turnstiles at rush hour . . .

SHE (*Seeing something in the distance*): Maybe it's just as well . . .

HE: And I've made you see nothing. (*He turns away*)

SHE: I want to be married. I like you. I'd like to be married to you . . . but I see people like her over there—that incredibly fat woman pushing those two —yes, two—incredibly fat children in that bright blue perambulator with that dog on the leash, and I say what's the use of being married. It obviously didn't make her happy . . . what's the good of marriage?

HE (*Crossing back to her and peering over her shoul-*

der, holding his breath): What incredibly fat woman?

SHE: You can't see her now. She just passed behind that rock. Why fall in love with anybody? You just get hurt. I'm young. I'm pretty. I don't need anybody (*He suddenly crouches down behind her, holding her legs, peeking out from around her hips*) What are you doing?

HE: That woman—what did you say she was pushing?

SHE: A bright blue perambulator with two enormous young . . . that's—that's your wife, isn't it? You weren't fooling . . .

HE: And what did you say she had on a leash?

SHE (*Squinting to see them in the distance*): A dog . . . a great Great Dane and look—it just bumped its head into that tree and she yanks it back and it falls down against a bench.

HE: The dog has no eyes, has it?

SHE: The dog has no eyes and the children are so ugly and your wife—you have to go home to that every night? (*He stands up and crosses to the bench*)

HE: We work together. Dogs that can see bite her. (*He sits down on the bench, back to audience*) Oh, I can't divorce her. You can divorce a pretty wife for a homely one, but you can't switch an ugly one for a beautiful one. (*She crosses to him and faces him hesitantly*)

SHE: Am I beautiful.

HE: You're very beautiful.

SHE: I really love you.

HE (*Pulls her down beside him*): Don't let her see us.

Under those two babies, she carries the blue rifle with the silencer on it. She'd shoot us if she saw us together.

SHE: And would that be any worse than you leaving me, me leaving you, you going back to her, me going back to my empty apartment? (*She turns away from him*) The last tenant left hundreds of murder mysteries and I'm afraid to read them. (*He turns her to him*)

HE: My wife's name is Maud. I'm going to call her. (*He kisses her. He stands up, calling*) Maud?

SHE (*Stands beside him, calls quietly*): Hey, Maud?

HE (*Louder*): Maud? Maud!

SHE (*Louder*): Hey, Maud!!!!

HE: She sees us! She's seen us! Hey, Maud! (*She kisses him all over his face so Maud will see, all the time they both keep waving and jumping up and down*)

SHE: Look! She's lifting the babies out and throwing them on the ground!

HE: The dog rears up and here comes the blue rifle. Hang on.
(*She is shot by the rifle with the silencer. She clutches her stomach in amazement. He is shot. They fall onto the bench, leaning over it, their knees almost on the ground*)

SHE (*Tapping him on the shoulder*): Hey, you really do have a sister Lucy, don't you.

HE (*In pain*): I do. (*They reach for each other, but both fall dead on either side of the bench. When their bodies hit the ground—*)
(*Blackout*)

La Turista (1966)

by SAM SHEPARD

Sam Shepard is our literary Yankee Doodle,
our Jesse James of letters, our Cowboy
Mouth. He speaks of and for the 60s generation which pushed itself out of bourgeois ag-
gression and failure, which ran itself ragged
on drugs and tripping out, which braced itself
for a life of inaction, terror, and disappointment. He is so accurate a sociologist, so pre-
cise a lexicographer, so connected a person that he has made art and history out of
a generation on the brink of the precipice.

La Turista (the first of three Shepard
plays produced at the American Place Theatre) is about the disappearance of the white
race: peeling away or burning up from sun-
burn, draining away from dysentery, sleeping away from drugs or sleeping sickness,
disappearing into death. Everything in the
play germinates from this central idea or
metaphor. Having said that, let me also say
that the situation in the play is real, beginning with a young married couple, Salem and
Kent (toxic cigarette brands), on vacation
in a poor Mexican town. Covered with sun-
burn, they sit up stiffly in their motel twin
beds, conversing in the cool deflated tone
of people tired of this world. Kent is afflicted
with the additional touristic malady, diarrhea.
Shepard himself has suggested, "The

term 'character' could be thought of in a different way when working on this play. Instead of the idea of a 'whole character' with logical motives behind his behavior which the actor submerges himself into, consider instead a fractured whole with bits and pieces of character flying off the central theme. In other words, more in terms of collage construction or jazz improvisation." Do not search for moment to moment motivation with Shepard. The actors should immerse themselves in the central need of these people to escape, to disappear, to "trip out"; they will find the playful, free, associative nature and energy of the roles and the play.

Two single beds with clean white sheets and pillows upstage center. Salem, a woman in panties and bra, sits on the stage left bed propped up with a pillow, facing the audience and reading Life *magazine. Kent, a man in underwear, sits in the same position on the stage right bed reading* Time *magazine. Both Salem and Kent have bright red skin. They continue reading as they talk.*

SALEM: The woman in—where was it? Puerto Juarez or something. The very rich Spanish woman. Remember? The young woman with her mother who spoke such good English. Very rich.

KENT: What did she say?

SALEM: She said the white of an egg is what you use for second- or third-degree burns. The pain is eased right away. What happens when the skin is burned? I mean what actually happens?

KENT: Well, the epidermis is actually cooked, fried like a piece of meat over a charcoal fire. The molecular structure of the fatty tissue is partially destroyed by the sun rays, and so the blood rushes to the surface to repair the damage.

SALEM: So your skin doesn't really turn red like magic, it's just the blood rushing to the surface.

KENT: Right.

SALEM: So Mexicans aren't really tan, are they. They just have darker skin, tougher skin with a tighter fatty molecular structure.

KENT: I think that's an anthropological argument now, where some say the dark-skinned people of the earth were born that way to begin with for camouflage reasons to protect them against death, and others say it was to protect them against the sun.

SALEM: It doesn't make much difference.

KENT: No. But the sun theory seems to make more sense. Well no, I guess the death theory makes more sense since Islandic people, people who live in snowy places, have light skin to match the snow. So I guess it has to do with camouflage, since camouflage has to do with deceiving death.

SALEM: What about Eskimos.

KENT: Eskimos are more on the yellow side, aren't they? More Mongoloid. Eskimos aren't really dark.

SALEM: Well, Mexicans are more Mongoloid than Negroid and you call them dark.

KENT: That's true. (*Kent jumps to his feet and starts for door and then stops short*)

SALEM: Que paso!

KENT: I started to feel it coming and then it stopped. I don't know whether it's coming or stopping.

SALEM: Que turista! No!

KENT: Speak English, will you. (*He starts again for the door and stops*)

SALEM: Is it dysentery?

KENT: I don't know. It starts and stops.

SALEM (*Like a nurse*): Cramps in the stomach?

KENT: Slight ones.

SALEM: Nausea?

KENT: Slight.

SALEM: Rumbling in the bowels?

KENT: A little.

SALEM: Esta turista? (*Kent starts to run for the door and stops again*)

KENT: You sound glad or something.

SALEM: No. Yo es muy simpatico.

KENT: We both ate the same food, you know, so you'll be getting it soon too.

SALEM: My metabolism is very high.
(*Kent returns to the bed, picks up the magazine, and continues to read*)

KENT: Relaxation is the thing you seek. You spend thousands of hours and dollars and plane rides to get to a place for relaxation. To just disappear for a while. And you wind up like this. With diarrhea.

SALEM: You came here to disappear?

KENT: That's right. Didn't you? To relax and disappear.

SALEM: What would you do if you did disappear?

KENT: Nothing. I'd be gone.

SALEM: I ask you that face to face. It deserves to be answered.

KENT: Do you know how soon it is before you can start peeling it?

SALEM: Not before it's dead, I can tell you that much. Right now it stings. That means it's alive and hurting. Pretty soon it itches. Then you know it's dying. Then it stops itching and you know it's dead. Then you can start peeling. Not before.

KENT: You can start peeling as soon as it begins to itch. I know that much. That's when you itch so you scratch it and that gets you peeling.

SALEM: You can't start before the itching stops.

KENT: Why not? You could even start while it's still stinging if you wanted. You could even start before it starts stinging and get a head start.

SALEM: And then really get burned. You'd be in sad shape then, boy.

KENT: Then you start peeling again.

SALEM: There's only three layers, you know. It doesn't go on forever.

KENT: Obviously you've never heard of the fourth-degree burn. A fourth-degree burn is unheard of because it's never happened, but one day it will, and doctors will be dismayed from coast to coast, and a new word will be born into their language. *The Fourth-Degree Burn!*

SALEM: What is it like! What is it like!
(*Kent rises on his bed and demonstrates for her*)

KENT: The fourth-degree burn comes about after the most extreme and excruciating process has taken its course. The first degree has already occurred and a layer has dropped away almost of its own accord. Effortlessly it floats to the floor at your feet and piles around your ankles like sheets of Kleenex. The second degree comes with a little more shock and a little more pain. It scrapes off like dust and covers the sheets.

SALEM: And now for the third!

KENT: Yes! But the third takes time. The third begins slowly and creeps along the surface, grabbing hold and easing up. Biting down and relaxing away until the spaces get fewer and the biting gets harder. Everything burns and everything you touch is as hot as the sun. You stand away from everything else. You stand in mid-air with space all around you. The ground is on fire. The breeze feels like boiling-hot water. The moon is just like the sun. You become a flame and dance in mid-air. The bottom is blue. The middle is yellow and changes to green. The top is red and changes to orange. The breeze dances with you. The flame reaches up and then shrinks and bursts into sparks. The ground bursts into flame and circles the breeze. The sparks dart through the breeze and dash back and forth hitting up against the flames, and——

(*The door opens, and a dark-skinned boy, but not Negro, enters with bare feet and carrying a shoe-shine kit. Both Salem and Kent scream and pull the top sheet of their beds over their bodies so just their heads are sticking out. The boy crosses in between the beds and just stares at them with his hand out.*)

FROM # The Carpenters (1970)

by STEVE TESICH

The Carpenters, which was first produced at the American Place Theatre, is one of the few plays dealing with the "generation gap" that does not collapse into inane and easy characterizations and solutions. As Richard Schotter says in an introduction to this work, "What distinguishes *The Carpenters* is Tesich's wry detachment and gentle irony, his very human and playful sense of the absurdity about 'togetherness' and mutual understanding. There are no villains . . . and no heroes either, only bemused human beings attempting to live together in peaceful coexistence by clinging tenaciously to familiar roles and illusions."

The play shows the crumbling of these fictions, leaving the members of the family disillusioned, frustrated, and trapped. Son Mark has returned from school (he has been thrown out) to bring home the truth about this family. Father is convinced that Mark has put a bomb in the cellar to blow up their home. Father believes that his life's purpose is to protect his home and his family, while they are convinced that *he* is the destroyer.

Mother and Father have several scenes in which the events are of little importance, but underneath their small talk is an immense amount of pain and hostility. Mother contains it; she is so blunted or dead that she reveals nothing. Another son, Waldo, says of her: "Keeping it all in, right, Ma? You just go around the house saying stuff like dinner's ready and lunch's on the table and keeping everything else in. . . . My mother's a balloon and my father's so full of hot air that one of these days, my mother'll blow up from it."

This scene must be played realistically. The dialogue, the situation, and the character's attitudes take care of the absurdity.

FATHER: I don't understand it . . . I just don't understand it.

MOTHER: What is it, dear?

FATHER: If you'd take your head out of that pot for a second you might be able to tell what it is . . . dear. My own son, our own son, our flesh and blood, is planning to kill me . . . planning to blow me up and you ask what is it.

MOTHER: How's he going to blow you up, dear?

FATHER: How? With a bomb, that's how.

MOTHER: What kind of bomb?

FATHER: What's that got to do with it? You want the color? It's a red bomb with a nasty black trim. It was in the basement this morning.

MOTHER: Why didn't you throw it out?

FATHER: It's not a bag of garbage, you know. I didn't know what to do with it. I went to look for it now and it was gone. I have no idea where it is now. It could be right here for all I know.

MOTHER: There's no bomb here.

FATHER: How do you know?

MOTHER: I just cleaned house and if there was a bomb anywhere I would have seen it.

FATHER: I really don't think you understand a thing. Not a thing.

MOTHER: I understand.

FATHER: If you understood you wouldn't be there peeling potatoes. What do I have to do to get it into your head that your son's planning to blow up the house?

MOTHER: If he was going to blow up the house I'd know about it.

FATHER: But you do know about it.

MOTHER: No, I don't.

FATHER: I just told you. What? I don't count. My word's no good. You have to hear it on the TV before you believe it.

MOTHER: No . . . it's just that I'd know about it. Nothing's happened here for so long that if something was going to happen I'd know about it. Remember . . . when you thought you had cancer and I said you didn't . . . that if you did I'd know about it . . . well, you didn't.

FATHER: You know what you're doing? . . . You're holding it against me for not having had cancer. Every time I say something you use that cancer business to prove me wrong. In order to be right I'd have to be dead. I'll tell you one thing, I'd rather die of cancer than have my own son kill me.

MOTHER: He's not going to kill you, dear.

FATHER: You're all on his side. You think I can't tell? I can tell. Everyone's taking sides all of a sudden and ole dad just isn't good enough anymore.

MOTHER: Nobody's taking sides, dear.

FATHER: No, of course not. They've already taken them.

MOTHER: It just seems like that to you because you're not used to being home during the day. If you went to work and came home tired like you always did you wouldn't worry about bombs and what not.

FATHER: Work! Work! I've been working for twenty-five years . . . a quarter of a century . . . when am I supposed to rest and spend some time with the family?

MOTHER: On weekends.

FATHER: I hate weekends. . . . I hate them . . . why can't I stay home during the week for a change?

MOTHER: Because we're not used to having you. Don't think I'm being harsh, dear, but it's really quite uncomfortable to have you around the house on weekdays. Usually I like to lie down during this time . . .

FATHER: Well go ahead. Lie down!

MOTHER: It's hard to lie down with you walking around the house.

FATHER: I'll lie down with you.

MOTHER: We tried that and it doesn't work.

FATHER: Now what the hell's that supposed to mean? If you think that I still can't . . . if you're trying to blame me . . .

MOTHER: You see? It's just uncomfortable. You're not tired enough. Waldo likes to pretend he's a bird or something and he's afraid you'll call him a retard if he does. Sissy and Mark . . . they'd like to do certain things and they can't because of you. We've had a nice comfortable schedule all these years and now nobody knows what to do because you're home all day long.

FATHER: Just pretend I'm not at home.

MOTHER: We can't do that, dear.

FATHER: Why not? Just pretend I'm not here.

MOTHER: If we pretended you weren't here you'd feel left out.

FATHER: We're all going crazy. Here I'm bickering with you and I completely forgot that there's a bomb in the house somewhere.

MOTHER: I told you you'd get used to it.

FATHER: You mean you knew all along it was here?

MOTHER: No, I still think there's nothing to worry about but even if there was you'd get used to it. It's only human nature.

FATHER: I feel like hitting you on the head. You know that? I feel like hitting you on the head with that pan.

MOTHER: Don't bother yourself, dear. Something hit me on the head long ago and I haven't felt a thing since. Let's just try to live the best we can.

FATHER: We can't live like this. Things have to change.

MOTHER: I think it'd be better if they stopped changing. Everything was fine until you changed the schedule.

FATHER: You don't understand a thing I'm telling you. My own son is planning to kill me.

MOTHER: If you really think he's got a bomb you should call the police.

FATHER: Call the police! Those idiots! What the hell do they know? Did they build my house? Did they raise my family? They know nothing about me. If they were so smart they'd find a way of keeping bombs from blowing up their stations. Call the police! Hand my son over to them! Never!

MOTHER: But you said he was trying to kill you.

FATHER: What's that got to do with police? I'll handle it in my own way. I don't care if I die but if you think I'm just going to stand by and let my own son commit a patricide, you're crazy. No policeman's going to come into my house. I'll not have strangers doing my work for me. That's what's brought us to this state . . . professionals. Whenever something comes up . . . call a pro. Instead of calling on each other we call them, and they don't know shit!

MOTHER: You're using foul language. What if Waldo hears you?

FATHER: If it takes foul language to get Waldo on my side I'll use foul language. Whatever it takes . . . I'll do it.

MOTHER: I think you should go to work and cool off.

FATHER: I am going to work. I'm going to work right here, in my own house, and I won't leave 'til I fix it up.

MOTHER: But if you use up your vacation we won't be able to go to Oregon.

FATHER: Too bad.

MOTHER: Waldo will be awfully disappointed.

FATHER: Not half as disappointed as I'll be if I get blown up.

MOTHER: Have it your way.

FATHER: Not my way. Our way. Starting now this family's going to have to start getting familiar with each other. We're going to have to start working together.

MOTHER: It won't work.

FATHER: It's got to work.

MOTHER: It won't work unless you go to work.

FATHER: Wife . . . you're stupid. It's no use talking to you. I'm going to have to go to the source of the problem. I'm going to have to talk to Mark.

MOTHER: He won't listen.

FATHER: Why not?

MOTHER: Because you've always said that children never listen.

FATHER: That's because we never had anything to tell them before. Now . . . it's different. Now there's a crisis. The house is falling apart. The family's falling apart. He'll listen. He'll listen to me this time.

Bad Habits (1971)

by TERRENCE McNALLY

Bad Habits is a two-play satire on topics current in the early 1970s—marriage counseling, health spas, offbeat therapeutic techniques, fame, and marriage itself. McNally's humor comes from caricatured, farcical characters, behaving outrageously as they compete with each other in heightened but real situations. Their caustic dialogue has the speed and sting of an electric barb. The forked tongue race is on!

The scene that follows is from the first play, *Ravenswood,* which is the name of a plush resort-like sanitarium for couples having marital problems. April and Roy Pitts, actors exhausted from their scramble for fame in the movie-theatre race, have come there to repair their egos and their marriage. The actors playing the scene should enjoy the repartee and move rapidly along without meaningful pauses or any search for underlying complexities. Have fun being mean.

ROY: Honey! You're blocking my sun.

APRIL: You're just gonna lie there like that?

ROY: Unh-hunh.

APRIL: So where's my reflector?

ROY: I told you to pack it if you wanted it.

APRIL: I want it.

ROY: You said you didn't want to get any darker.

APRIL: I'm starting to fade.

ROY: No, you're not.

APRIL: It's practically all gone. Look at you. You're twice as dark!

ROY: It's not a contest, honey.

APRIL: I mean what's the point of getting a tan if you don't maintain it? Roy!

ROY (*For Dr. Pepper's benefit, but without looking up from the reflector*): Do you believe this? I was with my agents all day and I'm supposed to be worried about a goddamn reflector!

APRIL: Just give me a couple of minutes with it.

ROY: It's the best sun time now.

APRIL: You know I've got that audition Wednesday.

ROY: No. N.O. (*April gives up, gets the tin of cocoa butter off the cart and begins applying it*) April's up for another new musical. They were interested in us both, actually, but I've got these film commitments.

APRIL: Tentative film commitments.

ROY: You're getting hostile, honey.

APRIL: What's hostile is you not packing my reflector.

ROY: I was busy with my agents. *You* are getting hostile.

APRIL: I've got a career, too, you know.

ROY (*Sitting up, he drops the reflector and motions for quiet*): Ssshh!

APRIL (*Grabbing the reflector*): Hello? Yes, we're checking on the availability of Roy Pitt for an Alpo commercial!

ROY: Shut up, April! (*He listens, disappointed*) Shit. (*Then he sees April*) Hold it. Stop it! (*He grabs the reflector and lies back*)

APRIL: Roy!

ROY: After that? You've gotta be kidding! I wouldn't give you this reflector if you whistled "Swanee River" out of your ass.

APRIL: I can, too.

ROY: I know. I've heard you.

APRIL: Just lie there and turn into leather.

ROY: I will.

APRIL: There are other things in the world more important than your sun tan, you know.

ROY: Like yours?

APRIL: For openers.

ROY: Like your career?

APRIL: Yes, as a matter of fact.

ROY: Will you stop competing with me, April? That's one of the reasons we came here. I can't help it if I'm hotter than you right now.

APRIL: That could change, Roy. Remember "Star Is Born."

ROY: Well, until it does, love me for what I am: Roy Pitt, the man. But don't resent me for my career.

APRIL: I know, Roy.

ROY: I love you for what you are: April James, the best little actress in New York City.

APRIL: What do you mean, "best little actress"?

ROY: I'm trying to make a point, honey!

APRIL: As opposed to what? A dwarf?

ROY: If we're going to have a good marriage and, April, I want that more than anything . . . !

APRIL: More than you wanted the lead in "Lenny"?

ROY: I didn't want "Lenny."

APRIL: He would've crawled through broken glass for that part!

ROY: I didn't want "Lenny." Now goddamit, shut up!

APRIL: I can't talk to you when you get like that.

ROY: Get like what? You haven't laid off me since we got in the car.

APRIL: You know I'm upset.

ROY: We've all been fired from shows.

APRIL: Before they went into rehearsal? I'm thinking of slitting the *two* wrists this time, Roy!

ROY: Actually, Heather MacNamara isn't a bad choice for that part.

APRIL: She's the pits!

ROY: We're the Pitts! (*Breaking himself up, then*) We liked her in "The Seagull."

APRIL: You liked her in "The Seagull." I'd like her in her coffin.

ROY: Obviously they're going ethnic with it.

APRIL: She isn't even ethnic. She's white bread. I'm ethnic. I want a hit, Roy. I need a hit. I'm going crazy for a hit. I mean, when's it my turn?

ROY: Honey, you're making a shadow.

APRIL: I'm sorry.

ROY: That's okay. Just stick with me, kid. We're headed straight for the top.

APRIL: Roy?

ROY: What, angel?

APRIL: Your toupe is slipping. (*Roy clutches at his hairpiece*) Roy wears a piece.

ROY: It's no secret. I've never pretended. It's not like your nose job!

APRIL: Don't speak to me. Just lie there and turn into naugahyde like your mother!

ROY: Honey! I almost forgot. Your agent called! They're interviewing hostesses for Steak & Brew.

APRIL: Give him skin cancer, God, give him skin cancer, please!

FROM Freeman (1972)

by PHILLIP HAYES DEAN

Freeman is one of three plays by Phillip
Hayes Dean originally produced at the American Place Theatre. Like many of his plays,
it is set in the fictional city of Moloch, which
resembles his birthplace, Pontiac, Michigan.
Dean has an uncommon instinct and knowl-
edge about the dynamics of plays. He writes
accessible, realistic works, often interfaced
with symbolic overtones.

 Freeman takes place in the home of the
Aquilas, a working-class Black family whose
lives are dominated by an automobile company—its factory, its economics, its smells,
and sounds. Freeman Aquila, in his 30s, is
the play's protagonist. It shows his frustrated
attempts to break out of the familial, social,
and political circumscriptions of his life.
Freeman's parents live routine lives, geared
to the factory; whatever complaints they have
are suppressed, and they seem to accept
their patterned existence. His wife, Osa Lee,
in her 20s and recently from the rural South,
feels protected by the security of these same
confines. Her horizons are quite clear. She
wants to have a home of her own for her un-
born child. She wants a working husband
whose job is secure. And when her mother
visits her from the South, it is most important

127

to her that she not be living with Freeman's parents.

Freeman, on the other hand, is caught between two life-styles. He has been programmed for a life in the factory, but his dreams take him into architecture, law, politics. He refuses to resign himself to what is expected of him and resists in outbursts of counterproductive, bravura behavior (defending a friend in court, running for political office). Complicated, gifted, yearning, but insufficiently educated and without the necessary credentials, Freeman is thwarted in all attempts at self-realization. In this scene, however, he is still heady with his own plans for a new way of life.

FREEMAN (*Moves to window as the sound of Teresa's car is heard starting off*): The job? . . .

OSA LEE (*Making eggs*): What did you say?

FREEMAN: Nothing.

OSA LEE: Why do you always do that to me? Always startin' t' say somethin' to me . . . then when I ask you what you're talkin' about . . . you say nothin'. (*Putting eggs on plate, then placing plate on table*) Freeman? . . . (*Pause*) I'm worried, Freeman.

FREEMAN (*Sitting down to eat eggs*): Worried? About what?

OSA LEE: Wish my mama could come here to be with me. Not that Miss Teresa ain't nice, but there ain't nobody like your own mother.

FREEMAN: She can come.

OSA LEE: No she can't. (*Pause*) Can't let her come up here an' see me livin' like this. Not doin' well. She'd have a fit.

FREEMAN (*Angry*): You're doing better now than you ever did before in your life.

OSA LEE: Ain't doin' as well as none of my brothers or sisters. My sister, Celestine . . . her husband got a good job over in Chicago. They're buying their own home.

FREEMAN: I don't care what Celestine and her husband are doing.

OSA LEE: My sister, Beth . . . her and her husband are both practical nurses like Miss Teresa . . . doin' real good.

FREEMAN: That's what you call doing good?

OSA LEE: My sister Sarah's husband . . . he's real smart. Owns two homes. One they live in an' th' other one they rent out. I'm the only one rooming.

FREEMAN: We ain't rooming.

OSA LEE: Just because it's your mama and daddy's house that don't change what it is. It's still rooming.

FREEMAN: That's how they suck you in.

OSA LEE: Huh?

FREEMAN: Get you to buy one of these shacks. Sell it to the niggers after the white folks move out. After they have worn it out. Slave your life away trying to pay for it. Then spend the rest of your life trying to fix it up.

OSA LEE: Gotta have some place to stay.

FREEMAN: We have a place to stay.

OSA LEE: It ain't ours.

FREEMAN: Think I'm going to sweat my life away out at Moloch Motors paying for one of these shacks? End up like my father? He's been in that foundry for thirty years . . . since he was twenty-two years old. And what's he got to show for it? A steel plate in his head and all the juices sucked out of him. Yeah, and a silver watch after twenty-five years. (*pause*) When I get myself a house . . . it's going to be one ain't nobody ever lived in before. One that I'll build myself. And it's going to be something. (*Takes a blueprint from attaché case*) This is the house we're going to have.

OSA LEE (*Looking at blueprint*): What is it?

FREEMAN: The house I'm going to build out in Blanchfield Hills.

OSA LEE: Ain't there where Dr. Coleman built his home?

FREEMAN: Yes.

OSA LEE: Who drew it?

FREEMAN: Designed! I did. Designed it myself. I probably could have been an architect . . . I took it downtown to one of those architectural firms and you know what? They thought a real architect had done it. He kept asking me what was the name of the architect that had designed it. Just couldn't believe that I had done it. (*Pause*) A twelve room house . . . brand new. Never been lived in by nobody else. See here . . . this is the downstairs. The living room is over there. The dining room will be here. The kitchen here . . . ranch style . . . all electric. The library and the den will be here . . . it'll also serve as my study. Some place I can get away and be alone to think. (*Another pause*) And the grounds will be landscaped beautifully . . . with a swimming pool for summer . . . Hot days you can just run out and take a dip in the pool.

OSA LEE: Where you gonna get th' money?

FREEMAN: I'll get it.

OSA LEE: Sure will be hard to keep clean.

FREEMAN: You'll have servants.

OSA LEE: Servants.

FREEMAN: Yes. We'll have servant quarters over the garage . . .

OSA LEE: I like them little houses over on Montana a heap mo' better.

FREEMAN (*Rolling up his blueprint*): You'll get use to it. (*Osa Lee moves toward stairs*) Where you going?

OSA LEE: Back to bed. I'm still sleepy. (*As she exits up the stairs*) Can't seem to get enough sleep. You goin' to th' Super Market with us after work?

FREEMAN: The Super Market?

OSA LEE: It's Friday! We always go to the Super Market on Fridays. Put your dishes in the sink.
(*She exits*)

part 2

Scenes for
Two Women

All My Sons (1947)

by ARTHUR MILLER

Miller's optimism about humankind and its ability to right itself if helped by consciousness and education is basic to all his plays. In *All My Sons,* the message is responsibility to the larger community. A straightforward, realistic play, conceived and written in wartime, it sharply contrasts human sacrifice with personal aggrandizement.

Like Ibsen, Miller brings his characters into the direct path of the moral consequences of their past choices and irrevocable deeds. And like Ibsen, he gives himself the dramatic problem of dramatizing the past, of making a dynamic of antecedent material.

All My Sons takes place in a small midwestern city in 1947 and focuses on the affluent Keller family. In this scene, we see the weight of the Kellers' recent history through its effect on a young neighbor, Ann. Ann's father was once Joe Keller's business partner, and Ann was engaged to marry Joe's son Larry. But Larry, an airman, was killed in the war, and Ann's father was indicted, together with Joe Keller, for supplying flawed airplane equipment to the military. Keller, however, was acquitted, while Ann's father was found guilty and sent to prison. Now Ann plans to marry Larry's brother, Chris Keller, who has recently returned from the service and works in his father's business.

Ann's father, who claims he was framed by Keller, feels she is betraying him. Larry's mother Kate is hostile to her. And, as the scene opens, Ann is awaiting the arrival of her brother George, who is also determined to stop the marriage. But Ann is resolute; she is determined to move on with her life, a life in which Chris is central. The pressures on her are enormous as she sits in this backyard, green with childhood memories, near a small tree stump, a sad reminder of Larry, the man she loved.

A neighbor approaches and agitates this interior conflict in Ann. Sue is a very practical, strong-minded woman in her early 30s. The clues for her resentment of the Keller family are revealed in the scene, as well as her immediate irritations. Like Joe and Kate Keller, Sue protects and preserves her family; nothing else matters.

"My intention in this play was to be as untheatrical as possible. To that end any metaphor, any figure of speech, however credible to me, was removed if it even slightly brought to consciousness the hand of the writer." This quote from Miller is an excellent guide to the kind of unadorned realistic acting these roles require. The actors' preparation must be full and accurate; all that is pertinent from the past must live meaningfully in the inner life of the characters.

Ann moves aimlessly, and then is drawn toward tree stump. She goes to it, hesitantly touches broken top in the hush of her thoughts. Sue enters from left, and calls, seeing Ann.

SUE: Is my husband . . . ?

ANN (*Turns, startled*): Oh!

SUE: I'm terribly sorry.

ANN: It's all right, I . . . I'm a little silly about the dark.

SUE: It is getting dark.

ANN: Are you looking for your husband?

SUE: As usual. (*Laughs tiredly*) He spends so much time here, they'll be charging him rent.

ANN: Nobody was dressed so he drove over to the depot to pick up my brother.

SUE: Oh, your brother's in?

ANN: Yeah, they ought to be here any minute now. Will you have a cold drink?

SUE: I will, thanks. My husband. Too hot to drive me to beach— Men are like little boys; for the neighbors they'll always cut the grass.

ANN: People like to do things for the Kellers. Been that way since I can remember.

SUE: It's amazing. I guess your brother's coming to give you away, heh?

ANN (*Giving her drink*): I don't know. I suppose.

SUE: You must be all nerved up.

ANN: It's always a problem getting yourself married, isn't it?

SUE: That depends on your shape, of course. I don't see why you should have had a problem.

ANN: I've had chances—

SUE: I'll bet. It's romantic . . . it's very unusual to me, marrying the brother of your sweetheart.

ANN: I don't know. I think it's mostly that whenever I need somebody to tell me the truth I've always thought of Chris. When he tells you something you know it's so. He relaxes me.

SUE: And he's got money. That's important, you know.

ANN: It wouldn't matter to me.

SUE: You'd be surprised. It makes all the difference. I married an interne. On my salary. And that was bad, because as soon as a woman supports a man he owes her something. You can never owe somebody without resenting them. (*Ann laughs*) That's true, you know.

ANN: Underneath, I think the doctor is very devoted.

SUE: Oh, certainly. But it's bad when a man always sees the bars in front of him. Jim thinks he's in jail all the time.

ANN: Oh ...

SUE: That's why I've been intending to ask you a small favor, Ann ... it's something very important to me.

ANN: Certainly, if I can do it.

SUE: You can. When you take up housekeeping, try to find a place away from here.

ANN: Are you fooling?

SUE: I'm very serious. My husband is unhappy with Chris around.

ANN: How is that?

SUE: Jim's a successful doctor. But he's got an idea he'd like to do medical research. Discover things. You see?

ANN: Well, isn't that good?

SUE: Research pays twenty-five dollars a week minus laundering the hair shirt. You've got to give up your life to go into it.

ANN: How does Chris?

SUE: Chris makes people want to be better than it's possible to be. He does that to people.

ANN: Is that bad?

SUE: My husband has a family, dear. Every time he has a session with Chris he feels as though he's compromising by not giving up everything for research. As though Chris or anybody else isn't compromising. It happens with Jim every couple of years. He meets a man and makes a statue out of him.

ANN: Maybe he's right. I don't mean that Chris is a statue, but . . .

SUE: Now darling, you know he's not right.

ANN: I don't agree with you, Chris . . .

SUE: Let's face it, dear. Chris is working with his father, isn't he? He's taking money out of that business every week in the year.

ANN: What of it?

SUE: You ask me what of it?

ANN: I certainly do ask you. You oughtn't cast aspersions like that. I'm surprised at you.

SUE: You're surprised at me!

ANN: He'd never take five cents out of that plant if there was anything wrong in it.

SUE: You know that.

ANN: I know it. I resent everything you've said.

SUE (*moving toward her*): You know what I resent, dear?

ANN: Please, I don't want to argue.

SUE: I resent living next door to the Holy Family. It makes me look like a bum, you understand?

ANN: I can't do anything about that.

SUE: Who is he to ruin a man's life? Everybody knows Joe pulled a fast one to get out of jail.

ANN: That's not true!

SUE: Then why don't you go out and talk to people? Go on, talk to them. There's not a person on the block who doesn't know the truth.

ANN: That's a lie. People come here all the time for cards and . . .

SUE: So what? They give him credit for being smart. I do, too. I've got nothing against Joe. But if Chris wants people to put on the hair shirt let him take off his broadcloth. He's driving my husband crazy with that phony idealism of his, and I'm at the end of my rope on it!

A Streetcar Named Desire (1947)

by TENNESSEE WILLIAMS

With this play, Mississippi-born Tennessee Williams established himself as a truly native theatre artist, master of the American idiom. Theme and action merge in his plays: death and loss try to snuff out desire and life within. Illusion, that fragile life support, crumbles in confrontation with physicality, primitivism, and reality.

Blanche Dubois, whose face shows the scars of despair and rejection, is about 30 years old, heir to a squandered plantation homestead. Cut from her genteel moorings, she is penniless, jobless, and loveless, but urges herself on through illusion and alcohol. Seeking refuge in the New Orleans home of her earthier, happily-married sister, she is confronted with the existence of her brother-in-law, Stanley Kowalski.

Williams tells us that Blanche is "a moth," skinless, covered only with veils and perfumes. Although she is totally vulnerable, she is also strong-willed, even dogmatic. She is ambivalent about her sister, Stella—"Stella for star"—who is younger, physically fulfilled, and satisfied with her life. She is especially disturbed by Stanley, a direct, uncomplicated working-class new American who vibrates with sexuality.

This scene takes place the morning after

a violent poker game. Stanley has smashed furniture, slapped Stella—and then immediately repented and reconciled with her. Blanche enters hysterical, partly from fear, partly from envy. She says she has been "half-crazy," giving the actress a clue to her highly-charged state. She is not to be thwarted; she knows what is right for Stella. She attacks.

In exquisite contrast, Stella is serene and tranquil, guiltless and giving, a happy woman who has life in her: she is pregnant. With ease and appreciation, she accommodates herself to her husband's life-style. She has no ulterior motives and simply reacts to Blanche and her progressive changes. When Stanley enters at the end of the scene, Stella embraces him fiercely in full view of Blanche.

BLANCHE: Stella?

STELLA (*Stirring lazily*): Hmmh?
(*Blanche utters a moaning cry and runs into the bedroom, throwing herself down beside Stella in a rush of hysterical tenderness*)

BLANCHE: Baby, my baby sister!

STELLA (*Drawing away from her*): Blanche, what is the matter with you?
(*Blanche straightens up slowly and stands beside the bed looking down at her sister with knuckles pressed to her lips*)

BLANCHE: He's left?

STELLA: Stan? Yes.

BLANCHE: Will he be back?

STELLA: He's gone to get the car greased. Why?

BLANCHE: Why! I've been half crazy, Stella! When I found out you'd been insane enough to come back in here after what happened—I started to rush in after you!

STELLA: I'm glad you didn't.

BLANCHE: What were you thinking of? (*Stella makes an indefinite gesture*) Answer me! What? What?

STELLA: Please, Blanche! Sit down and stop yelling.

BLANCHE: All right, Stella. I will repeat the question quietly now. How could you come back in this place last night? Why, you must have slept with him! (*Stella gets up in a calm and leisurely way*)

STELLA: Blanche, I'd forgotten how excitable you are. You're making much too much fuss about this.

BLANCHE: Am I?

STELLA: Yes, you are, Blanche. I know how it must have seemed to you and I'm awful sorry it had to happen, but it wasn't anything as serious as you seem to take it. In the first place, when men are drinking and playing poker anything can happen. It's always a powder keg. He didn't know what he was doing. . . . He was as good as a lamb when I came back and he's really very, very ashamed of himself.

BLANCHE: And that—that makes it all right?

STELLA: No, it isn't all right for anybody to make such a terrible row, but—people do sometimes. Stanley's always smashed things. Why, on our wedding night —soon as we came in here—he snatched off one of my slippers and rushed about the place smashing the lightbulbs with it.

BLANCHE: He did—*what?*

STELLA: He smashed all the lightbulbs with the heel of my slipper! (*She laughs*)

BLANCHE: And you—you *let* him? Didn't *run*, didn't *scream*?

STELLA: I was—sort of—thrilled by it. (*She waits for a moment*) Eunice and you had breakfast?

BLANCHE: Do you suppose I wanted any breakfast?

STELLA: There's some coffee left on the stove.

BLANCHE: You're so—matter of fact about it, Stella.

STELLA: What other can I be? He's taken the radio to get it fixed. It didn't land on the pavement so only one tube was smashed.

BLANCHE: And you are standing there smiling!

STELLA: What do you want me to do?

BLANCHE: Pull yourself together and face the facts.

STELLA: What are they, in your opinion?

BLANCHE: In my opinion? You're married to a madman!

STELLA: No!

BLANCHE: Yes, you are, your fix is worse than mine is! Only you're not being sensible about it. I'm going to *do* something. Get hold of myself and make myself a new life!

STELLA: Yes?

BLANCHE: But you've given in. And that isn't right, you're not old! You can get out.

STELLA: I'm not in anything I want to get out of.

BLANCHE: What—Stella?

STELLA: I said I am not in anything that I have a desire to get out of. Look at the mess in this room! And those empty bottles! They went through two cases last night! He promised this morning that he was going to quit having these poker parties, but you know how long such a promise is going to keep. Oh, well, it's his pleasure, like mine is movies and bridge. People have got to tolerate each other's habits, I guess.

BLANCHE: I don't understand you. (*Stella turns toward her*) I don't understand your indifference. Is this a Chinese philosophy you've—cultivated?

STELLA: Is what—what?

BLANCHE: This—shuffling about and mumbling— 'One tube smashed—beer bottles—mess in the kitchen!' —as if nothing out of the ordinary has happened! (*Stella laughs uncertainly and picking up the broom, twirls it in her hands*)

BLANCHE: Are you deliberately shaking that thing in my face?

STELLA: No.

BLANCHE: Stop it. Let go of that broom. I won't have you cleaning up for him!

STELLA: Then who's going to do it? Are you?

BLANCHE: I? I!

STELLA: No, I didn't think so.

BLANCHE: Oh, let me think, if only my mind would function! We've got to get hold of some money, that's the way out!

STELLA: I guess that money is always nice to get hold of.

BLANCHE: Listen to me. I have an idea of some kind. (*Shakily she twists a cigarette into her holder*) Do you remember Shep Huntleigh? (*Stella shakes her head*) Of course you remember Shep Huntleigh. I went out with him at college and wore his pin for a while. Well—

STELLA: Well?

BLANCHE: I ran into him last winter. You know I went to Miami during the Christmas holidays?

STELLA: No.

BLANCHE: Well, I did. I took the trip as an investment, thinking I'd meet someone with a million dollars.

STELLA: Did you?

BLANCHE: Yes. I ran into Shep Huntleigh—I ran into him on Biscayne Boulevard, on Christmas Eve, about dusk . . . getting into his car—Cadillac convertible; must have been a block long!

STELLA: I should think it would have been—inconvenient in traffic!

BLANCHE: You've heard of oil wells?

STELLA: Yes—remotely.

BLANCHE: He has them, all over Texas. Texas is literally spouting gold in his pockets.

STELLA: My, my.

BLANCHE: Y'know how indifferent I am to money. I think of money in terms of what it does for you. But he could do it, he could certainly do it!

STELLA: Do what, Blanche?

BLANCHE: Why—set us up in a—shop!

STELLA: What kind of a shop?

BLANCHE: Oh, a—shop of some kind! He could do it with half what his wife throws away at the races.

STELLA: He's married?

BLANCHE: Honey, would I be here if the man weren't married? (*Stella laughs a little. Blanche suddenly*

springs up and crosses to phone. She speaks shrilly)
How do I get Western Union?—Operator! Western
Union!

STELLA: That's a dial phone, honey.

BLANCHE: I can't dial. I'm too—

STELLA: Just dial O.

BLANCHE: O?

STELLA: Yes, "O" for Operator! *(Blanche considers a
moment; then she puts the phone down)*

BLANCHE: Give me a pencil. Where is a slip of paper?
I've got to write it down first—the message, I mean
. . . *(She goes to the dressing table, and grabs up
a sheet of Kleenex and an eyebrow pencil for writing
equipment)* Let me see now . . . *(She bites the pencil)* 'Darling Shep. Sister and I in desperate situation.'

STELLA: I beg your pardon!

BLANCHE: 'Sister and I in desperate situation. Will explain details later. Would you be interested in—?'
(She bites the pencil again) 'Would you be—interested—in . . .' *(She smashes the pencil on the table
and springs up)* You never get anywhere with direct
appeals!

STELLA *(With a laugh)*: Don't be so ridiculous, darling!

BLANCHE: But I'll think of something, I've *got* to think
of—*some*thing! Don't, don't laugh at me, Stella!
Please, please don't—I—I want you to look at the
contents of my purse! Here's what's in it! Sixty-five
measly cents in coin of the realm!

STELLA *(Crossing to bureau)*: Stanley doesn't give me
a regular allowance, he likes to pay bills himself, but

—this morning he gave me ten dollars to smooth things over. You take five of it, Blanche, and I'll keep the rest.

BLANCHE: Oh, no. No, Stella.

STELLA: I know how it helps your morale just having a little pocket money on you.

BLANCHE: No, thank you—I'll take to the streets!

STELLA: Talk sense! How did you happen to get so low on funds?

BLANCHE: Money just goes—it goes places. (*She rubs her forehead*) Sometime today I've got to get hold of a bromo!

STELLA: I'll fix you one now.

BLANCHE: Not yet—I've got to keep thinking!

STELLA: I wish you'd just let things go, at least for a—while ...

BLANCHE: Stella, I can't live with him! You can, he's your husband. But how could I stay here with him, after last night, with just those curtains between us?

STELLA: Blanche, you saw him at his worst last night.

BLANCHE: On the contrary, I saw him at his best! What such a man has to offer is animal force and he gave a wonderful exhibition of that! But the only way to live with such a man is to—go to bed with him! And that's your job—not mine!

STELLA: After you've rested a little, you'll see it's going to work out. You don't have to worry about anything while you're here. I mean—expenses ...

BLANCHE: I have to plan for us both, to get us both —out!

STELLA: You take it for granted that I am in something that I want to get out of.

BLANCHE: I take it for granted that you still have sufficient memory of Belle Reve to find this place and these poker players impossible to live with.

STELLA: Well, you're taking entirely too much for granted.

BLANCHE: I can't believe you're in earnest.

STELLA: No?

BLANCHE: I understand how it happened—a little. You saw him in uniform, an officer, not here but—

STELLA: I'm not sure it would have made any difference where I saw him.

BLANCHE: Now don't say it was one of those mysterious electric things between people! If you do I'll laugh in your face.

STELLA: I am not going to say anything more at all about it!

BLANCHE: All right, then, don't.

STELLA: But there are things that happen between a man and a woman in the dark—that sort of make everything else seem—unimportant. (*Pause*)

BLANCHE: What you are talking about is brutal desire —just—Desire!—the name of that rattletrap streetcar that bangs through the Quarter, up one old narrow street and down another . . .

STELLA: Haven't you ever ridden on that streetcar?

BLANCHE: It brought me here—Where I'm not wanted and where I'm ashamed to be . . .

STELLA: Then don't you think your superior attitude is a bit out of place?

BLANCHE: I am not being or feeling at all superior, Stella. Believe me I'm not! It's just this. This is how I look at it. A man like that is someone to go out with—once—twice—three times when the devil is in you. But live with? Have a child by?

STELLA: I have told you I love him.

BLANCHE: Then I *tremble* for you! I just—*tremble* for you. . . .

STELLA: I can't help your trembling if you insist on trembling! (*There is a pause*)

BLANCHE: May I—speak—*plainly?*

STELLA: Yes, do. Go ahead. As plainly as you want to.

BLANCHE: Well—if you'll forgive me—he's *common!*

STELLA: Why, yes, I suppose he is.

BLANCHE: Suppose! You can't have forgotten that much of our bringing up, Stella, that you just *suppose* that any part of a gentleman's in his nature! *Not one particle, no!* Oh, if he was just—*ordinary!* Just *plain*—but good and wholesome, but—*no.* There's something downright—*bestial*—about him! You're hating me saying this, aren't you?

STELLA: Go on and say it all, Blanche.

BLANCHE: He acts like an animal, has an animal's habits! Eats like one, moves like one, talks like one! There's even something—subhuman—something not quite to the stage of humanity yet! Yes, something —apelike about him, like one of those pictures I've seen in—anthropological studies! Thousands and thousands of years have passed him right by, and there he is—Stanley Kowalski—survivor of the Stone Age! Bearing the raw meat home from the kill in the jungle! And you—*you* here—*waiting* for him! Maybe he'll strike you or maybe grunt and kiss you! That is, if kisses have been discovered yet! Night falls and the other apes gather! There in the front of the cave, all grunting like him, and swilling and

gnawing and hulking! His poker night!—you call it
—this party of apes! Somebody growls—some creature snatches at something—the fight is on! *God!*
Maybe we are a long way from being made in God's
image, but Stella—my sister—there has been *some*
progress since then! Such things as art—as poetry
and music—such kinds of new light have come into
the world since then! In some kinds of people some
tenderer feelings have had some little beginning!
That we have got to make *grow!* And *cling* to, and
hold as our flag! In this dark march toward whatever
it is we're approaching. . . . *Don't—don't hang back
with the brutes!*

FROM

FROM The Autumn Garden (1951)
by LILLIAN HELLMAN

The Autumn Garden, considered by many to be Lillian Hellman's best play, is set in a summer resort in Louisiana, September, 1949. The title also describes most of the characters, who are in the autumn of their lives and now have to harvest the seeds which they have sown.

The exception is 18-year-old Sophie, whose American father died during World War II. Sophie lived in Europe with her French mother until the end of the war, when she was brought to the United States by an affluent American aunt. The aunt wished to educate and "improve" her, but Sophie has been unhappy and wants to return to France.

Now she seizes an opportunity to get the money she needs. An incident which she did not design, but allowed to happen, gives her the basis for blackmail. The previous night, Nina's husband Nick, a charming dilettante, got drunk and made advances to her, finally falling asleep in her bed. She remained in the room. Sophie, outwardly shy, is a tough-minded realist, a matter-of-fact and determined young woman who values her dignity. She can pressure Nina because she knows Nina is bound to Nick and to the unbreakable patterns of her middle-aged life.

152

At the moment when this scene begins, Nina is enjoying the warm feelings of her latest reconciliation with Nick. She would like to keep her self-respect as well as feel she is helping Sophie; Sophie's well-being will make the whole situation acceptable. While the scene seems to be about money, it is really about the need of both women to maintain self-respect. We should see in Nina the erosive force of a life spent clinging to romantic illusions. Sophie, in contrast, is young and fresh and has no illusions.

SOPHIE: You are a pretty woman, Mrs. Denery, when your face is happy.

NINA: And you think my face is happy *this* morning?

SOPHIE: Oh, yes. You and Mr. Denery have had a nice reconciliation.

NINA: Er. Yes, I suppose so.

SOPHIE: I am glad for you. That is as it has been and will always be. (*She sits down*) Now could I speak with you and Mr. Denery?

NINA: Sophie, if there was anything I can do— Er. Nick isn't here. I thought it best for us all—

SOPHIE: Ah. Ah, my aunt will be most sad.

NINA: Sophie, there's no good my telling you how sorry, how— What can I do?

SOPHIE: You can give me five thousand dollars, Mrs. Denery. American dollars, of course. (*Demurely; her accent from now on grows more pronounced*) I have been subjected to the most degrading experience from which no young girl easily recovers. (*In French*) A most degrading experience from which no young girl easily recovers—

NINA: It sounds exactly the same in French.

SOPHIE: Somehow sex and money are simpler in French. Well. In English, then, I have lost or will lose my most beloved fiancé; I cannot return to school and the comrades with whom my life has been so happy; my aunt is uncomfortable and unhappy in the only life she knows and is now burdened with me for many years to come. I am utterly, utterly miserable, Mrs. Denery. I am ruined. (*Nina bursts out laughing. Sophie smiles*) Please do not laugh at me.

NINA: I suppose I should be grateful to you for making a joke of it.

SOPHIE: You make a mistake. I am most serious.

NINA: Are you? Sophie, it is an unpleasant and foolish incident and I don't wish to minimize it. But don't you feel you're adding considerable drama to it?

SOPHIE: No, ma'am. I did not say that is the way I thought of it. But that is the way it will be considered in this place, in this life. Little is made into very much here.

NINA: It's just the same in your country.

SOPHIE: No, Mrs. Denery. You mean it is the same in Brussels or Strasbourg or Paris, with those whom you would meet. In my class, in my town, it is not so. In a poor house if a man falls asleep drunk—and certainly it happens with us each Saturday night—he is not alone with an innocent young girl because the young girl, at my age, is not so innocent and because her family is in the same room, not having any other place to go. It arranges itself differently; you have more rooms and therefore more troubles.

NINA: Yes. I understand the lecture. (*Pauses*) Why do you want five thousand dollars, Sophie?

SOPHIE: I wish to go home.

NINA: Then I will be happy to give it to you. Happier than you know to think we can do something.

SOPHIE: Yes. I am sure. But I will not accept it as largesse—to make you happy. We will call it a loan, come by through blackmail. One does not have to be grateful for blackmail money, nor think of oneself as a charity girl.

NINA: Blackmail money?

SOPHIE: Yes ma'am. You will give me five thousand dollars because if you do not I will say that Mr. Denery seduced me last night. (*Nina stares at her, laughs*) You are gay this morning, madame.

NINA: Sophie, Sophie. What a child you are. It's not necessary to talk this way.

SOPHIE: I wish to prevent you from giving favors to me.

NINA: I intended no favors. And I don't like this kind of talk. Nick did not seduce you and I want no more jokes about it. Suppose we try to be friends—

SOPHIE: I am not joking, Mrs. Denery. And I do not wish us to be friends.

NINA (*Gets up*): I would like to give you the money. And I will give it to you for that reason and no other.

SOPHIE: It does not matter to me what you would like. You will give it to me for my reason—or I will not take it.
(*Angrily, Nina goes toward door, goes into the room, then turns and smiles at Sophie*)

NINA: You are serious? Just for a word, a way of calling something you would hurt my husband and me?

SOPHIE: For me it is more than a way of calling something.

NINA: You're a tough little girl.

SOPHIE: Don't you think people often say other people are tough when they do not know how to cheat them?

NINA: I was not trying to cheat you of anything—

SOPHIE: Yes, you were. You wish to be the kind lady who most honorably stays to discharge—within reason—her obligations. And who goes off, as she has gone off many other times, to make the reconciliation with her husband. How would you and Mr. Denery go on living without such incidents as me? I have been able to give you a second, or a twentieth, honeymoon.

NINA: Is that speech made before you raise your price?

SOPHIE (Smiles): No. A blackmail bargain is still a bargain.

FROM Picnic (1953)

by WILLIAM INGE

"You meet the talent of William Inge, the true and wonderful talent which is for offering, first, the genial surface of common American life, and then not ripping but quietly dropping the veil that keeps you from seeing yourself as you are."—Tennessee Williams

Underneath whatever modest bravura Inge's people may demonstrate, there exists in all of them quiet frustration and yearning. In this play, characteristically with Inge, the father is absent. We see a society of women, modest in every way, except in their desire for men. This appetite—and the characters' efforts to control it—dominates the action. It is Labor Day weekend, time for the annual picnic, the big event. And there is a new arrival in town: Hal, the perfect macho hero of the 1950s, T-shirted, muscular, rough hewn but altogether appealing.

The night before the picnic, the following scene takes place between two teenaged sisters, Madge, 18, and Millie, 16. Although Madge is clearly the "belle" of this community, she suffers from a deep inferiority; she feels that no one treats her seriously. Her sister Millie is quite the contrary—intelligent, ungainly, boisterous but likable. Her basic shyness is disguised by her outward assertiveness. She is forever mocking her sister

157

and the wiles of the female. However, she
now wants some education in the techniques
of attracting a male. She has a date with Hal
for the picnic, and she is admitting her excitement. Madge, on the other hand, is stuck
with boring, acceptable, rich Alan Seymour,
and she is feeling irritable and self-absorbed.
It will help the actress to use a small physical
activity like filing her nails to give her a
detached, uninterested air. Millie could reveal her exuberance by practicing dance
steps. Underneath the text is the everpresent
sibling rivalry, distorting any possible bond
or support. Remember, also, that Inge is
never harsh. His is a gentle, forgiving voice
even in its sadness.

---

*It is late afternoon. The sun is beginning to set and
fills the atmosphere with radiant orange. When the curtain goes up, Millie is on the porch alone. She has per-
mitted herself to "dress up" and wears a becoming,
feminine dress in which she cannot help feeling a little
strange. She is quite attractive. Piano music can be
heard off stage, somewhere past Mrs. Potts's house, and
Millie stands listening to it for a moment. Then she
begins to sway to the music and in a moment is dancing
a strange, impromptu dance over the porch and yard.
The music stops suddenly and Millie's mood is broken.
She rushes upstage and calls off, left.*

MILLIE: Don't quit now, Ernie! (*She cannot hear Ernie's reply*) Huh? (*Madge enters from kitchen. Millie
turns to Madge*) Ernie's waiting for the rest of the
band to practice. They're going to play out at the
park tonight.

MADGE (*Sitting on chair*): I don't know why you
couldn't have helped us in the kitchen.

MILLIE (*Lightly, giving her version of the sophisticated belle*): I had to dress for the ball.

MADGE: I had to make the potato salad and stuff the eggs and make three dozen bread-and-butter sandwiches.

MILLIE: I had to *bathe*—and dust my limbs with powder—and slip into my frock . . .

MADGE: Did you clean out the bathtub?

MILLIE: Yes, I cleaned out the bathtub. (*She becomes very self-conscious*) Madge, how do I look? Now tell me the truth.

MADGE: You look very pretty.

MILLIE: I feel sorta funny.

MADGE: You can have the dress if you want it.

MILLIE: Thanks. (*A pause*) Madge, how do you talk to boys?

MADGE: Why, you just talk, silly.

MILLIE: How d'ya think of things to say?

MADGE: I don't know. You just say whatever comes into your head.

MILLIE: Supposing nothing ever comes into my head?

MADGE: You talked with him all right this morning.

MILLIE: But now I've got a *date* with him, and it's *different!*

MADGE: You're crazy.

MILLIE: I think he's a big showoff. You should have seen him this morning on the high diving board. He did real graceful swan dives, and a two-and-a-half gainer, and a back flip—and kids stood around clapping. He just ate it up.

MADGE (*Her mind elsewhere*): I think I'll paint my toenails tonight and wear sandals.

MILLIE: And he was braggin' all afternoon how he used to be a deep-sea diver off Catalina Island.

MADGE: Honest?

MILLIE: And he says he used to make hundreds of dollars doin' parachute jumps out of a balloon. Do you believe it?

MADGE: I don't see why not.

MILLIE: You never hear Alan bragging that way.

MADGE: Alan never jumped out of a balloon.

MILLIE: Madge, I think he's girl crazy.

MADGE: You think every boy you see is something horrible.

MILLIE: Alan took us into the Hi Ho for Cokes and there was a gang of girls in the back booth—Juanita Badger and her gang. (*Madge groans at hearing this name*) When they saw him, they started giggling and tee-heeing and saying all sorts of crazy things. Then Juanita Badger comes up to me and whispers, "He's the cutest thing I ever saw." Is he, Madge?

MADGE: I certainly wouldn't say he was "the cutest thing I ever *saw*."

MILLIE: Juanita Badger's an old floozy. She sits in the back row at the movie so the guys that come in will see her and sit with her. One time she and Rubberneck Krauss were asked by the management to leave —and they weren't just kissin', either!

MADGE: I never even speak to Juanita Badger.

MILLIE: Madge, do you think he'll like me?

MADGE: Why ask me all these questions? You're supposed to be the smart one.

MILLIE: I don't really care. I just wonder.

A Young Lady of Property (1953)

by HORTON FOOTE

Horton Foote was one of the better television writers of the 1950s, and this play is a fine example of the intimate character study set in a small town (here, Harrison, Texas), designed for the small screen and supported by naturalistic acting performances.

Wilma, a lonely girl of fifteen whose mother deeded her property in her will, seeks a family, an identity, some roots. In this scene, she confesses this to her best friend, Arabella, while they are both pretending to prepare for a movie career. Their Hollywood dream is a bubble that breaks easily because it is not what they really want. The scene ends with each recognizing her own deeper needs.

The girls are quite different. Wilma is forceful, spirited, haughty, stubborn, with a well-hidden insecurity. Arabella holds back, is shy, gullible, frightened of losing Wilma's friendship. Arabella is a follower, Wilma, a leader. The characters reveal themselves in the writing and should be played with subtle and detailed behavior. Discover little actions and reactions as the scene is rehearsed. It must never lose its spontaneity and believability.

The front porch and yard of a lovely old Victorian cottage. It has not had too good care, but it still has retained its charm. Wilma is seated in a swing in the yard. She is rocking back and forth singing "Birmingham Jail" in her hillbilly style. Arabella comes running onto the porch.

WILMA: Hey, Arabella. Come sit and swing.

ARABELLA: All right. Your letter came.

WILMA: Whoopee. Where is it?

ARABELLA: Here.

WILMA: "Dear Miss Thompson: Mr. Delafonte will be glad to see you anytime next week about your contemplated screen test. We suggest you call the office when you arrive in the city and we will set an exact time. Yours truly, Adele Murray." Well . . . Did you get yours?

ARABELLA: Yes.

WILMA: What did it say?

ARABELLA: The same.

WILMA: Exactly the same?

ARABELLA: Yes.

WILMA: Well, let's pack our bags. Hollywood, here we come.

ARABELLA: Wilma . . .

WILMA: Yes?

ARABELLA: I have to tell you something . . . well . . . I . . .

WILMA: What is it?

ARABELLA: Well . . . promise me you won't hate me, or stop being my friend.

WILMA: Oh, my cow. Stop talking like that. I'll never stop being your friend. What do you want to tell me?

ARABELLA: Well . . . I don't want to go to see Mr. Delafonte, Wilma . . .

WILMA: You don't?

ARABELLA: No. I don't want to be a movie star. I don't want to leave Harrison or my mother or father . . . I just want to stay here the rest of my life and get married and settle down and have children.

WILMA: Arabella . . .

ARABELLA: I'd die if I had to go to see Mr. Delafonte. Why, I even get faint when I have to recite before the class. I'm not like you. You're not scared of anything.

WILMA: Why do you say that?

ARABELLA: Because you're not. I know.

WILMA: Oh, yes, I am. I'm scared of lots of things.

ARABELLA: What?

WILMA: Getting lost in a city. Being bitten by dogs. Old lady Leighton taking my daddy away . . .
(*A pause*)

ARABELLA: Will you still be my friend?

WILMA: Sure. I'll always be your friend.

ARABELLA: I'm glad. Oh, I almost forgot. Your Aunt Gert said for you to come on home.

WILMA: I'll go in a little. (*A pause. She swings back and forth*) I love to swing in my front yard. Mama and I used to come out here and swing together.

Some nights when Daddy was out all night gambling I'd wake up and hear her out here swinging away. Sometimes she'd let me come and sit beside her. We'd swing until three or four in the morning. (*A pause. She looks out into the yard*) The pear tree looks sickly, doesn't it? The fig trees are doing nicely though. I was out in back and the weeds are near knee high, but fig trees just seem to thrive in the weeds. The freeze must have killed off the banana trees . . . (*A pause. Wilma stops swinging*) Maybe I won't leave either. Maybe, I won't go to Hollywood after all.

ARABELLA: You won't?

WILMA: No. Maybe, I shouldn't. That just comes to me now. You know sometimes this old house looks so lonesome it tears at my heart. I used to think it looks lonesome just whenever it had no tenants, but now it comes to me it has looked lonesome ever since Mama died and we moved away, and it will look lonesome until some of us move back here. Of course, Mama can't, and Daddy won't. So it's up to me. (*A pause*) Maybe I'll stay in Harrison and finish school and live with Aunt Gert and keep on renting the house until I meet some nice boy with good habits and steady ways, and marry him. Then we'll move here and have children and I bet this old house won't be lonely anymore. I'll get Mama's old croquet set and put it out under the pecan trees and play croquet with my children, or sit in this yard and swing and swing and wave to people as they pass by.

ARABELLA: Oh, I wish you would. Mama says that's a normal life for a girl, marrying and having children. She says being an actress is all right, but the other's better.

WILMA: Maybe I've come to agree with your mama. Maybe I was going to Hollywood out of pure lonesomeness. Aunt Gert says nobody is lonesome with a house full of children, so maybe that's what I just ought to stay here and have . . .

ARABELLA: Have you decided on a husband yet?

WILMA: No.

ARABELLA: Mama says that's the bad feature of being a girl, you have to wait for the boy to ask you and just pray that the one you want wants you. Tommy Murray is nice, isn't he?

WILMA: I think so.

ARABELLA: Jay Godfrey told me once he wanted to ask you for a date, but he didn't dare because he was afraid you'd turn him down.

WILMA: Why did he think that?

ARABELLA: He said the way you talked he didn't think you would go out with anything less than a movie star.

WILMA: Maybe you'd tell him different . . .

ARABELLA: All right. I think Jay Godfrey is very nice. Don't you?

WILMA: Yes, I think he's very nice and Tommy is nice . . .

ARABELLA: Maybe we could double-date sometimes.

WILMA: That might be fun.

ARABELLA: Oh, Wilma. Don't go to Hollywood. Stay here in Harrison and let's be friends forever . . .

WILMA: All right. I will.

ARABELLA: You will?

WILMA: Sure, why not? I'll stay here. I'll stay and marry and live in my house.

ARABELLA: Oh, Wilma. I'm so glad. I'm so very glad.

FROM A Roomful of Roses (1955)
by EDITH SOMMER

A Roomful of Roses is a fine example of the 50s play of personal relationships. We are concerned with the life adjustment of 15-year-old Bridget, whose parents divorced eight years ago when her mother fell in love with her fantasy hero, a war correspondent. The rejected father takes Bridget away to South America, far from her "scandalous" mother. He now seeks a new marriage and has sent Bridget back to visit her happily remarried mother for the first time.

Bridget, conflicted and deeply wounded, is unyielding and obtuse. She wants to show her mother she is indifferent to her and doesn't really need her. This is the actress's overt intention. Underneath, her feelings are very mixed. While she really loves her mother and wants her mother to love her, she also needs to hurt her, to punish her for the years of separation. Her love for her mother, her need for family and place are masked behind the appearance of imperviousness and hate.

Nancy, the mother, yearns to connect with her daughter. Both guilty and loving, she expresses her deepest feelings with grace and clarity. She desperately wants her daughter's affection and also wants to help her become a whole person who can more fully relate to others. The scene illuminates the mother and daughter's search for one another.

BRIDGET: I don't know why everybody gets so excited, just because it turns out I won't be here for an old dance.

NANCY: So you've decided to leave next Saturday.

BRIDGET: Why not? My three weeks are up.

NANCY: Are they? I hadn't realized.

BRIDGET: Well, they're not actually up till Monday. But I hope you're not going to hold me over on a technicality.

NANCY: Would you find that so dreadful?

BRIDGET: Are you joking?

NANCY: No, I'm not.

BRIDGET: You're going to try to make me stay?

NANCY: Darling, don't misunderstand —I'm not going to try to make you do anything. I thought you would know that by now.

BRIDGET: That's good. Of course. You haven't any rights at all, as far as I am concerned.

NANCY: I don't know that my "rights"—or lack of them—has anything to do with it, Bridie——

BRIDGET: Please.

NANCY: I'm sorry—Bridget. (*Reaching toward her in an impulsive gesture of affection*) Darling, I do want you to stay. More than anything in the world, I want you to stay. We all want you—won't you think about it? Just during the next few days, think about it. Hard.

BRIDGET: No! It's utterly impossible!

NANCY: Are you so happy at home?

BRIDGET: Why do you ask me that?

NANCY: I want you to be happy somewhere. If not with me, then somewhere else.

BRIDGET: You don't have to worry about that. I *am* happy. Terribly.

NANCY: And you like your school?

BRIDGET: I love it. The only thing I don't like—I don't like this conversation. And if it's all right with you, I'll dress for dinner now.

NANCY: Oh, baby—you don't have to be so lonely.

BRIDGET: Listen! Don't say a thing like that to me. Don't you dare to be sorry for me!

NANCY: Bridget!

BRIDGET: Don't you dare! You have no right! (*She starts up the stairs*)

NANCY: *Bridie!* You come back here. Don't ever speak to me in that tone again. I don't care what you think I have done to you, you are never to speak to me in that way again. Do you understand?

BRIDGET: Yes.

NANCY: All right. Now come over here and sit down.

BRIDGET: I have nothing to say.

NANCY: But I have something to say. I've been waiting a long time to say it, so I hope . . . I want you to understand, that no matter how you feel toward me, you are a deep and important part of my life. I love you very much.

BRIDGET: Is that all?

NANCY: No. No, it isn't. There is something else. I knew—you would feel resentful and hurt. . . . But I didn't dream it would be like this. I've tried in every way I know to reach you. I've stayed awake nights trying to think of a way—some way—of reaching you. . . .

BRIDGET: Of breaking me down, you mean.

NANCY: Yes, if you want to put it that way. Bridie, you're a little girl still. In many ways a very little girl. But soon—you will be a young woman. (*Bridget starts to rise*) Now wait! It's for your own sake I'm saying this. It's for *you*. Bridie, don't let the fact that there was something very bad in your life once be the most important thing about you. Don't blame everyone you meet for something that happened a long time ago.

BRIDGET: May I go to my room now?

NANCY: Do you really hate me so much?

BRIDGET: No, I don't hate you. I don't feel anything about you at all. Just blankness. And I want to keep it that way.

NANCY: Bridie, it wasn't all my fault—what happened wasn't all *my* fault! I've never told you this before, but your father was— Oh, God.

BRIDGET: I don't care *whose* fault it was! You were the one who ran away!

NANCY: Not from you! I wanted you with me. I tried —you know I tried—I didn't run away from you.

BRIDGET: You ran away from Dad and me. Why? Because you liked Jay better?

NANCY: No—things aren't that simple. . . .

BRIDGET: Then *why?*

NANCY: Bridie, listen—there are things you won't understand until you are older, but try—try to understand this—the love I have for Jay is love your father did not want from me. And it has nothing whatever to do with the love I feel for you.

BRIDGET: You're too late, Mother. I don't care anymore. That's funny. I call you Mother. But it's only because I don't know what else to call you. To me you aren't my mother. As far as I'm concerned, my mother is dead. And I used to wish you *had* died. Oh, how I wished . . . I'd lie awake in bed at night and pretend that you had died. Sometimes it seemed so real—and I'd cry . . . All right, now you know what I really feel about you. Do you still want me to stay?

NANCY: More than ever.

BRIDGET: You're crazy! . . . (*She turns and runs up the stairs*)

FROM The Middle of the Night (1956)

by *PADDY CHAYEFSKY*

Starting in the early 1950s with realistic, tender stories for television, Paddy Chayefsky has contributed a large body of work to TV, film, and the theatre, including his Academy Award-winning screenplay for *Network* in 1977. His early work, like the famous television script and film *Marty* and this play, *Middle of the Night,* dealt with the unfulfilled inner lives and yearnings of ordinary urban Americans. He captures their average ideas, average talk, and quiet emotion in accurate, sensitive dialogue.

In this scene, the Girl, Betty, is considering a divorce from her husband, a musician who is frequently away from home. While they still attract one another physically, she feels that the marriage is incomplete. She has taken up with the more emotionally generous Mr. Kingsley, a lonely widower in his 50s. He makes her feel wanted, and their relationship has flowered into love. But Betty is uncertain about her decision and needs to confide in someone—in this case, the Girl Friend, Marilyn.

The acting should be as naturalistic as possible, and the actresses must make the past experiences and needs of their characters exist specifically and truthfully.

THE GIRL (*Entering from bedroom in slip with hose in hand*): Would you close the door please, Marilyn?

THE GIRL FRIEND: Oh sure. Well, how do you feel?

THE GIRL: Fine.

THE GIRL FRIEND: What's new?

THE GIRL: Nothing. What's new with you?

THE GIRL FRIEND: Nothing. I was down at Macy's, so Frank's taking the kids over to his mother's and you know how I can't stand her, so I told him as long as I'm downtown, I'll go in to a downtown movie.

THE GIRL: I've got a date tonight.

THE GIRL FRIEND: Yes, I know. You hear anything from George?

THE GIRL (*Puts on hose*): Oh, he called three times last week all the way from Las Vegas. Three o'clock in the morning he called once.

THE GIRL FRIEND: What did he have to say?

THE GIRL: Well, I wrote him a letter about a week ago. I asked him for a divorce. I finally went up to see this lawyer last week. You remember Carol McKeever? Her brother, he's a lawyer. So he told me the cheapest way to get a divorce is to go to Mexico. So I said: "Oh, boy." So it really isn't so complicated. It costs about seven hundred and fifty dollars, the plane tickets and everything. So I wrote George and asked him for a divorce. I sent the letter registered, air mail, special delivery so it would get there quick. The next night, I swear to God, George was on the phone from Las Vegas. So we must have talked about twenty minutes. Oh, boy, I wonder what he paid for that call. So he called again about three o'clock in the morning after the last show. (*Rises;*

fastens hose) You know what was bothering him. He didn't even care why I wanted the divorce. He just thought the whole thing was a big personal insult. So he finally said he wouldn't contest the divorce and that's the last I heard from him. That was last Thursday, no, Friday.

THE GIRL FRIEND: Are you really going to go through with this divorce?

THE GIRL: Don't tell my mother because she doesn't know about it.

THE GIRL FRIEND: I'm your friend, Betty, and I'm going to tell you something right from the shoulder. You're making a big mistake.

THE GIRL (*Crosses to closet; takes out dress*): I know you feel that way, Marilyn.

THE GIRL FRIEND: What do you figure, to marry this man?

THE GIRL: Yes, if he asks me. I think I'm happy, Marilyn. I can't tell you how I feel in so many words, but life seems very pleasant to me right now. I— even get along with my mother. I think I'm in love.

THE GIRL FRIEND: Oh Betty!

THE GIRL: Seriously in love. I feel so full sometimes, it just wells up in me, my feeling for him. He went away for three days on a business trip to Detroit, and I thought I would die before he came back.

THE GIRL FRIEND: Boy, he must be some operator, this guy.

THE GIRL: You want to know something? (*Rises; steps into dress*)
(*Girl friend rises and helps her; zips up back*)
In the whole three months, he hasn't touched me once. I know what my mother thinks. She thinks I walk out of this door, I head straight for a hotel.

I told you what we do. We go dancing. We go driving. Mostly we talk. He hasn't put a hand on me in the whole three months.

THE GIRL FRIEND: Is that good?

THE GIRL: No, it isn't good, and it worries me, if you want to know. I think he's afraid of getting too involved with me.

THE GIRL FRIEND: What I mean is, do you think he's going to be able to satisfy you sexually?
(*Pause. The girl goes to closet; takes slippers*)
Well now, Betty, you're jumping into a marriage and you have to be a little realistic too. In ten years, he's going to be sixty-three and you're going to be thirty-four. Do you think you're going to be happy with a sixty-three-year-old husband in ten years? Think about that a minute. A sixty-three-year-old husband with white hair. You're a kid, you know that? You really are. What do you think life is, a Street and Smith Love Story Magazine? You had a good marriage with George. You paid the rent and you went to bed. What are you looking for?

THE GIRL: I'm looking for more than that, Marilyn.

THE GIRL FRIEND: You want to know what life is? You live, that's all. That's life. You get married, you have kids—you get up in the morning and you go to sleep at night. Frank goes bowling every Thursday, and I manage to get down to Macy's once a week, and that's it, and it's not so bad. I don't know what you mean by happiness. You had a good marriage with George. At least he was hungry for you all the time. It was all over his face. That's more than most of us can say about our husbands.

THE GIRL: Are you having trouble with Frank, Marilyn?

THE GIRL FRIEND: Frank and me? We get along

fine. We're perfectly happy. He stays out of my way and I stay out of his. You know I envy you George, you know that. You have a husband who's crazy about you. Sure, he has his faults. He's a little selfish. He's a little conceited. But he doesn't go bowling on Thursday nights or stay up reading a magazine all night long. And one thing you know for sure, he isn't going to be sixty-three in ten years. You're going to want to have children, Betty. How do you know he's going to be able to give you kids? Because after a couple of years, that's all there really is—the kids.

THE GIRL: You don't mean that, Marilyn.

THE GIRL FRIEND: Yes, I do.

FROM All the Way Home (1961)

by TAD MOSEL

All the Way Home is based on James Agee's
luminious novel *A Death in the Family,* about
an American family in the years just before
World War I. Both the novel and the play
won the Pulitzer Prize.

Mary Follett is a young mother who is
able to endure the terror and grief of her
husband's death and still continue to give
support and nourishment to her family. Her
strength is in part built-in, in part the product
of her religious faith. I have chosen a wonderful acting scene from the play which reveals Mary and her Aunt Hannah just after
Mary learns of her husband Jay's car accident. A call has come saying that the accident was very serious, requiring no doctor
but the presence of a male member of the
family. Mary and Aunt Hannah must wait.
They talk, they hide their fear of the truth;
a little of it is spoken, then pushed aside.
They make tea, they repeat the known facts,
always side-stepping the dreaded possibility.
They touch each other, they pray a little, they
wait.

In this scene, what is *unspoken,* the sub-
text, is extremely important. The emotions
are held down, revealing themselves in many
small ways as the characters try to prepare,
cope, avoid breaking down. They must fill

177

in the silences which would otherwise give
space to thoughts which would crumple their
containment. The actors should find the full
emotion in early rehearsals so that they can
later suppress feelings that are real to them.

MARY: What time is it, Aunt Hannah?

HANNAH: About ten twenty-five.

MARY: Let's see, Andrew drives pretty fast, though not
so fast as Jay, but he'll be driving better than usual
tonight, and it's just over twelve miles. That would
be—supposing he goes thirty miles an hour, that's
twelve miles—let's see, six times four is twenty-four,
six times five's thirty, twice twelve is twenty-four
—sakes alive, I was always dreadful at figures.

HANNAH: It's only twelve miles. We should hear very
soon.

MARY: Let's have some tea.

HANNAH: Why not let me— (*She stops*)

MARY: What?

HANNAH: Just let me know if there's anything I can
help with.

MARY: Not a thing, thank you. (*She goes into the kitch-
en, and during the following lights the stove, puts
the kettle on to boil, takes down the box of tea, finds
the strainer, the cups, and saucers. Hannah watches,
her hands folded*) We'll make up the downstairs bedroom. Remember he stayed there when his poor
back was sprained. It's better than upstairs, near the
kitchen and the bathroom and no stairs to climb.
He's always saying we must get the bathroom upstairs but we never do. And of course, if need be,
that is if he needs a nurse, we can put her in the
dining room and eat in here, or even set up a cot

right in the room with him and put up a screen. Or if she minds that, why she can just sleep on the living-room davenport and keep the door open in between. Don't you think so?

HANNAH: Certainly.

MARY: Of course it's very possible he'll have to be taken straight to a hospital. The man did say it was serious, after all. Sugar and milk—(*She gets them*) —or lemon? I don't know if I have any lemons, Aunt Hannah—

HANNAH: Milk is fine for me.

MARY: Me too. Would you like some Zuzus? (*She gets them from the cupboard*) Or bread and butter, or toast? I could toast some.

HANNAH: Just tea will do.

MARY: Well, here are the Zuzus. (*She puts them on the table*)

HANNAH: Thank you.

MARY: Goodness sakes, the watched *pot!* (*She stands by the stove, motionless*)

HANNAH: I hope you didn't really mind my giving Rufus that cap, Mary.

MARY (*Vaguely*): Heavens no, you were good to do it.

HANNAH: I'm sure if you had realized how much he wanted one, you'd have given it to him yourself long ago.

MARY (*Forcing concentration*): Of course. Oh, yes. But *Harbisons,* isn't that where you got it? I hear it's so tough, how did you ever dare go *in?*

HANNAH: Fortunately, I'm so blind I couldn't see what might hurt me. I just sailed up to the nearest man

and said, "Where do I go, please, to find a cap for
my nephew?" And he said, "I'm no clerk, Ma'am,
I'm a customer myself." And I said, "Then why
aren't you wearing a hat?" He had no answer to
that, of course, so—

MARY: Why didn't he tell me!

HANNAH: Who?

MARY: That man on the telephone? Why didn't I ask!
I didn't even ask! *How* serious! *Where* is he hurt!
Papa noticed it!

HANNAH: You couldn't think.

MARY: Is he living or dead?

HANNAH: That we simply have to wait and find out.

MARY: Of course we have to wait! That's what's so
unbearable!

HANNAH: Try if you can to find a mercy in it.

MARY: A *mercy*—?

HANNAH: A little time to prepare ourselves.

MARY: I'm sorry, Aunt Hannah, you're quite right. Did
Rufus pick out the cap all by himself?

HANNAH: You don't think I chose that monstrosity, do
you? (*She laughs*) At first he picked a very genteel
little serge, but I smelled the hypocrisy behind it, and
forgive an old woman, Mary, but I said, "Do you
really like that one or do you just think it will please
your mother?" Then he revealed his true taste. But
I was switched if I was going to boss him.

MARY: Either he's badly hurt but he'll live. Or he is
so terribly hurt that he will die from it, maybe after
a long, terrible struggle, maybe breathing his last at
this very minute and wondering where I am, why I'm
not there. Or he was already gone when the man

called. Of course it's just what we have no earthly business guessing about. And I'm not going to say he's dead until I know for sure that he is.

HANNAH: Certainly not.

MARY: But I'm all but certain that he is, all the same. (*After a moment*) Oh I do beseech my God that it be not so! (*Turning to Hannah, lost, scared*) Aunt Hannah, can we kneel down for a moment? (*Hannah does not respond*) Aunt *Hannah—?*

HANNAH: No, Mary.

MARY: Why not—?

HANNAH: It's too easy. As you say, it's one thing or the other. But no matter what it is, there's not one thing in this world or the next that we can do or hope or guess at or wish or pray that can change it one iota. Because whatever it is, *is*. That's all. And all there is now is to be ready for it, strong enough for it, whatever it may be. That's all that matters because it's all that's possible.

MARY: I'm *trying* to be ready—!

HANNAH: Your beliefs have never been truly tested. God has come easily to you. He's going to come harder now. But if you wait until you can't go on without Him, you'll find Him. When you *have* to pray, we'll pray.

MARY: Goodness sakes, why don't I get his room ready?

The Effect of Gamma Rays on Man-in-the-Moon Marigolds (1970)

by PAUL ZINDEL

This play, closely focused on a mother and her teenaged daughters, recalls the intimate dramas of the 1950s. Indeed, it was written many years prior to its 1970 off-Broadway production which won it the Pulitzer Prize, an Obie, and the New York Drama Critics Award. The roles have great appeal to actors because of their strong emotional under-currents and psychological complexity.

The girls' mother has been abandoned by her husband. She is loveless and desper-ately unhappy; she takes out her pain and frustration on her daughters, and embrasses them with her eccentric appearance and be-havior. The younger daughter, Tillie, escapes the painful realities of her family life by put-ting all her energies into scientific experi-ments. Ruth, the older and prettier sister, is much more highly strung and temperamental and cannot match Tillie's scholastic achieve-ment.

In the scene that follows, Tillie is pre-paring to go to her high school's science fair to accept a prize for her experiment with

man-in-the-moon marigolds. She is groom-
ing herself for her acceptance speech, trying to overcome her self-consciousness, her
shyness, her insecurity about her looks and
articulateness. Ruth, on the other hand,
needs to upset Tillie. She is jealous of her
and wants her to fail. She tries to intensify
Tillie's insecurities while Tillie tries to hold
herself together.

While Tillie doesn't have much to say,
she has a great deal of acting to do to project her inner preoccupations. This sub-
textual acting is extremely important throughout the scene, as well as the accuracy with
which the actors do their physical business.
We must believe that Ruth is really feeding a
rabbit and that Tillie is really assembling her
experiment.

RUTH: The only competition you have to worry about
is Janice Vickery. They say she caught it near Prin-
cess Bay Boulevard and it was still alive when she
took the skin off it.

TILLIE (*Taking some plants from Ruth*): Let me do
that, please, Ruth.

RUTH: I'm sorry I touched them, really.

TILLIE: Why don't you feed Peter?

RUTH: Because I don't feel like feeding him . . . Now
I feel like feeding him.
(*She gets some lettuce from a bag*)
I heard that it screamed for three minutes after she
put it in because the water wasn't boiling yet. How
much talent does it take to boil the skin off a cat
and then stick the bones together again? That's what
I want to know. Ugh. I had a dream about that, too.
I figure she did it in less than a day and she ends up

as one of the top five winners . . . and you spend
months growing atomic flowers.

TILLIE: Don't you think you should finish getting ready?

RUTH: Finish? This is it!

TILLIE: Are you going to wear that sweater?

RUTH: Look, don't worry about me. I'm not getting up
on any stage, and if I did I wouldn't be caught dead
with a horrible bow like that.

TILLIE: Mother put it—

RUTH: They're going to laugh you off the stage again
like when you cranked that atom in assembly . . .
I didn't mean that . . . The one they're going to laugh
at is Mama.

TILLIE: What?

RUTH: I said the one they're going to laugh at is Mama
. . . Oh, let me take that bow off.

TILLIE: It's all right.

RUTH: Look, just sit still. I don't want everybody making fun of you.

TILLIE: What made you say that about Mama?

RUTH: Oh, I heard them talking in the Science Office
yesterday. Mr. Goodman and Miss Hanley. She's
getting $12.63 to chaperon the thing tonight.

TILLIE: What were they saying?

RUTH: Miss Hanley was telling Mr. Goodman about
Mama . . . when she found out you were one of the
five winners. And he wanted to know if there was
something wrong with Mama because she sounded
crazy over the phone. And Miss Hanley said she
was crazy and she always has been crazy and she

can't wait to see what she looks like after all these years. Miss Hanley said her nickname used to be *Betty the Loon.*

TILLIE (*As Ruth combs her hair*): Ruth, you're hurting me.

RUTH: She was just like you and everybody thought she was a big weirdo. There! You look much better! (*She goes back to the rabbit*)
Peter, if anybody stuck you in a pot of boiling water I'd kill them, do you know that? . . .
(*Then to Tillie*)
What do they call boiling the skin off a cat? I call it murder, that's what I call it. They say it was hit by a car and Janice just scooped it up and before you could say *bingo* it was screaming in a pot of boiling water . . .

Do you know what they're all waiting to see? Mama's feathers! That's what Miss Hanley said. She said Mama blabs as though she was the Queen of England and just as proper as can be, and that her idea of getting dressed up is to put on all the feathers in the world and go as a bird. Always trying to get somewhere, like a great big bird.

TILLIE: Don't tell Mama, please. It doesn't matter.

RUTH: I was up there watching her getting dressed and sure enough, she's got the feathers out.

TILLIE: You didn't tell her what Miss Hanley said?

RUTH: Are you kidding? I just told her I didn't like the feathers and I didn't think she should wear any. But I'll bet she doesn't listen to me.

TILLIE: It doesn't matter.

RUTH: It doesn't matter? Do you think I want to be laughed right out of the school tonight, with Chris Burns there, and all? Laughed right out of the school, with your electric hair and her feathers on that stage, and Miss Hanley splitting her sides?

TILLIE: Promise me you won't say anything.

RUTH: On one condition.

TILLIE: What?

RUTH: Give Peter to me.

TILLIE (*Ignoring her*): The taxi will be here any minute and I won't have all this stuff ready. Did you see my speech?

RUTH: I mean it. Give Peter to me.

TILLIE: He belongs to all of us.

RUTH: For me. All for me. What do you care? He doesn't mean anything to you anymore, now that you've got all those crazy plants.

TILLIE: Will you stop?

RUTH: If you don't give him to me I'm going to tell Mama that everybody's waiting to laugh at her.

TILLIE: Where are those typewritten cards?

RUTH: I MEAN IT! Give him to me!

TILLIE: Does he mean that much to you?

RUTH: Yes!

TILLIE: All right.

FROM Bad Habits (1971)

by TERRENCE McNALLY

Dunelawn is the second play of Terrence McNally's *Bad Habits.* Like *Ravenswood,* it lampoons psychotherapy and self-improvement carried to an extreme. Dunelawn is a place where people go to become perfect and seek to get rid of their bad habits.

The head of Dunelawn is Dr. Toynbee whom Nurse Benson, his chief aide, deeply admires because he has already achieved "perfection." (The character never speaks except gibberish at the end of the play.) Nurse Benson is striving for "perfection" herself and seems to be well on her way. ("Perfection," as you might have guessed, is whatever you wish; it is a person's self-image.) She is purposeful and energetic, very bossy and certain she knows what is absolutely right for everybody. Nurse Hedges, her co-worker and friend, is the opposite. She is preoccupied with her feelings of inferiority and snivels all the time. Nurse Hedges needs encouragment and advice in her quest for perfectability; Nurse Benson needs to reinforce her confidence by using Hedges as a less-perfect person who needs the advice and encouragement only she is able to give. They satisfy each other's needs, absurd as they may be.

The actresses need not look for complexity in these roles. Portray each character boldly and keep experimenting until it feels like fun. This is very much a duo scene; accurately playing off each other and finding exactly the right rhythms are extremely important.

HEDGES: I admire you so much!

BENSON: Becky Hedges!

HEDGES: You can help me to get rid of my faults until you're blue in the face, but I'll never be the beauty you are.

BENSON: You're an adorable person, Becky.

HEDGES: I'm not talking about adorable. I'm talking about beauty. No one ever told Elizabeth Taylor she was adorable.

BENSON: Do I have to say it? Beauty is skin deep. Besides, Elizabeth has a lot of faults.

HEDGES: You're changing the subject. Ruth, look at me.

BENSON: Yes?

HEDGES: Now tell me this is a beautiful woman you see.

BENSON: What are you driving at, Becky?

HEDGES: Nothing. I just wish I were beautiful like you. And I don't want you to just *say* I am.

BENSON: I wouldn't do that to you.

HEDGES: Thank you.

BENSON: I said you were adorable.

HEDGES: And I said you were beautiful.

BENSON: It's out of my hands.

HEDGES: It's out of mine, too.

BENSON: You're sniveling again.

HEDGES: I know.

BENSON (*She pulls Hedges over to the bench and sits her down*): Becky, listen to me. You think I'm beautiful. Thank you. I can accept a compliment. I know I'm beautiful. I can't lie to myself anymore. But what good did it do me as far as Hugh Gumbs was concerned?

HEDGES: Such a beautiful name!

BENSON: There you go again, Becky.

HEDGES: I didn't snivel that time.

BENSON: You made a stupid, flattering, self-serving, Minnie Mouse remark, which is much worse. Hugh Gumbs is not a beautiful name and you know it.

HEDGES: I'm sorry. I'll be good. I'll be better. Finish your story.

BENSON: I don't even remember where I was.

HEDGES: You were talking about your beauty and how little good it did you as far as Hugh Gumbs was concerned.

BENSON: That man wouldn't even look at me. Looks had nothing to do with it. I know that now. Ask Hugh Gumbs! And I know I'm more beautiful than that hussy he abandoned me for. In my heart of hearts, I know that Mildred Canby is not a beautiful woman.

HEDGES: Mildred who?

BENSON: Mildred Canby.

HEDGES: What a horrible name, too.

BENSON: Attractive, yes. Beautiful, no. Now what Hugh Gumbs wanted in a woman, what every man wants in any woman, is something deeper than beauty. He wants character. He wants the traditional virtues. He wants womanly warmth.

HEDGES: You can say that again.

BENSON: Believe me, Hugh Gumbs is a very unhappy man right now. How could he not be? Mildred Canby had even less character and more faults than I did. And less beauty, too. I knew that marriage wouldn't last. (*She takes out her compact*)

HEDGES: Don't cry, Ruth.

BENSON: Me? Cry? Why should I cry?

HEDGES: Because you lost Hugh?

BENSON: I'm grateful to him! He broke my heart, I don't deny it, but if it hadn't been for Hugh I would never have been forced into the soul-searching and self-reevaluation that ended up with the 118-pound, trim-figured woman you say is so beautiful standing in front of you. No, when I think back on Ruth Benson then and compare her to Ruth Benson now, I thank my lucky stars for Hugh.

HEDGES (*As Benson continues to gaze at herself in the compact mirror*): You're so wise, Ruth.

BENSON: Am I?

HEDGES: Wise about love.

BENSON: I wonder.

HEDGES: You are.

BENSON: We'll see.

HEDGES: I'm not.

BENSON: Hmmmmmmm?

HEDGES: Wise about love. I'm downright dumb about it. If I weren't, I'd be married to Tim Taylor right this very minute. What I wouldn't give for another chance at him!

BENSON: Buck up, Hedges.

HEDGES: Oh I will, Ruth. I'm just feeling a little sorry for myself. I don't know why. If you want to know the truth, I haven't thought of Tim Taylor one way or the other for a long time.

BENSON: I should hope not. A man who smokes is a very bad emotional risk.

HEDGES: Tim didn't smoke.

BENSON: But he drank. It's the same thing. Rummies, every last one of them.

HEDGES: Did Hugh Gumbs drink?

BENSON: Among other things.

HEDGES: It must have been awful for you.

BENSON: It was heck. Sheer unadulterated heck.

HEDGES: That sounds funny.

BENSON: Believe me, it wasn't.

HEDGES: No, what you just said. About it being heck. I'm still used to people saying the other.

BENSON: It won't seem funny after a while. You'll see. (*Dr. Toynbee strolls across the stage, smiling benignly, reading a book*) Good morning, Dr. Toynbee!

HEDGES: Good morning, Dr. Toynbee! That man is so good, Ruth!

BENSON: I worship the ground he walks on.

HEDGES: Oh me, too, me, too! I'd give anything to be just like him.

BENSON: Goodbye, Dr. Toynbee! And thank you!

HEDGES: Goodbye, Dr. Toynbee! And thank you! (*Dr. Toynbee exits down the aisle, waving*) Ruth?

BENSON: What?

HEDGES: I know it's none of my business, but I've seen that look in your eyes whenever Dr. Toynbee passes.

BENSON: What look?

HEDGES: You know.

BENSON: The only look, as you put it, in my eyes when Dr. Toynbee passes is one of sheer and utter respect. Certainly not the look you're so grossly alluding to. You're out of line, don't you think, Hedges? You're certainly in extremely bad taste.

HEDGES: You're not sweet on the good doctor?

BENSON: Dr. Toynbee is above that.

HEDGES: I know, but are you? (*Benson slaps her*) Is any woman? (*Benson slaps her again and they fall into each other's arms crying*) I'm sorry, Ruth, I didn't mean to hurt you. You've been so good to me! I'm such a different person since I've been with you! I don't even know who I am anymore and I say these silly, dreadful, awful things! I don't recognize myself in the mirror in the morning. I've changed so much it scares me.

BENSON: You haven't changed. You've improved, re-

fined, what was already there. I always had this figure, don't you see? Even when I weighed all that
weight, I still had this figure.

HEDGES: Even when you were up to 230?

BENSON: I was never 230.

HEDGES: You told me you were ...

BENSON: I was never 230! Now shut up and listen, will
you?

HEDGES: I'm sorry, Ruth.

BENSON: I didn't change anything. People are born
without any faults, they simply fall into bad habits
along life's way. Nobody's trying to *change* anybody,
Becky. It's the real them coming out, that's all.

HEDGES: The real them!

BENSON: Look, face it, you've got big thighs, that's the
real you. Now I've got nice thighs, as it turns out,
but I didn't always know that.

HEDGES: I don't think I can get any thinner.

BENSON: I'm not talking about diets. I'm talking about
the real you and your G.D. big thighs!

HEDGES: That's exactly what Tim Taylor didn't like
about me. And now that I'm getting thinner they
look even bigger. I *know!* I'm sniveling again! I don't
know what to do about them, Ruth! (*She is desper-
ately hitting her thighs*)

BENSON: Wear longer skirts!

HEDGES: Now you really are cross with me!

BENSON: You can be so dense sometimes. I mean really, Hedges, I'm talking about a whole other thing

and you start sniveling about diets. You can diet all you want and you're still going to end up with big thighs. That's not the point.

HEDGES: What is it, then?

BENSON: Oh there's no point in talking to you about it!

HEDGES: I'm sorry.

BENSON: And stop that horrible sniveling!

HEDGES: I'm never going to get any better. I have just as many bad habits as when I came here. We just keep pretending I'm improving when the real truth is, I'm getting worse! (*She races to the medical cart and hysterically prepares one of the syringes*)

BENSON: What are you doing?

HEDGES: Why shouldn't I? I'm no better than anyone of them and I'm supposed to work here!

BENSON: Give me that! (*They struggle*)

HEDGES: Let me do it, Ruth!

BENSON: Have you lost your mind?

HEDGES: I wish I was dead! (*Benson topples Hedges, who falls in a heap, and takes away the syringe. Almost without realizing, she reaches inside her blouse and takes a package of cigarettes out of her bosom, puts one in her mouth and strikes a match. Hedges raises her head at the sound*) Ruth!

BENSON: Oh my God! I wasn't thinking!

HEDGES: You of all people!

BENSON: I wasn't going to smoke one!

HEDGES: It's a full pack.

BENSON: It's a courtesy pack. In case I run into someone. They're not mine. I've given it up. I swear to God I have. You've got to believe me.

HEDGES: I don't know what to think.

BENSON: Becky, please!

HEDGES: If you say so, Ruth.

part 3

Scenes for Two Men

FROM The Strike (1954)

by ROD SERLING

This is an excellent example of the socially conscious drama done so well on television in the 1950s, written by one of the most accomplished social-activist writers of the period for one of the more consistent programs, Studio One.

The Strike is a play in documentary style about the unrelieved anguish and guilt of war. It takes place in the battlefield operations post, a cellar, in Korea in 1951. Major Gaylord, in his late thirties, is dressed in a war-torn uniform with the face and posture to match it. He has decided to risk the death of a platoon of 20 men in an attempt to save the remaining 500. The wounded Lt. Jones, who is in direct command of the 20, has just learned of Major Gaylord's decision. Although he shares the numbing tiredness of war, he cannot stand by while his men are being sacrificed for strategic military considerations.

Jones' youth, with its deliberate assurance and persistence, is in direct contrast to the Major's authority and weary sense of responsibility. Jones is dominated by one thought: his men must be saved. The Major is occupied with the many details of command; he can only intermittently give Jones his attention. Develop business that will make

clear his preoccupation and Jones's re-
peated efforts to break through and confront
him.

_____

JONES: Major Gaylord? I'm Jones, sir. A Company.

GAYLORD: So?

JONES: You sent a platoon of my company out yesterday afternoon. On a patrol.

GAYLORD: We're trying to make contact now.

JONES: You haven't heard from them, then?

GAYLORD: Not yet
(*He lights a cigarette, turns his back*)

JONES: May I ask the purpose of that patrol?

GAYLORD: You're out of line, Lieutenant. (*Turns to
him*) It should be quite obvious why a patrol is sent
out in a situation like ours.

JONES: To ascertain the strength and location of the
enemy? You mean you don't know . . . sir?

GAYLORD: You concerned about 'em, are you, Jones?

JONES: They're twenty of my men.

GAYLORD: I didn't know that. Your brand wasn't on
them. Had I known I'd have sent out three ROK's
and a platoon of army nurses.

JONES: Major Gaylord—those men don't stand a
chance across that river—and I want to know whose
decision it was to send 'em across.

GAYLORD: My decision. Are you satisfied?

JONES: How about another patrol to hunt for 'em?

GAYLORD: Negative.

JONES: Just a couple of men . . . and myself, then.

GAYLORD: Negative. We can't spare a couple of men now.

JONES: You could spare twenty yesterday afternoon!

GAYLORD: That was yesterday afternoon.

JONES: Begging your pardon, sir—

GAYLORD: Don't beg my pardon. Speak your piece and get back to your company.

JONES: My company is five effectives, forty litter cases —and the rest of 'em are face down for three miles up the road.

GAYLORD: What do you want, Jones? Taps and an invocation? At 0600 we're moving back . . . straight back. There's three miles of open country. If artillery's been brought up across the river we couldn't be a better target if we got painted with red, white and blue lines with a dot in the forehead. That's why a patrol went across to find out.

JONES: It did a lot of good, didn't it?

GAYLORD (*Looks at him for a long time*: Jonesy— this whole stinking war doesn't seem to be doing much good. But if it makes you happy—I'm sweatin' those boys of yours out like each one was a kid brother.

JONES: But not enough to send somebody out to save their necks.

GAYLORD: That'll do it.

JONES: And when we move out, do we leave 'em out there?

GAYLORD: I said that'll do it!

JONES (*A pause, and then very quietly*): Yessir. (*He turns and goes out*)

FROM **A Hatful of Rain** (1955)

by MICHAEL V. GAZZO

(See previous notes on this play, p. 31.)

In this scene, Johnny's action is to get $20 from Polo to pay his gangster creditors for a fix. Although his feelings about his brother are uncomplicated, his immediate goal is pursued with some indirection. He asks for pity, he promises reform, and finally resorts to revealing that there are threats on his life. Polo, on the other hand, is burdened with love-hate feelings toward his brother. He has taken the blame for the loss of his father's money, which in fact Johnny spent on drugs. Polo has now decided that he will not give in to his brother's entreaties, he will not be made to feel guilty, he will stay in control. The scene plays out the interaction of their divergent needs and desires. The actors should develop the physical life of the scene (Polo prepares the laundry and Johnny finds different business) so that they don't play everything as a direct confrontation.

It is about ten in the morning. As the lights dim up, Johnny is seen coming down the fire escape. Halfway down, he slips; panicked, he grabs the railing and stops his fall. He steadies himself and then climbs down to the hall. He opens the door and enters the kitchen. The door to Polo's room is ajar.

JOHNNY: Polo! Hi!

POLO: Welcome home.

JOHNNY: Celia go to work?

POLO: It's ten o'clock in the morning. She starts at nine . . . she's not here, so figure it out for yourself.

JOHNNY: The old man wanted you to have those shirts. How do they fit?

POLO: I haven't put it on yet.

JOHNNY: I was out all night.

POLO: No kidding. Your wife wants you to get these things for supper.

JOHNNY: Where are you going?

POLO: I'm going to take the laundry out. . . .

JOHNNY: You know what's happening . . . ?

POLO: I read the papers. Where you been?

JOHNNY: All over.

POLO: Where's all over?

JOHNNY: All over . . . Harlem, Lower East Side . . . everybody's disappeared.

POLO: It'll all blow over in a few weeks. . . .

JOHNNY: No. No . . . they dropped the net, Polo . . . they're starting to tie the knot. Every pusher in the city's vanished. . . . Look, Polo. . . . I was lucky. I met Ginnino. I told him to hold some for me . . . I have to get to him in fifteen minutes.

POLO: Who fixed you last night?

JOHNNY: Chuchie . . . I stopped over his place. He gave me half of his . . . enough to carry me through the night . . . but I'm thin now, Polo.

POLO: I told you yesterday, Johnny, the cupboard's bare. I'm out of the box and that's all there is to it. If I inherited the Chrysler building right now I wouldn't give you another dime. Try to understand that.

JOHNNY: Don't start lecturing me now. All I need is twenty bucks—and he won't do business on credit.

POLO: Take the kitchen set down and sell it to the Salvation Army. This linoleum isn't in bad shape. If you sell it at night in the dark, maybe you can get a few bucks for it. . . .

JOHNNY: Polo, you know I never sold a thing out of this house and I never will.

POLO: Try to listen, Johnny, try to hear me. I felt great refusing the old man that twenty-five hundred because I know the money went to a good cause. . . . It's only something he wanted all his life. You were right in the middle when he shouted, "Where? Where did it go?"

JOHNNY: Yeh, I was right in the middle. And I almost said, "Here!" It went here. (*Thrusting his arm forward*)

POLO: You went through that twenty-five hundred like grease through a tin horn. . . . I'm afraid to park my car out front . . . you might steal it some night.

JOHNNY: I'm quitting tomorrow. Tomorrow I'm quitting. . . .

POLO: It's been tomorrow for months, Johnny, the calendar never moves.

JOHNNY: Polo! This is the last time I'll ask you . . . I need twenty bucks. . . .

POLO: Twenty bucks, twice a day.

JOHNNY: Where am I gonna get it?

POLO: Get yourself a black felt hat, cut holes in it for eyes, and go down in the men's room of the subway like Apples does and clobber some poor bastard over the head. . . .

JOHNNY: The answer is no?

POLO: You look tired. . . .

JOHNNY: Here. . . . (*Tosses gun on bed*) I almost used it four times last night . . . I picked dark streets and I waited. Four times . . . and they were set-ups. An old guy . . . must have been eighty years old . . . all alone. A guy and his girl, a young kid coming home from a dance drunk . . . some woman. Four times I left the doorway—I was on top of them . . . They weren't even afraid of me. I asked for a match, which way Fifty-sixth Street was . . . and would you give me a light please. Dust—that's all. Tired feet, tired eyes, and jammed up log tight.

POLO: Where did you get this . . . ?

JOHNNY: The lousy bastards told me it wasn't loaded. I'm into them for seven or eight hundred . . . on top of your twenty-five hundred cash. They want their money today . . . They'll be coming for me.

POLO: What do you mean?

JOHNNY: What do you think I mean?

POLO: It's not going to be Mother and Apples alone . . . they know I'm here, they'll bring company. Put those shoes on and let's get out of here.

JOHNNY: No more running, Polo. I'm through running. I can't run anymore. If they don't get me today, they'll get me tomorrow.

POLO: You saw what happened to Willy DeCarlo . . .

JOHNNY: I'm not running away from them . . . and that's that! I'm going to stay right here. . . .

POLO: You're crazy, you're going crazy!

JOHNNY: I'm not moving. . . .

POLO: I haven't got seven or eight hundred dollars, Johnny . . . there's nothing I can do.

JOHNNY: Take the laundry out . . . and go to a movie or something.

POLO: What are you going to do?

JOHNNY: I'm going to wait for them . . .

POLO: You going to fight back . . . ?

JOHNNY: Well, I'm not going to stand still while they beat the hell out of me. . . .

POLO: You can't win . . . they'll kick your ribs in.

FROM **A Memory of Two Mondays** (1955)

by ARTHUR MILLER

This long one-act play was first produced
with another, *A View from the Bridge,* which
was the generic title for the evening. Set in an
automobile parts warehouse in the 1930s, it
is a memory without a plot, a memory of
people whose lives are filled with loss, small
victories, and the inexorable pressures of
mean, hard times.

This scene is between two of the more
articulate workers, 18-year-old Bert, who is
leaving the next day to go to college, and the
young man he considers his intellectual superior, 26-year-old Kenneth. Kenneth, an
Irish immigrant, is romantic about life itself,
but very realistic about life's limited possi-
bilities for himself. He knows he has nowhere
to go, so he has stopped yearning and has
taken to drink. They will soon be separated,
Ken to stick fast to his own despair, and Bert
to go forward unheralded but resolute.

Their conversation is an intimate inter-
lude in which each character confides his
fears, frustrations, and hopes. The scene has
no one dramatic issue; it is a montage of a
relationship with many transitions. An over-
abundance of naturalistic details will reduce
and clutter the acting and interfere with its
evocativeness.

KENNETH: Bert? How would you feel about washing these windows—you and I—once and for all? Let a little of God's light in the place?

BERT: Would you?

KENNETH: Well, I would if you would.

BERT: Okay, come on! Let's do a little every day; couple of months it'll all be clean! Gee! Look at the sun!

KENNETH: Hey, look down there!
See the old man sitting in a chair?
And roses all over the fence!
Oh, that's a lovely back yard!
(*A rag in hand, Bert mounts the table; they make one slow swipe of the window before them and instantly all the windows around the stage burst into the yellow light of summer that floods into the room*)

BERT: Boy, they've got a tree!
And all those cats!

KENNETH: It'll be nice to watch the seasons pass.
That pretty up there now, a real summer sky
And a little white cloud goin' over?
I can just see autumn comin' in
And the leaves falling on the gray days.
You've got to have a sky to look at!
(*Gradually, as they speak, all light hardens to that of winter, finally*)

BERT: Kenny, were you ever fired from a job?

KENNETH: Oh, sure; two-three times.

BERT: Did you feel bad?

KENNETH: The first time, maybe. But you have to get used to that, Bert. I'll bet you never went hungry in your life, did you?

BERT: No, I never did. Did you?

KENNETH: Oh, many and many a time. You get used to that too, though.

BERT: That tree is turning red.

KENNETH: It must be spectacular out in the country now.

BERT: How does the cold get through these walls?
Feel it, it's almost a wind!

KENNETH: Don't cats walk dainty in the snow!

BERT: Gee, you'd never know it was the same place—
How clean it is when it's white!
Gus doesn't say much anymore, y'know?

KENNETH: Well, he's showin' his age. Gus is old.
When do you buy your ticket for the train?

BERT: I did. I've got it.

KENNETH: Oh, then you're off soon!
You'll confound all the professors, I'll bet!
(*He sings softly*)
    "The minstrel boy to the war has gone . . ."
(*Bert moves a few feet away; thus he is alone. Kenneth remains at the window, looking out, polishing, and singing softly*)

BERT: There's something so terrible here!
There always was, and I don't know what.
Gus, and Agnes, and Tommy and Larry, Jim and Patricia—
Why does it make me so sad to see them every morning?
It's like the subway;
Every day I see the same people getting on
And the same people getting off,
And all that happens is that they get older. God!
Sometimes it scares me; like all of us in the world
Were riding back and forth across a great big room,
From wall to wall and back again,

And no end ever! Just no end!
(*He turns to Kenneth, but not quite looking at him,
and with a deeper anxiety*)
Didn't you ever want to be anything, Kenneth?

KENNETH: I've never been able to keep my mind on
it, Bert. . . .
I shouldn't've cut a hole in me shoe.
Now the snow's slushin' in, and me feet's all wet.

BERT: If you studied, Kenneth, if you put your mind
to something great, I know you'd be able to learn
anything, because you're clever, you're much smarter
than I am!

KENNETH: You've got something steady in your mind,
Bert;
Something far away and steady.
I never could hold my mind on a far-away thing . . .
(*His tone changes as though he were addressing a
group of men; his manner is rougher, angrier, less
careful of proprieties*)
She's not giving me the heat I'm entitled to.
Eleven dollars a week room and board,
And all she puts in the bag is a lousy pork sandwich,
The same every day and no surprises.
Is that right? Is that right now?
How's a man to live.
Freezing all day in this palace of dust
And night comes with one window and a bed
And the streets full of strangers
And not one of them's read a book through,
Or seen a poem from beginning to end
Or knows a song worth singing.
Oh, this is an ice-cold city, Mother,
And Roosevelt's not makin' it warmer, somehow.
(*He sits on the table, holding his head*)
And here's another grand Monday!
(*They are gradually appearing in natural light now,*

*but is a cold wintry light which has gradually sup-
planted the hot light of summer. Bert goes to the
hook for a sweater)*

Jesus, me head'll murder me. I never had the head-
ache till this year.

BERT: You're not taking up drinking, are you?

KENNETH (*He doesn't reply. Suddenly, as though to
retrieve something slipping by, he gets to his feet,
and roars out*):

"The Ship of State," by Walt Whitman!
"O Captain! my Captain! our fearful trip is done!
    The ship has weathered every wrack,
    The prize we sought is won . . ."

Now what in the world comes after that?

BERT: I don't know that poem.

KENNETH: Dammit all! I don't remember the bloody
poems anymore the way I did! It's the drinkin' does
it, I think. I've got to stop the drinkin'!

BERT: Well, why do you drink, Kenny, if it makes you
feel—

KENNETH: Good God, Bert, you can't always be doin'
what you're better off to do! There's all kinds of
unexpected turns, y'know, and things not workin' out
the way they ought! What in hell *is* the next stanza
of that poem? "The prize we sought is won . . ."
God, I'd never believe I could forget that poem! I'm
thinkin', Bert, y'know—maybe I ought to go on to
the Civil Service. The only trouble is there's no jobs
open except for the guard in the insane asylum. And
that'd be a nervous place to work, I think.

BERT: It might be interesting, though.

KENNETH: I suppose it might. They tell me it's only

the more intelligent people goes mad, y'know. But it's sixteen hundred a year, Bert, and I've a feelin' I'd never dare leave it, y'know? And I'm not ready for me last job yet, I think. I don't want nothin' to be the last, yet. Still and all . . .

The Zoo Story (1959)

by EDWARD ALBEE

Edward Albee wrote his first play, *The Zoo Story,* as a "sort of thirtieth birthday present" to himself. Rejected by American producers, it was first performed in Germany, followed by an American production a year later. Albee believes that all his work is an effort to illuminate man's condition as it really is, without flattery, or reassurance, or pandering.

Jerry is in his thirties, an outsider, a "permanent transient," a prototype of the violent and alienated characters of the 1960s. The play begins after he has walked all the way up Fifth Avenue in New York City on a summer Sunday and has arrived in Central Park. Almost at the end of his own history, designing his own suicide-murder, he confronts Peter, an ordinary looking man in his early forties who has a proper job, a proper family with pets, a proper life.

As this scene begins, Jerry is moving with increased agitation to the final stages of his quest; he must bring this confrontation to a climax and reach a resolution to his caged existence. Jerry says to Peter, "You have everything in the world you want." Indeed, Peter has established himself comfortably and wants to keep things that way;

he will, when challenged, defend his home, family—and his park bench—to the death.

Albee's dialogue is highly charged and filled with dramatic energy; do not let the exhilarating feeling of "acting" which it provides lull you into thinking you have it. Work on making the meaning, the truth of the lines, and drives of the characters alive in you. Your acting ability should also suggest the lethalness of the object you use as a weapon. Do not use a real knife.

JERRY: You have everything in the world you want; you've told me about your home, and your family, and *your own* little zoo. You have everything, and now you want this bench. Are these the things men fight for? Tell me, Peter, is this bench, this iron and this wood, is this your honor? Is this the thing in the world you'd fight for? Can you think of anything more absurd?

PETER: Absurd? Look, I'm not going to talk to you about honor, or even try to explain it to you. Besides, it isn't a question of honor; but even if it were, you wouldn't understand.

JERRY (*Contemptuously*): You don't even know what you're saying, do you? This is probably the first time in your life you've had anything more trying to face than changing your cats' toilet box. Stupid! Don't you have any idea, not even the slightest, what other people *need*?

PETER: Oh, boy, listen to you; well, you don't need this bench. That's for sure.

JERRY: Yes; yes, I do.

PETER (*Quivering*): I've come here for years; I have hours of great pleasure, great satisfaction, right here. And that's important to a man. I'm a responsible person, and I'm a GROWNUP. This is my bench, and you have no right to take it away from me.

JERRY: Fight for it, then. Defend yourself; defend your bench.

PETER: You've *pushed* me to it. Get up and fight.

JERRY: Like a man?

PETER (*Still angry*): Yes, like a man, if you insist on mocking me even further.

JERRY: I'll have to give you credit for one thing: you *are* a vegetable, and a slightly nearsighted one, I think . . .

PETER: THAT'S ENOUGH. . . .

JERRY: . . . but, you know, as they say on TV all the time—you know—and I mean this, Peter, you have a certain dignity; it surprises me. . . .

PETER: STOP!

JERRY (*Rises lazily*): Very well, Peter, we'll battle for the bench, but we're not evenly matched. (*He takes out and clicks open an ugly-looking knife.*)

PETER (*Suddenly awakening to the reality of the situation*): You *are* mad! You're stark raving mad! YOU'RE GOING TO KILL ME!
(*But before Peter has time to think what to do, Jerry tosses the knife at Peter's feet*)

JERRY: There you go. Pick it up. You have the knife and we'll be more evenly matched.

PETER (*Horrified*): No!

JERRY (*Rushes over to Peter, grabs him by the collar; Peter rises; their faces almost touch*): Now you pick up that knife and you fight with me. You fight for your self-respect; you fight for that goddamned bench.

PETER (*Struggling*): No! Let . . . let go of me! He . . . Help!

JERRY (*Slaps Peter on each "fight"*): You fight, you miserable bastard; fight for that bench; fight for your parakeets; fight for your cats, fight for your two daughters; fight for your wife; fight for your manhood, you pathetic little vegetable. (*Spits in Peter's face*) You couldn't even get your wife with a male child.

PETER (*Breaks away, enraged*): It's a matter of genetics, not manhood, you . . . you monster. (*He darts down, picks up the knife and backs off a little; he is breathing heavily*) I'll give you one last chance; get out of here and leave me alone! (*He holds the knife with a firm arm, but far in front of him, not to attack, but to defend*)

JERRY (*Sighs heavily*): So be it!
(*With a rush he charges Peter and impales himself on the knife. Tableau: For just a moment, complete silence, Jerry impaled on the knife at the end of Peter's still firm arm. Then Peter screams, pulls away, leaving the knife in Jerry. Jerry is motionless, on point. Then he, too, screams, and it must be the sound of an infuriated and fatally wounded animal. With the knife in him, he stumbles back to the bench that Peter had vacated. He crumbles there, sitting, facing Peter, his eyes wide in agony, his mouth open*)

PETER (*Whispering*): Oh my God, oh my God, oh my God. . . . (*He repeats these words many times, very rapidly*)

JERRY (*Jerry is dying; but now his expression seems to change. His features relax, and while his voice varies, sometimes wrenched with pain, for the most part he seems removed from his dying. He smiles*): Thank you, Peter. I mean that, now; thank you very much. (*Peter's mouth drops open. He cannot move; he is transfixed*) Oh, Peter, I was so afraid I'd drive you away. (*He laughs as best he can*) You don't know how afraid I was you'd go away and leave me. And now I'll tell you what happened at the zoo. I think . . . I think this is what happened at the zoo . . . I think. I think that while I was at the zoo I decided that I would walk north . . . northerly, rather . . . until I found you . . . or somebody . . . and I decided that I would talk to you . . . I would tell you things . . . and things that I would tell you would . . . Well, here we are. You see? Here we *are*. But . . . I don't . . . could I have planned all this? No . . . no, I couldn't have. But I think I did. And now I've told you what you wanted to know, haven't I? And now you know all about what happened at the zoo. And now you know what you'll see in your TV, and the face I told you about . . . you remember . . . the face I told you about . . . my face, the face you see right now. Peter . . . Peter? . . . Peter . . . thank you. I came unto you (*He laughs, so faintly*) and you have comforted me. Dear Peter.

PETER (*Almost fainting*): Oh my God!

JERRY: You'd better go now. Somebody might come by, and you don't want to be here when anyone comes.

PETER (*Does not move, but begins to weep*): Oh my God, oh my God.

JERRY (*Most faintly, now; he is very near death*): You won't be coming back here anymore, Peter; you've been dispossessed. You've lost your bench, but you've defended your honor. And Peter, I'll tell you something now; you're not really a vegetable; it's all right, you're an animal. You're an animal, too. But you'd better hurry now, Peter. Hurry, you'd better go . . . see? (*Jerry takes a handkerchief and with great effort and pain wipes the knife handle clean* of fingerprints) Hurry away, Peter. (*Peter begins to stagger away*) Wait . . . wait, Peter. Take your book . . . book. Right here . . . beside me . . . on your bench . . . my bench, rather. Come . . . take your book. (*Peter starts for the book, but retreats*) Hurry . . . Peter. (*Peter rushes to the bench, grabs the book, retreats*) Very good, Peter . . . very good. Now . . . hurry away. (*Peter hesitates for a moment, then flees*) Hurry away. . . . (*His eyes are closed now*) Hurry away, your parakeets are making the dinner . . . the cats . . . are setting the table . . .

PETER (*Off stage, a pitiful howl*): OH MY GOD!

JERRY: (*His eyes still closed, he shakes his head and speaks; a combination of scornful mimicry and supplication*): Oh . . . my . . . God.
(*He is dead*)
(*Curtain*)

All the Way Home (1961)

by TAD MOSEL

(See previous notes on this play, p. 177.)

In this scene two brothers reveal their ambivalent sibling relationship. Both men are in their mid-30s. Jay is the more stable, helped by his wife Mary and her strength. He works in his father-in-law's law office and is presently awaiting the birth of his second child. With patience and responsibility, Jay tries to supply Ralph with a ballast, a gentle hand to lead him out of the abyss of alcoholism. Ralph too is married and has a son, but he is an undertaker who carries with him the deathly smell of formaldehyde. He is undermined by his insecurities, his feelings of inferiority, his terrible fever of competitiveness and jealousy toward his brother. Here he seeks reassurance that he is equal to Jay and like him in many ways.

Playing "drunk" can be a trap if the actor just stumbles around and slurs his speech. Rather, very specific feelings and attitudes are released by drunkenness; they usually come out with some degree of exaggeration, and there are rapid transitions of mood. Ralph goes from defending himself with complaints, to expressions of warmth for Jay, to self-pity. The actor should feel these things and then release them with the letting-go licensed by being drunk.

RALPH: Smell my hands, Jay, go ahead, smell 'em.

JAY: Now there's nothin' on your hands, Ralph.

RALPH: Yes there is, Jay, it's that f'maldehyde. *I* can't smell it but ever'body else can. I scrub 'em and scrub 'em, and I can't ever get rid of that smell. Why last night I went t'the picture show, and I was sittin' there next t'this girl and she got up and moved. It was that smell, Jay, don't you think?

JAY: Go on, Ralph, you're the worst tail chaser in La-Follette!

RALPH: It was 'at smell made her move, I tell yuh! It's terrible t'work with it ever' day of your life, and then even when you go out for a good time t'have it go along with yuh. The picture show was good though. Charlie. You like Charlie?

JAY: Sure do.

RALPH: Last night he put a bag of eggs in the seat of his pants and then forgot and sat on 'em. (*He panto-mimes this and sits in chair at the table*)

JAY (*Laughing*): Rufus and I seen that one.

RALPH (*Laughing with him*): You 'n' I like lotsa the same things, Jay, maybe we're more brothers than we seem.

JAY: I reckon people'd know we was brothers.

RALPH: Thank yuh for that. (*Taking up the bottle*) Well, outside they're thinkin' he's been in there long enough for two drinks, and I've only had one. If that's what they're goin' to think, I might's well *have* two!

JAY: You sure can hold it, Ralph.

RALPH: He'p yourself.

JAY: Ever'body's waitin' on us, Ralph!

RALPH: Go on, Jay, Mary can't see. I tell you what, I'll keep watch for yuh!

JAY: It ain't that. (*He shoves the bottle at Ralph who grabs it from him*)

RALPH: So God-damned reformed, ain't you!

JAY: I'm just thinkin' of you. If you keep pullin' away at that bottle, it ain't goin' to last you through the day. And I know that feelin' when the bottle's empty and you ain't full.

RALPH: I want it to be empty, Jay. I'm no good when I'm like this. No good at all. I'm mean and I'm reckless. I'm not even real. *I wish this bottle was empty!*
(*After a short silence, Jay grabs the bottle from him, drinks the last of the whiskey and drops the bottle loudly into the trash can*)

JAY: Empty. Now are you ready to go?

RALPH: How's it make you feel, Jay?

JAY: That little bit don't make me feel anything.

RALPH: If you had a lot?

JAY: Come on, Ralph, it's gettin' late. If we're going to get to Great-Granmaw's and back before dark, we got to start.

RALPH: I ain't movin' from this spot till you tell me how it makes you feel!

JAY: Well, if I had as much as you, Ralph, I'd go quiet. So quiet, I could hear the tickin' of the earth. And I'd be young as ever I could remember, and nothin' bad had ever happened to me or ever would. I wouldn't dare talk to no one, of course, for fear they'd show me the lie. And after a while it'd get lonesome in there all by myself, and I'd go off like a firecracker. If you happened to be standin' by, you'd get a few powder burns, let me tell you.

RALPH: What made you change, Jay? Was it Mary's religion?

JAY: Mary's religion is her own.

RALPH: How'd you do it, then?

JAY: I made a vow to myself. I said if I ever get drunk again, I'll kill myself.

RALPH: Oh Jay. That's a strong vow.

JAY: Couldn't afford to leave myself any loopholes.

RALPH: Don't y'ever get thirsty?

JAY: There's too many reasons why I don't want to kill myself.

RALPH: What reasons?

JAY: There's two of 'em right out in the yard. (*Grinning*) As a matter of fact, two'n a half. (*His patience beginning to go*) Now come on, Ralph, I promised them an outing today! They been lookin' forward to it for weeks, and I'm not goin' to disappoint them!

RALPH: I got reasons out in the yard too, don't I, Jay?

JAY (*Giving him a towel, briskly*): Now wipe off your face. You worked yourself into a sweat.

RALPH: I could take that vow of yours, couldn't I, Jay?

JAY: Nobody's goin' to try and stop you!

RALPH: I'm takin' that vow this minute! Stand back! (*He stands up and straightens himself*) Or Jay, maybe I could just take a vow that if ever I get drunk again I'll take your vow.

JAY: You better think on it, Ralph, that's a pretty serious step!

RALPH: All right, Jay, I tell you what! I hereby take a vow—to think on it!

FROM The Old Glory (1964)

by ROBERT LOWELL

In his trilogy *The Old Glory,* Robert Lowell analyzes the American character by looking back into our history and literature. His sources are Hawthorne and Melville, but the work is totally his own, invested with his acute historical sense and written in his elegant and purposeful verse. It is America's major poetic epic. It was the opening production of the American Place Theatre and was presented again as our Bicentennial celebration.

Benito Cereno is the most mysterious and immediately appealing of the three plays. It takes place around the year 1800, when America is sensing her destiny and beginning to have a presence on the world scene. Cocksure and arrogant, intent on sloughing off her puritan provincialism, magnanimous in a manner only wild optimism and unlimited resources allow, America steps into her future.

Captain Delano is the prototypical American, confident in his virtue, good intentions, and good health. Yet he lacks the insight to deal with the forces of change, failure, and decay, and he is put profoundly off-balance by the presence of Blacks. *Benito Cereno* dramatizes this deep immaturity in the American character, but in this opening

224

scene, the prevailing feeling must still be "all is very, very well."

Delano's bosun, John Perkins, is at the beginning of his career and wants to prove himself to the captain as a fit, observant, and knowledgeable young officer. Delano needs to demonstrate his worldliness and superior ability to perceive what is going on, not just in America but all over the world. He relishes the opportunity to educate his pupil, the puritanical Perkins.

Since the play is in verse, the actors must be attentive to the rhythms and give full value to the resonant language, but avoid surface elocution. The intentions, the relationships, the attitudes are real.

About the year 1800, an American sealing vessel, the President Adams, *at anchor in an island harbor off the coast of Trinidad. The stage is part of the ship's deck. Everything is unnaturally clean, bare and ship-shape. To one side, a polished, coal-black cannon. The American captain, Amasa Delano from Duxbury, Massachusetts, sits in a cane chair. He is a strong, comfortable-looking man in his early thirties who wears a spotless blue coat and white trousers. Incongruously, he has on a straw hat and smokes a corncob pipe. Beside him stands John Perkins his bosun, a very stiff, green young man, a relative of Delano's. Three sailors, one carrying an American flag, enter. Everyone stands at attention and salutes with machinelike exactitude. Then the three sailors march off stage. Delano and Perkins are alone.*

DELANO: There goes the most beautiful woman in South America.

PERKINS: We never see any women, Sir;
   just this smothering, overcast Equator,

a seal or two,
the flat dull sea,
and a sky like a gray wasp's nest.

DELANO: I wasn't talking about women,
I was calling your attention to the American flag.

PERKINS: Yes, Sir! I wish we were home in Duxbury.

DELANO: We are home. America is wherever her flag
flies.
My own deck is the only place in the world
where I feel at home.

PERKINS: That's too much for me, Captain Delano.
I mean I wish I were at home with my wife;
these world cruises are only for bachelors.

DELANO: Your wife will keep. You should smoke, Perkins.
Smoking turns men into philosophers
and swabs away their worries.
I can see my wife and children or not see them
in each puff of blue smoke.

PERKINS: You are always tempting me, Sir!
I try to keep fit,
I want to return to my wife as fit as I left her.

DELANO: You're much too nervous, Perkins.
Travel will shake you up. You should let
a little foreign dirt rub off on you.
I've taught myself to speak Spanish like a Spaniard.
At each South American port, they mistake me for a
Castilian Don.

PERKINS: Aren't you lowering yourself a little, Captain?
Excuse me, Sir, I have been wanting to ask you a
question.

Don't you think our President, Mr. Jefferson, is
    lowering himself
by being so close to the French?
I'd feel a lot safer in this unprotected place
if we'd elected Mr. Adams instead of Mr. Jefferson.

DELANO: The better man ran second!
    Come to think of it, he rather let us down
by losing the election just after we had named this
    ship.
the *President Adams*. Adams is a nervous dry fellow.
When you've travelled as much as I have,
you'll learn that that sort doesn't export, Perkins.
Adams didn't get a vote outside New England!

PERKINS: He carried every New England state;
    that was better than winning the election.
I'm afraid I'm a dry fellow, too, Sir.

DELANO: Not when I've educated you!
    When I am through with you, Perkins,
you'll be as worldly as the Prince Regent of En-
    gland,
only you'll be a first class American officer.
I'm all for Jefferson, he has the popular touch.
Of course he's read too many books,
but I've always said an idea or two won't sink
    our Republic.
I'll tell you this, Perkins,
Mr. Jefferson is a gentleman and an American.

PERKINS: They say he has two illegitimate Negro chil-
    dren.

DELANO: The more the better! That's the quickest way
    to raise the blacks to our level.
Surprised you swallow such Federalist bilge, Perkins!
I told you Mr. Jefferson is a gentleman and an Amer-
    ican,
when a man's in office, Sir, we all pull behind him!

PERKINS: Thank God our Revolution ended where the
French one began.

DELANO: Oh the French! They're like the rest of the
Latins.
they're hardly white people,
they start with a paper republic
and end with a toy soldier, like Bonaparte.

PERKINS: Yes, Sir. I see a strange sail making for the
harbor.
They don't know how to sail her.

DELANO: Hand me my telescope.

PERKINS: Aye, aye, Sir!

DELANO (*With telescope*): I see an ocean undulating
in long scoops of swells;
it's set like the beheaded French Queen's high wig;
the sleek surface is like waved lead,
cooled and pressed in the smelter's mould.
I see flights of hurried gray fowl,
patches of fluffy fog.
They skim low and fitfully above the decks,
like swallows sabering flies before a storm.
This gray boat foreshadows something wrong.

PERKINS: It does, Sir!
They don't know how to sail her!

DELANO: I see a sulphurous haze above her cabin,
the new sun hangs like a silver dollar to her stern;
low creeping clouds blow on from them to us.

PERKINS: What else, Sir?

DELANO: The yards are woolly
the ship is furred with fog.
On the cracked and rotten head-boards,
the tarnished, gilded letters say, the *San Domingo*.
A rat's-nest messing up the deck,

black faces in white sheets are fussing with the ropes.
I think it's a cargo of Dominican monks.

PERKINS: Dominican monks, Sir! God help us,
I thought they were outlawed in the new world.

DELANO: No, it's nothing. I see they're only slaves.
The boat's transporting slaves.

PERKINS: Do you believe in slavery, Captain Delano?

DELANO: In a civilized country, Perkins,
everyone disbelieves in slavery,
everyone disbelieves in slavery and wants slaves.
We have the perfect uneasy answer;
in the North, we don't have them and want them;
Mr. Jefferson has them and fears them.

PERKINS: Is that how you answer, Sir,
when a little foreign dirt has rubbed off on you?

DELANO: Don't ask me such intense questions.
You should take up smoking, Perkins.
There was a beautiful, dumb English actress—
I saw her myself once in London.
They wanted her to look profound,
so she read Plato and the Bible and Benjamin Frank-
lin,
and thought about them every minute.
She still looked like a moron.
Then they told her to think about nothing.
She thought about nothing, and looked like Socrates.
That's smoking, Perkins, you think about nothing
and look deep.

PERKINS: I don't believe in slavery, Sir.

DELANO: You don't believe in slavery or Spaniards
or smoking or long cruises or monks or Mr. Jefferson!
You are a Puritan, all faith and fire.

PERKINS: Yes, Sir.

DELANO: God save America from Americans!
(*Takes up the telescope*)
I see octogonal network bagging out
from her heavy top like decayed beehives.
The battered forecastle looks like a raped Versailles.
On the stern-piece, I see the fading arms of Spain.
There's a masked satyr, or something
with its foot on a big white goddess.
She has quite a figure.

PERKINS: They oughtn't to be allowed on the ocean!

DELANO: Who oughtn't? Goddesses?

PERKINS: I mean Spaniards, who cannot handle a ship,
and mess up its hull with immoral statues.

DELANO: You're out of step. You're much too dry.
Bring me my three-cornered hat.
Order some men to clear a whaleboat.
I am going to bring water and fresh fish to the
San Domingo.
These people have had some misfortune, Perkins!

PERKINS: Aye, aye, Sir.

DELANO: Spaniards? The name gets you down,
you think their sultry faces and language
make them Zulus.
You take the name *Delano*—
I've always thought it had some saving
Italian or Spanish virtue in it.

PERKINS: Yes, Sir.

DELANO: A Spaniard isn't a Negro under the skin,
particularly a Spaniard from Spain—
these South American ones mix too much with the
Indians.

Once you get inside a Spaniard,
he talks about as well as your wife in Duxbury.

PERKINS (*Shouting*): A boat for the captain! A whaleboat for Captain Delano!

FROM **The Odd Couple** (1965)

by NEIL SIMON

Neil Simon is Broadway's most successful playwright because he creates characters and situations that are accessible, identifiable, and above all funny. *The Odd Couple* went on from Broadway to success as a TV series. Felix and Oscar are middle-aged men separated from their wives and sharing an apartment. Felix is nervous, compulsively meticulous, continually straightening and cleaning. Oscar is easy-going and quite the opposite. Their conflicts of personality, lifestyle and aspirations are rich comic material, and Simon makes the most of them.

The cause of the tension in this scene is stated by Oscar in the speech beginning, "I'll tell you exactly what it is." As he unleashes his stored-up feelings, allow for an explosiveness in the acting, a letting go, so that what comes from the character's mouth is not thought out, but rather boils over. The trap with Simon is to deliver the lines as a series of jokes. Rather the actors must play the reality of the characters' intentions and circumstances. If the actors are true to their characters, both the humor of the lines and the underlying human comedy will come to life.

Felix comes out of the kitchen carrying a tray with a steaming dish of spaghetti. As he crosses behind Oscar to the table, he indicates that it smells delicious and passes it close to Oscar to make sure Oscar smells the fantastic dish he's missing. As Felix sits and begins to eat, Oscar takes a can of aerosol spray from the bar, and circling the table, sprays all around Felix, then puts the can down next to him and goes back to his newspaper.

FELIX (*Pushing the spaghetti away*): All right, how much longer is this gonna go on?

OSCAR (*Reading his paper*): Are you talking to me?

FELIX: That's right, I'm talking to you.

OSCAR: What do you want to know?

FELIX: I want to know if you're going to spend the rest of your life not talking to me. Because if you are, I'm going to buy a radio. Well? I see. You're not going to talk to me. All right. Two can play at this game. If you're not going to talk to me, I'm not going to talk to you. I can act childish too, you know. I can go on without talking just as long as you can.

OSCAR: Then why the hell don't you shut up?

FELIX: Are you talking to me?

OSCAR: You had your chance to talk last night. I begged you to come upstairs with me. From now on I never want to hear a word from that shampooed head as long as you live. That's a warning, Felix.

FELIX: I stand warned. Over and out!

OSCAR (*Gets up, takes a key out of his pocket and slams it on the table*): There's a key to the back

door. If you stick to the hallway and your room, you won't get hurt.
(*He sits back down on the couch*)

FELIX: I don't think I gather the entire meaning of that remark.

OSCAR: Then I'll explain it to you. Stay out of my way.

FELIX (*Picks up the key and moves to the couch*): I think you're serious. I think you're really serious. Are you serious?

OSCAR: This is my apartment. Everything in my apartment is mine. The only thing here that's yours is you. Just stay in your room and speak softly.

FELIX: Yeah, you're serious. Well, let me remind you that I pay half the rent and I'll go into any room I want.
(*He gets up angrily and starts toward the hallway*)

OSCAR: Where are you going?

FELIX: I'm going to walk around your bedroom.

OSCAR (*Slams down his newspaper*): You stay out of there.

FELIX: Don't tell me where to go. I pay a hundred and twenty dollars a month.

OSCAR: That was off-season. Starting tomorrow the rates are twelve dollars a day.

FELIX: All right. (*He takes some bills out of his pocket and slams them down on the table*) There you are. I'm paid up for today. Now I'm going to walk in your bedroom.
(*He starts to storm off*)

OSCAR: Stay out of there! Stay out of my room!
(*He chases after him. Felix dodges around the table as Oscar blocks the hallway*)

FELIX (*Backing away, keeping the table between them*)
Watch yourself! Just watch yourself, Oscar!

OSCAR (*With a pointing finger*): I'm warning you. You
want to live here, I don't want to see you, I don't
want to hear you and I don't want to smell your
cooking. Now get this spaghetti off my poker table.

FELIX: Ha! Ha, ha!

OSCAR: What the hell's so funny?

FELIX: It's not spaghetti. It's linguini!
(*Oscar picks up the plate of linguini, crosses to the
doorway and hurls it into the kitchen*)

OSCAR: Now it's garbage!
(*He paces by the couch*)

FELIX: You are crazy! I'm a neurotic nut but *you are
crazy!*

OSCAR: *I'm* crazy, heh? That's really funny coming
from a fruitcake like you.

FELIX (*Goes to the kitchen door and looks in at the
mess. Turns back to Oscar*): I'm not cleaning that
up.

OSCAR: Is that a promise?

FELIX: Did you hear what I said? I'm not cleaning it
up. It's your mess. (*Looking into the kitchen again*)
Look at it. Hanging all over the walls.

OSCAR (*Crosses to the landing and looks in the kitchen
door*): I like it.
(*He closes the door and paces around*)

FELIX: You'd just let it lie there, wouldn't you? Until
it turns hard and brown and . . . Yich, it's disgusting.
I'm cleaning it up.
(*He goes into the kitchen. Oscar chases after him.
There is the sound of a struggle and falling pots*)

OSCAR: *Leave it alone!* You touch one strand of that linguini—and I'm gonna punch you right in your sinuses.

FELIX (*Dashes out of the kitchen with Oscar in pursuit. He stops and tries to calm Oscar down*): Oscar, I'd like you to take a couple of phenobarbital.

OSCAR: Go to your room! Did you hear what I said? *Go to your room!*

FELIX: All right, let's everybody just settle down, heh? (*He puts his hand on Oscar's shoulder to calm him but Oscar pulls away violently from his touch*)

OSCAR: If you want to live through this night, you'd better tie me up and lock your doors and windows.

FELIX (*Sits at the table with a great pretense of calm*): All right, Oscar, I'd like to know what's happened?

OSCAR (*Moves toward him*): What's *happened?*

FELIX (*Hurriedly slides over to the next chair*): That's right. Something must have caused you to go off the deep end like this. What is it? Something I said? Something I did? Heh? What?

OSCAR: It's nothing you said. It's nothing you did. It's *you!*

FELIX: I see. Well, that's plain enough.

OSCAR: I could make it plainer but I don't want to hurt you.

FELIX: What is it, the cooking? The cleaning? The crying?

OSCAR (*Moving toward him*): I'll tell you exactly what it is. It's the cooking, cleaning and crying. It's the talking in your sleep, it's the moose calls that open your ears at two o'clock in the morning. I can't take it anymore, Felix. I'm crackin' up. Everything you

do irritates me. And when you're not here, the things
I know you're gonna do when you come in irritate
me. You leave me little notes on my pillow. I told
you a hundred times, I can't stand little notes on
my pillow. "We're all out of Corn Flakes. F.U." It
took me three hours to figure out that F.U. was Felix
Ungar. It's not your fault, Felix. It's a rotten combination.

FELIX: I get the picture.

OSCAR: That's just the frame. The picture I haven't
even painted yet. I got a typewritten list in my office
of the "Ten Most Aggravating Things You Do That
Drive Me Berserk." But last night was the topper.
Oh, that was the topper. Oh, that was the ever-loving
lulu of all times.

FELIX: What are you talking about, the London broil?

OSCAR: No, not the London broil. I'm talking about
those two lamb chops. (*He points upstairs*) I had
it all set up with that English Betty Boop and her
sister, and I wind up drinking tea all night and telling
them *your* life story.

FELIX (*Jumps up*): Oho! So *that's* what's bothering
you. That I loused up your evening!

OSCAR: After the mood you put them in, I'm surprised
they didn't go out to Rockaway and swim back to
England.

FELIX: Don't blame me. I warned you not to make the
date in the first place.
(*He makes his point by shaking his finger in Oscar's face*)

OSCAR: Don't point that finger at me unless you intend
to use it!

FELIX (*Moves in nose to nose with Oscar*): All right,
Oscar, get off my back. Get off! Off!

(Startled by his own actions, Felix jumps back from Oscar, warily circles him, crosses to the couch and sits)

OSCAR: What's this? A display of temper? I haven't seen you really angry since the day I dropped my cigar in your pancake batter.
(He starts toward the hallway)

FELIX: Oscar, you're asking to hear something I don't want to say. But if I say it, I think you'd better hear it.

OSCAR *(Comes back to the table, places both hands on it and leans toward Felix)*: If you've got anything on your chest besides your chin, you'd better get it off.

FELIX *(Strides to the table, places both hands on it and leans toward Oscar. They are nose to nose)*: All right, I warned you. You're a wonderful guy, Oscar. You've done everything for me. If it weren't for you, I don't know what would have happened to me. You took me in here, gave me a place to live and something to live for. I'll never forget you for that. You're tops with me, Oscar.

OSCAR *(Motionless)*: If I've just been told off, I think I may have missed it.

FELIX: It's coming now! You're also one of the biggest slobs in the world.

OSCAR: I see.

FELIX: And completely unreliable.

OSCAR: Finished?

FELIX: Undependable.

OSCAR: Is that it?

FELIX: And irresponsible.

OSCAR: Keep going. I think you're hot.

FELIX: That's it. I'm finished. *Now* you've been told off. How do you like that?
(*He crosses to the couch*)

OSCAR (*Straightening up*): Good. Because now I'm going to tell *you* off. For six months I lived alone in this apartment. All alone in eight rooms. I was dejected, despondent and disgusted. Then *you* moved in—my dearest and closest friend. And after three weeks of close, personal contact—I am about to have a nervous breakdown! Do me a favor. Move into the kitchen. Live with your pots, your pans, your ladle and your meat thermometer. When you want to come out, ring a bell and I'll run into the bedroom. (*Almost breaking down*) I'm asking you nicely, Felix—as a friend. Stay out of my way!
(*And he goes into the bedroom*)

FELIX (*Is hurt by this, then remembers something. He calls after him*): Walk on the paper, will you? The floors are wet. (*Oscar comes out of the door. He is glaring maniacally, as he slowly strides back down the hallway. Felix quickly puts the couch between him and Oscar*) Awright, keep away. Keep away from me.

OSCAR (*Chasing him around the couch*): Come on. Let me get in one shot. You pick it. Head, stomach or kidneys.

FELIX (*Dodging about the room*): You're gonna find yourself in one sweet lawsuit, Oscar.

OSCAR: It's no use running, Felix. There's only eight rooms and I know the short cuts.
(*They are now poised at opposite ends of the couch. Felix picks up a lamp for protection*)

FELIX: Is this how you settle your problems, Oscar? Like an animal?

OSCAR: All right. You wanna see how I settle my problems. I'll show you. (*Storms off into Felix's bedroom. There is the sound of falling objects and he returns with a suitcase*) I'll show you how I settle them. (*Throws the suitcase on the table*) There! That's how I settle them!

FELIX: Where are you going?

OSCAR: Not me, you idiot! You. You're the one who's going. I want you out of here. Now! Tonight!
(*He opens the suitcase*)

FELIX: What are you talking about?

OSCAR: It's all over, Felix. The whole marriage. We're getting an annulment! Don't you understand? I don't want to live with you anymore. I want you to pack your things, tie it up with your Saran Wrap and get out of here.

FELIX: You mean actually move out?

OSCAR: Actually, physically and immediately. I don't care where you go. Move into the Museum of Natural History. (*Goes into the kitchen. There is the crash of falling pots and pans*) I'm sure you'll be very comfortable there. You can dust around the Egyptian mummies to your heart's content. But I'm a human, living person. (*Comes out with a stack of cooking utensils which he throws into the open suitcase*) All I want is my freedom. Is that too much to ask for? (*Closes it*) There, you're all packed.

FELIX: You know, I've got a good mind to really leave.

OSCAR (*Looking to the heavens*): Why doesn't he ever listen to what I say? Why doesn't he hear me? I know I'm talking—I recognize my voice.

FELIX: Because if you really want me to go, I'll go.

OSCAR: Then go. I want you to go, so go. When are you going?

FELIX: When am I going, huh? Boy, you're in a bigger hurry than Frances was.

OSCAR: Take as much time as she gave you. I want you to follow your usual routine.

FELIX: In other words, you're throwing me out.

OSCAR: Not in other words. Those are the perfect ones. (*Picks up the suitcase and holds it out to Felix*) I am throwing you out.

FELIX: All right, I just wanted to get the record straight. Let it be on *your* conscience.
(*He goes into his bedroom*)

OSCAR: What? What? (*Follows him to the bedroom doorway*) Let what be on my conscience?

FELIX (*Comes out putting on his jacket and passes by Oscar*): That you're throwing me out. (*Stops and turns back to him*) I'm perfectly willing to stay and clear the air of our differences. But you refuse, right?

OSCAR (*Still holding the suitcase*): Right! I'm sick and tired of you clearing the air. That's why I want you to leave!

FELIX: Okay, as long as I heard you say the words, "Get out of the house." Fine. But remember, what happens to me is your responsibility. Let it be on *your* head.
(*He crosses to the door*)

OSCAR (*Follows him to the door and screams*): Wait a minute, damn it! Why can't you be thrown out like a decent human being? Why do you have to say things like, "Let it be on your head"? I don't want it on my head. I just want you out of the house.

FELIX: What's the matter, Oscar? Can't cope with a little guilt feelings?

OSCAR (*Pounding the railing in frustration*): Damn you. I've been looking forward to throwing you out all day long, and now you even take the pleasure out of that.

FELIX: Forgive me for spoiling your fun. I'm leaving now—according to your wishes and desires.
(*He starts to open the door*)

OSCAR (*Pushes by Felix and slams the door shut. He stands between Felix and the door*): You're not leaving here until you take it back.

FELIX: Take what back?

OSCAR: "Let it be on your head." What the hell is that, the Curse of the Cat People?

FELIX: Get out of my way, please.

OSCAR: Is this how you left that night with Frances? No wonder she wanted to have the room repainted right away. (*Points to Felix's bedroom*) I'm gonna have yours dipped in bronze.

FELIX (*Sits on the back of the couch with his back to Oscar*): How can I leave if you're blocking the door?

OSCAR: Felix, we've been friends a long time. For the sake of that friendship, please say, "Oscar, we can't stand each other; let's break up."

FELIX: I'll let you know what to do about my clothes. Either I'll call—or someone else will. I'd like to leave now.
(*Oscar, resigned, moves out of the way. Felix opens the door*)

OSCAR: Where will you go?

FELIX (*Turns in the doorway and looks at him*): Where? (*He smiles*) Oh, come on, Oscar. You're not really interested, are you?
(*He exits. Oscar looks as though he's about to burst with frustration. He calls after Felix*)

OSCAR: All right, Felix, you win. (*Goes out into the hall*) We'll try to iron it out. Anything you want. Come back, Felix. Felix? *Felix?* Don't leave me like this—you louse! (*But Felix is gone. Oscar comes back into the room closing the door. He is limp. He searches for something to ease his enormous frustration. He throws a pillow at the door, and then paces about like a caged lion*) All right, Oscar, get a hold of yourself! He's gone! Keep saying that over and over. He's gone. He's really gone! (*He holds his head in pain*) He did it. He put a curse on me. It's on my head. I don't know what it is, but something's on my head.

FROM We Bombed in New Haven (1968)

by JOSEPH HELLER

This play by Joseph Heller is part of a small
body of work generated by protest against
war, senseless, abstract killing, personal
loss, and its timeless repetition. Written in
the style of Heller's famous novel, *Catch-22,*
it is a lampoon filled with dark ironies and
black humor.

By using the stage as the world of the
play, by having the actors announce that they
are actors playing roles, not the characters
themselves, Heller creates a universal metaphor. Both life and war are games. Relationships are empty, emotions are fluid and
fading, life is turned into death either by
whim or by an unseen order of things.

The scene which follows is a good example of the play's perversities. Henderson,
a mocking and arrogant young sergeant, has
disappeared just at the time his group is
scheduled to depart to bomb Minnesota. ("I
want to blow Minnesota off the map before
someone else does," says the Major.) Sergeant Henderson is also scheduled to die in
the takeoff, or so the Major assures us. The
Major is characteristically confident that
these inevitabilities will occur and that by
using his authority he can bring them about.
His subordinate Captain Starkey is an easy-

going man; he frequently questions the senselessness of what's going on but ends up following orders and enforcing them.

The fact that the audience is continually reminded that the soldiers are really actors encourages a freer, bolder style of playing than in representational, realistic drama. In addition, the actors often step out of their roles to talk directly to the audience, as in Starkey's final speech here. The actor must make a quick transition and give his personal response to what has just happened; these inner responses must be powerfully felt, so that the actor feels compelled to step forward and express them.

The Major, alone with Starkey in front of the curtain shows a trace of anxiety, weariness, and despair.

MAJOR: They've got to be watched. I never really trust them. I bet they're horsing around and complaining right now. I'll bet they're even smoking. They've always got to be watched.

STARKEY: Should I go back and watch them?

MAJOR: I want you to find Henderson.

STARKEY: Suppose he's already gone?

MAJOR (*Tiredly, and with a touch of sadness*): He has to be somewhere. Find Henderson and bring him back. I'm tired. I work hard, too.

STARKEY: I never heard you talk like *that* before.

MAJOR: That's because you never listen. You're always so busy with your wife and your donuts.

STARKEY: I do my job, don't I?

MAJOR: You do it very well. Go find Henderson.

STARKEY: What will you do with him?

MAJOR: I'm gonna kill him.

STARKEY: No, I mean it.

MAJOR: So do I. I'm going to kill him.

STARKEY: You can't *kill* him, really.

MAJOR: Why not?

STARKEY: Are you kidding?

MAJOR: Are you?

STARKEY: You can't just kill people.

MAJOR: Why not?

STARKEY: Because you just—well, can't.

MAJOR: And just what do you think we've been doing?

STARKEY: Are you serious?

MAJOR (*Turning away*): Go find Henderson and bring him back so I can kill him and get it over with.

STARKEY: You really think you're going to kill him?

MAJOR: If I have to.

STARKEY: Right here? Right out in front of all these people? In front of all these witnesses?

MAJOR: If I have to.

STARKEY: Oh, no. They won't let you. They won't just sit there and let you kill him.

MAJOR: Yes, they will.

STARKEY: Listen. Do you mean it when you say that?

MAJOR: Do *you* mean it when you ask that?

STARKEY: Oh, God! Why won't you ever answer a question?

MAJOR: Why won't you?

STARKEY: Goddammit, are you trying to make a fool out of me now ... out here ... with everyone watching?

MAJOR: Don't shout at me.

STARKEY: I'm sorry.

MAJOR: Don't swear at me.

STARKEY: I'm sorry.

MAJOR: Don't contradict me.

STARKEY: I'm sorry.

MAJOR: And don't challenge my authority.

STARKEY: I'm sorry. I am sorry, but ... are you acting now? Or do you really mean everything you're saying?

MAJOR: It doesn't matter. Can't you see that? All that does matter is what happens. That's the thing you don't realize. And that's the reason you're always so aimless and wishy-washy in just about everything you do.

STARKEY: Hey, wait a minute! You start talking that way to me and I'll quit, too.

MAJOR: No, you won't quit. You haven't got the character to quit. Popping off in front of a lot of people like this is just about as far as you'll ever go.

STARKEY: Don't you be so sure.

MAJOR: I am sure. Quit, if you think you can. Go ahead, quit.

STARKEY: I quit! (*Starkey starts away, while The Major watches confidently. Starkey slows after a few steps, hesitates, and comes to a stop, hanging his head with shame*)

MAJOR: No, you won't quit. You're a captain, and captains don't quit. Captains obey. You're conditioned to agree and you're trained to do as you're told. You like the pay and the prestige, and you do enjoy your job here, remember? So you'll stay right where you are, do just what you're supposed to, and continue reciting your lines exactly on cue—just as you're doing right now.

STARKEY: No, I'm not! I am not! Goddammit, I'm not!

MAJOR: Yes, you are. Should I show you? (*He holds open the script and points to a page*) You can shout it out to them even louder one more time, if it makes you feel so free, and honest, and independent. You can even go on pretending to yourself that you have convictions—but only for another few seconds. And after that you will have to go on saying and doing exactly what you're supposed to, because *that's* what you are—let's face it—that's *all* you are, a captain. And also, because you're afraid of this. (*Holds up his hand, his fingers outstretched*) Do you know what this is?

STARKEY: A hand.

MAJOR: No. (*Bending his fingers to clench them*) It's a fist. You're afraid it can smash you to bits, and it can. And you also know that I can summon a whole army of people with guns and clubs just by blowing on this marvelous little military whistle of mine. (*The Major reaches into his pocket, pulls out his baby pacifier, and begins munching on it. Starkey laughs*)

STARKEY: That's not a whistle. It's a baby's pacifier.

MAJOR: It's a whistle, if I say it is. And if I do say it is, do you know what you'd better say?

STARKEY: Yes, sir.

MAJOR: What do you say?

STARKEY: Yes, sir!

MAJOR: It's a whistle.

STARKEY (*Saluting*): Yes, sir!

MAJOR: Good. Find Henderson and bring him to me.

STARKEY: Yes, sir!
(*The Major has won and is satisfied, and his air of antagonism leaves him. He speaks in a tone that is suddenly soft and almost apologetic, appealing to Starkey for understanding and forgiveness*)

MAJOR: My friend—I really don't want to talk to you this way.

STARKEY: No?

MAJOR: But I must. Do you understand?

STARKEY: Yes, sir.

MAJOR: Thank you. (*The Major leaves, carrying his script. Starkey stares after him with resentment*)

STARKEY: Yes, sir. (*He turns and shuffles forward step or two to address the audience*)
I am a man.
I'm not a thing.
I'm a modern, contemporary, adult human being.
I'm a very decent and respectable and sensitive hu-
  man being.
I'm married now and have children, and I
  work for a living, just like you—you all
  know that.
I've got pride and character and dignity, and
  I have a wish and a determination to main-
  tain my self-respect.
I do have convictions.
I have very deep convictions and very gen-
  uine and powerful feelings that I want to
  give voice to in loud, rolling sentences like:

"Was this the face that launched a thousand
ships and burnt the topless towers of Ilium?
Sweet Helen, make me immortal with a kiss."
(*With a wistful smile*)
I want to make long speeches like that.
(*With even greater longing*)
I want to play tragedy.
(*Turning grave again*)
That's why I'm really not so happy here right
now.
The part I have is too . . . limited.
I'm not sure I like it here anymore,
Squeezed in between the curtain
And the edge of the stage,
Squeezed into this small narrow role,
Pressed into a tight uniform,
Between the curtain
And edge of the stage,
And forced to say,
"Yes, sir."

FROM **Feiffer's People** (1968)

by *JULES FEIFFER*

Jules Feiffer is a well-known and widely published cartoonist and a successful playwright
with three plays (*Little Murders, The White
House Murder Case,* and *Knock Knock*) to
his credit. Although he often writes about human failures, people with hang-ups, blocks,
anger, frustrations, and hopelessness, the
scene which follows creates an unusual
Feiffer character—a success, no problems, in
control, sure of himself. He is encountered on
the street by a former co-worker, Eddie, who
is somewhat older, full of hyperbole and vain
gestures. Eddie spouts pointless advice to
the younger Harry, masking his own failure
and self-doubt behind bluster and pomp.
They make a sharp and poignant contrast.

It might be helpful to act the scene as if
it were raining, using the behavior and objects (umbrellas, wet clothes) to avoid over-
direct, face-to-face playing.

---

*Harry and Eddie enter from opposite sides. Harry is
young, conservatively dressed, carries attaché case. Eddie is dressed similarly but not as well. He is bigger,
beefier and quite obviously older.*

EDDIE (*Facing front*): Taxi! (*Harry spots him, tries
to back off. Eddie spots him*) Harry! Howsa kid! You

251

makin' any money? (*Pumps Harry's slightly reluctant hand*)

HARRY: I can't complain, Eddie. I can't complain.

EDDIE (*Still clasping hand*): Son of a gun, you're looking good. Been a long time, huh? Damn glad to get rid of us, I bet, huh? Gave you a rough time down in the shop, didn't we?

HARRY (*Trying to disengage hand*): Ancient history, Eddie. Ancient history.

EDDIE (*Holding on*): You kids. Hot shots. Want to make the world over in a day. I bet we knocked that out of you, Harry, huh, boy? Hey, not that I don't sympathize. *I* used to be a rebel in my youth. But I learned. Just the way you'll learn. I get along with everybody. Been with the firm fifteen years that way. Tell the boss jokes on the office staff. Tell the office staff jokes on the boss. Know what they call me? Mr. Sunshine. (*Holds him tighter*) I seen fellows like you come and go. You're still not too old to take a little advice.

HARRY (*Trying to free hand*): Well look, Eddie—

EDDIE (*In a conspiratory whisper*): Never trust anybody! (*Looks nervously around*) The sons of bitches are out to get you!

HARRY (*Humoring him*): Nobody's coming.

EDDIE (*Putting his arm around him*): Develop sincerity! Notice my handshake? Sincere.

HARRY: Eddie, how come I always feel that you're standing closer to me than I am to you?

EDDIE (*In a hoarse whisper*): Don't do favors! Nice guys finish *last!* Never expect too much and you won't be disappointed! Never play around with executive secretaries.

HARRY (*Trying to free his hand*): You're hurting me.

EDDIE: You still with Plutocrat Corporate?

HARRY: Still with them.

EDDIE: Don't let it bother you. You'll do better. Use your head. That's my only advice to you. What did they start you with? Seventy-five hundred?

HARRY: They did all right by me, Eddie—

EDDIE: Less, huh? I don't want to know your secrets. What? Fifty-five hundred? You don't have to be ashamed with me.

HARRY: Well—I'm buying a house on the island, Eddie.

EDDIE: No kidding. Nice little house, huh? Very good idea. Cute little house. Two—three rooms. Comfortable enough. Then when you're making a little more you can add a wing so your wife can move in with you.

HARRY: It's twenty-five rooms, Eddie. We're happy with it.

EDDIE (*Long, stunned pause*): Hey, what did you pay for that suit?

HARRY: It's a pretty good suit, Eddie.

EDDIE: Listen, if I'm being nosey, tell me to mind my own business.

HARRY: It's a pretty good suit.

EDDIE: *That* much. (*Inspects him carefully*) I like those cuff links you're wearing.

HARRY: Comfortable.

EDDIE (*Turns him around like a model at a fashion show*): Very nice. (*Inspects his shoes. Lifts one trouser*) Those English?

HARRY: English.

EDDIE: They look like very expensive shoes. You mind holding your shoe up in the light so I can see better? (*Harry complies*)

HARRY: They're comfortable.

EDDIE (*Punches him dispiritedly on shoulder*): I've been thinking lately about going out on my own. You stay in one place too long they don't appreciate you.

HARRY: To each his own, Eddie.

EDDIE: That's a very nice briefcase. I guess you got lots of important papers in that briefcase.

HARRY: It's good health that counts, Eddie.

EDDIE: Yeah? I got a bad stomach.

HARRY: It's not good to overdo it, kid.

EDDIE: Yeah? Well, I'll tell you. A lot of it is pure luck. My break will come.

HARRY: I wouldn't worry.

EDDIE: I'm a slow starter. We're not as glamorous as some people but when we get moving we . . . get moving.

HARRY: Slow and steady wins the race, Eddie.

EDDIE: You notice I don't stand so straight anymore. An old taxicab accident. I could've sued but when you're a nice guy you're a nice guy. You subject to migraine?

HARRY: Can't say that I am.

EDDIE: You're a very lucky boy. It's not what you know it's who you know. I never *could* make the right contacts. Sincerity isn't the best business trait in the world. I guess you learned that quick enough, Harry.

HARRY: It's all in the way you look at it, kid.

EDDIE: You missed the war, didn't you?

HARRY: Too young.

EDDIE (*Smiles ruefully*): Yeah. (*Begins to cough. Harry steps toward him*) I'm OK. I'm OK. (*Harry offers him pocket handkerchief. Eddie stares at it. Unfolds it. It is long, bordered in gold thread with a large ornate monogram in the center. Eddie examnines it sadly, refolds it and puts it in his own pocket. Then from another pocket, he takes out a Kleenex and blows his nose*) Got to be going, Harry.

HARRY: Good seeing you, Eddie. (*Turns away*)

EDDIE: Hey! (*Harry exits. Eddie shouts after him*) What did you pay for your tie? (*Long pause while he waits for reply. Coughs*) Hey, do you know a good doctor? (*He waits for reply as lights fade*)

(See previous notes on this play, p. 127.)

This scene between Freeman and Rex occurs towards the end of the play. Rex had been adopted by Freeman's parents, the Aquilas, and they grew up together as brothers and friends. However, they haven't seen each other much in recent years. Rex went on to college and medical school and became a prosperous doctor; he lives in an expensive and exclusive neighborhood and is regarded as one of the outstanding people in the Black community.

At this point in the play, Freeman has failed in all his various schemes. He has lost his job and his wife has just given birth to his son. Now he must take a job as a "Sanitation Engineer," a euphemism for janitor. All illusions have been stripped away, but he struggles to hold on to his dignity. He is trying to bring himself to accept the job, but as always he must be true to himself. When his inner feelings overflow, he expresses them honestly.

Rex is trying to carry out what he feels is his responsibility to the Aquila family. He is determined to see Freeman reconciled to the job he has arranged for him; he knows it is Freeman's last resort. Underneath the text, there lurks an additional intention for

Rex—to finally break off the relationship with Freeman. But he must make it seem as if Freeman is the one making the break.

The lights come up on Rex standing in the kitchen drinking coffee. It is morning. Rex crosses to stove and fills his cup again.

FREEMAN (*Entering from the upstairs. He is dressed in the uniform of a maintenance man*): Where's mama and dad?

REX: They left a few minutes ago for work.

FREEMAN (*Sits down at table*): I didn't hear them.

REX: Want some coffee? (*He gets coffeepot and pours Freeman a cup of coffee*) I looked in on Osa Lee and your boy yesterday morning. Sure looks like you.

FREEMAN: Looks like dad to me.

REX: Hard pair of lungs.

FREEMAN: I guess he takes that from me.

REX: Big fellow. You're going to have to move to keep up with him. Osa Lee is due to bring him home tomorrow, isn't she?

FREEMAN: Unhuh.

REX: Soon as you finish your coffee, I'll drive you over to the Coleman Community Center.

FREEMAN: I can walk.

REX: I'll drive you over. Introduce you around.

FREEMAN: Introduce me around?

REX: See to it that you get started on the right foot. I want you and Burt Callahan to get off to a fresh start.

FREEMAN: Burt Callahan?

REX: He's the Director of the center.

FREEMAN: Oh, you mean, that little white fag that runs the center.

REX: Why do you call him a fag, Freeman?

FREEMAN: Because that's what he is.

REX: How do you know? How do you know that he's a fag?

FREEMAN: The way he switches.

REX: You're not going over there calling him a fag, I hope.

FREEMAN: I ain't gonna call him nothing. Don't wanna have anythin' to do with th' fag.

REX: You'll be working under him, Freeman. He's the Director of the center.

FREEMAN: He's the Director! A switching, little, white fag.

REX: He has a Master's degree in Social Work.

FREEMAN: You know, maybe I can do some good over there. Help some of those people.

REX: You're not being hired to do that.

FREEMAN: I'm being hired to mop the floor.

REX: Don't go over there trying to run the place.

FREEMAN: I'll read up on Social Work.

REX: Freeman, you're the Sanitation Engineer. And Mr. Callahan . . .

FREEMAN: Mr. Callahan!

REX: Yes, Mr. Callahan . . . the Director of the Coleman Community Center.

FREEMAN: So I have to call him Mr. Callahan. What does he call me? Boy?

REX: He'll call you by your name.

FREEMAN: Freeman.

REX: Freeman.

FREEMAN: He calls me Freeman and I call him Mr. Callahan. What do I call you, Rex? Doctor Coleman?

REX: I don't care what you call me.

FREEMAN: You want me to call you Doctor Coleman when you come into the center?

REX: Would that kill you?

FREEMAN: What does mama call you out at the hospital?

REX: Doctor Coleman.

FREEMAN: And what do you call her?

REX: Aquila.

FREEMAN: Aquila.

REX: It's just a formality.

FREEMAN: I'm going to check 'em out over there carefully. And when I catch them doing anything funny I'll report to you.

REX: No. You're not going to report anything to me. You're going over there and do your job. Period.

FREEMAN: O.K.

REX : I mean that, Freeman. You're on probation over there.

FREEMAN: Probation?

REX: You have to prove to those people there that you can do the job.

FREEMAN: I don't prove anything to anybody. I don't have to.

REX: Yes you do.

FREEMAN: To Callahan?

REX: And to me.

FREEMAN: You?

REX: I want you to be the best Sanitation Engineer anyone ever saw. Ten times better! And I want you to keep your mouth shut. Just do what you're told. Don't give them any arguments. They ask you to do something you don't want to do . . . you do it. And then come see me. If you have a legitimate gripe I'll take it up.

FREEMAN: Man, you better get on outta my face. What do you think I am!

REX: I'll tell you what you are. You're a man with a family . . . a wife and a newborn child to support.

FREEMAN: And because of that I should take shit.

REX: Because of that you have to take shit.

FREEMAN: Man, you're talking to Freeman.

REX: I want you to use a little tact.

FREEMAN: Shall I scratch my head and show my teeth?

REX: I'm not asking you to do that.

FREEMAN: That's exactly what you're asking me to do.

REX: All I am asking you to do is to use a little finesse. You can get anything you want if you go about it the right way.

FREEMAN: What way is that?

REX: You know what I mean.

FREEMAN: No, I don't.

REX: Man . . .

FREEMAN: Why don't you teach me? Teach me how to bullshit.

REX: The world buys bullshit. They buy it by the ton!

FREEMAN: Then show me how to do it.

REX: You have contempt for me, don't you, Freeman?

FREEMAN: Do I?

REX: Why? Because I did something with my life? You have contempt for me! You better come down to earth, boy. I have letters in front of my name. What do you have? Numbers!

FREEMAN: At least I have my self-respect.

REX: And that's about all you have. I make seventy-five thousand dollars a year!

FREEMAN: So you make seventy-five thousand dollars a year. So what!

REX: That's an accomplishment.

FREEMAN: If that's what you want. Willing to do what you had to do to get it.

REX: Your opinion of me doesn't mean a damn thing. I don't give a good goddamn what you think about me.

FREEMAN: Then what are you so upset about?

REX: Because I'm getting tired of your abuse.

FREEMAN: What's wrong, Rex? You can't take honesty?

REX: Honesty.

FREEMAN: I'm direct.

REX: You and your honesty. I forgot you're the only honest man in the world.

FREEMAN: That bothers you, doesn't it?

REX: It bothers me for you. You're going to destroy yourself with your honesty. Yourself and everybody around you.

FREEMAN: Like you do with bullshit! You're a bullshit artist, Rex.

REX: You think you're perfect, don't you? Self-perfection!

FREEMAN: I'm an honest man . . .

REX: About other people. You use your honesty as a weapon against people. Cut them to pieces with your honesty. Ned. Teresa. Osa Lee. And you've done it all your life. I wonder what would happen if you turn that honesty on yourself.

FREEMAN: I live by it.

REX: Do you?

FREEMAN: Damn straight.

REX: Then what are you, Freeman? Can you, with any degree of honesty, say who and what you are? You're right, I'm a bullshit artist. I learned that to survive. How are you going to survive? How are you going to make that honesty work for you?

FREEMAN: I don't know what you mean.

REX: What skills do you have, Freeman?

FREEMAN: Skills? . . .

REX: What can you do? I can bullshit. What can you do?

FREEMAN: ... nothing.

REX: I know how hard it is for you to take this ...

FREEMAN: Go on, man.

REX: What are the choices open to you? You're an honest man. What are they?

FREEMAN: The janitor ...

REX: I won't try to influence you. But I'm going to lay it right on the line. Do you want the job? I mean I can call it off, like that. But if I do, that's it. Think about it. Think about Osa Lee coming home with that child tomorrow.

FREEMAN (*After a pause*): All right, I want it.

REX: And you have to accept it! And everything that goes with it.

FREEMAN: Say it, Rex. (*Long pause*) I guess it's all over between me and you.

REX: I didn't say that.

FREEMAN: But it's true. You and me ...

REX: We'll always be friends.

FREEMAN: No. No, we won't. I don't think we really have for a long time. We just ... remembered we used to be friends. Funny, we're never friends when we talk about now. Only time I get a friendly feeling coming from you is when we talk about old times.

REX: I'm sorry you feel that way.

FREEMAN: I won't call you anymore. No more message left on your service ... for you to call me. No more hairbrained schemes that I'm trying to involve you in.

REX: I never mind.

FREEMAN: You won't have to worry about me showing up at your house for parties. It was something that was and is no more.

REX: If you feel that way ...

FREEMAN: Yeah, I feel that way.

REX: I hate to rush you but ...

FREEMAN: We better be getting over there.

REX (*Putting the dishes in the sink*): Better put these things in the sink ...

FREEMAN: I always forget.
   (*He exits followed by Rex*)

part 4

Monologues
for Women

Orpheus Descending (1957)

by TENNESSEE WILLIAMS

"She is past thirty, lacking prettiness, she has an odd, fugitive beauty which is stressed, almost to the point of fantasy, by a style of make-up . . . the face and lips powdered white, the eyes outlined and exaggerated with black pencil, and the lids tinted blue. Her family name is the oldest and most distinguished in the county . . . the quality of her voice is curiously clear and childlike."

Thus Tennessee Williams describes his fragile character who calls for life in a corrupt society that pecks away at small, bewildered beings.

In this monologue, Carol Cutrere is trying to provoke a younger man's sexual desire. Provoke is the accurate word here, because she is driven to do bizarre and extreme things in her desperate attempt to feel alive. She senses a kindred spirit in the handsome vagabond Val. He is a fresh figure in her life and she's particularly excited with this encounter.

Carol is a complex character, terribly vulnerable while highly aggressive, poetic and sensual, and could be described by one of the earlier titles of this play, "Something Wild in the Country."

CAROL: I used to be what they call a Christ-bitten reformer. You know what that is?—A kind of benign
exhibitionist. . . . I delivered stump speeches, wrote
letters of protest about the gradual massacre of the
colored majority in the county. I thought it was
wrong for pellagra and slow starvation to cut them
down when the cotton crop failed from army worm
or boll weevil or too much rain in summer. I wanted
to, tried to, put up free clinics, I squandered the
money my mother left me on it. And when that Wil-
lie McGee thing came along—he was sent to the
chair for having improper relations with a white
whore—(*Her voice is like a passionate incantation*)
I made a fuss about it. I put on a potato sack and
set out for the capitol on foot. This was in winter.
I walked barefoot in this burlap sack to deliver a
personal protest to the Governor of the State. Oh,
I suppose it was partly exhibitionism on my part,
but it wasn't completely exhibitionism; there was
something else in it, too. You know how far I got?
Six miles out of town—hooted, jeered at, even spit
on!—every step of the way—and then arrested!
Guess what for? Lewd vagrancy! Uh-huh, that was
the charge, "lewd vagrancy," because they said that
potato sack I had on was not a respectable garment.
. . . Well, all that was a pretty long time ago, and
now I'm not a reformer anymore. I'm just a "lewd
vagrant." And I'm showing the "S.O.B.'s" how lewd
a "lewd vagrant" can be if she puts her whole heart
in it like I do mine! All right. I've told you my story,
the story of an exhibitionist. Now I want you to do
something for me. Take me out to Cypress Hill in
my car. And we'll hear the dead people talk. They
do talk there. They chatter together like birds on Cypress Hill, but all they say is one word and that one
word is "live," they say "Live, live, live, live, live!"
It's all they've learned, it's the only advice they can
give—Just live. . . . (*She opens the door*) Simple!—
a very simple instruction. . . .

Lady is one of Tennessee Williams' lovely and loveless heroines who futilely seeks life in surroundings dominated by the forces of death. One of these forces is her husband, who at this point is dying. She has hired an itinerant musician, the Orpheus figure of the title, to help run their business and has an affair with him. Near the end of the play she learns she is pregnant (life); she thought she was barren (death).

To reach the ecstatic peak called for by the author in this speech, the actress must feel behind it the lifetime of terror and struggling against dying. It's a final burst of exuberance, based on the illusion that she has at last conquered death, just before her husband shoots her.

LADY: When a woman's been childless as long as I've been childless, it's hard to believe that you're still able to bear!—We used to have a little fig tree between the house and the orchard. It never bore any fruit, they said it was barren. Time went by it, spring after useless spring, and it almost started to—die. . . . Then one day I discovered a small green fig on the tree they said wouldn't bear! (*She is clasping a gilt paper horn*) I ran through the orchard. I ran through the wine garden shouting, "Oh, Father, it's going to bear, the fig tree is going to bear!"—It seemed such a wonderful thing, after those ten barren springs, for the little fig tree to bear, it called for a celebration—I ran to a closet, I opened a box that we kept Christmas ornaments in!—I took them out, glass bells, glass birds, tinsel, icicles, stars. . . . And I hung the little tree with them, I decorated the fig tree with glass bells and glass birds, and silver icicles and stars, because it won the battle and it would bear! (*Rises, ecstatic*) Unpack the box! Unpack the box with the Christmas ornaments in it, put them on me, glass bells and glass birds and stars and tinsel and snow! (*In a sort of delirium she thrusts the conical gilt paper hat on her head and runs to the foot of the stairs with the paper horn. She blows the horn over and over, grotesquely mounting the stairs, as Val tries to stop her. She breaks away from him and runs up to the landing, blowing the paper horn and crying out*) I've won, I've won, Mr. Death, I'm going to bear! (*Then suddenly she falters*)

Ludlow Fair (1965)

by LANFORD WILSON

Most of Wilson's plays concern people gentle but confused by their interior conflicts and their unsettling exterior conditions. *Ludlow Fair* takes place in Greenwich Village and is the story of two female roommates: Rachel —glamorous, fun-loving, fast-living, over-romantic, over-dramatic; and Agnes—plain, shy, ironic, self-deprecating, unpopular. Agnes has the following monologue after she has comforted Rachel to sleep. Now she can think about herself and the date she has tomorrow. She mocks Charles to protect herself; she recognizes her real yearning and admits her resentment of Rachel and her successes. She dreams of husband and children, but she never allows herself to give up completely to romance—the consequences are too painful. She saves herself with jokes and objectivity. We have more compassion for her than she shows herself.

AGNES: I'm going to be a mess tomorrow. I probably won't make it to work, let alone lunch. A casual lunch, my God. I wonder what he'd think—stupid Charles—if he knew I was putting up my hair for him; catching pneumonia. No lie, I can't wait till summer to see what kind of sunglasses he's going

to pop into the office with. Probably those World's
Fair charmers. A double unisphere. (*Turns*) Are you
going to sleep? (*Pause. No reply*) Well, crap. (*Turning back to mirror*) I may be tendering my notice,
anyway. You've gone through six men while I sit
around and turn to fungus. It's just not a positive
atmosphere for me, honey. Not quite. You're out
with handsome Val or someone and I'm wondering
if the boss's skinny, bony son will come up to the
water cooler if I . . . (*Trails off, becomes interested
in the roller. Now to someone—as at dinner*) No.
No Stroganoff. No, I'm on a diet. (*Correcting herself*) No. I will not admit that. Good or bad if he
says Stroganoff and baked potatoes; it's Stroganoff
and baked potatoes. And sour cream. And beer.
He's probably on a diet himself. He could fill out,
God knows. (*Turning to Rachel*) You know what
Charles looks like? (*Pause*) He looks like one of
those little model men you make out of pipe cleaners
when you're in grade school. (*Turning*) Remember
those? If I ever saw Charles without his clothes, he's
so pale and white, I swear to God I'd laugh myself
silly. (*As if directly to someone, over lunch. Casual-
ly*) You know, Charles, you've got nice eyes. You
really have. Deep. I like brown eyes for a man. I
don't like blue eyes, they always look weak or
weepy. Either that or cold. You know? Brown eyes
are warm; that's good. They're gentle. (*Quickly*)
Not weak, but gentle. (*Half to herself. Lightly*) I
used to want to have a girl; a little girl with blue
eyes. For a girl that's good. So I used to always picture—God, idealize, really—very heavy-set, blond
men. Swiss types, you know. (*Back to Charles*) But
a son I'd want to have brown eyes. That's better for
boys. (*Looks at the sleeve of her robe*) You think?
(*Almost embarrassed*) I don't know anymore——
Oh, yes; I got it at Saks. It was on sale, I believe.
(*Breaking off, disgusted*) Now, what the hell does

he care where I got it? And it wasn't on sale, knucklehead. And it wasn't Saks. (*Concentrating on her hair*) It was Bonds. Not that he'd know the damn difference.

La Turista (1966)
by SAM SHEPARD

(See previous notes on this play, p. 109.)
    This monologue by Salem is preceded
and followed by events and speeches which
inform it. Kent is spit upon by a "poor Mexican boy" whom he has characterized in a
litany of liberal cliches. As Kent rushes to the
bathroom to wash away the contamination,
Salem is reminded of this story about her
father. Afterwards, Kent emerges restored
and dressed in shiny cowboy clothes. He
comments, "That's the trouble with the
States, you know. Everything's so clean and
pure and immaculate up there that a man
doesn't even have a chance to build up his
own immunity. . . . An isolated land of purification."
    Salem is telling us how the "purification"
began, and how each family keeps it alive.
Cleanliness is maintained as part of the authority structure that supports order. The
speech should flow out without any attempt
to break it up into realistic details (such as
pausing to remember), or any support of the
text with physical illustration. It is a report,
not an emotional experience.

SALEM: When I was about ten I think, little boy, I'd
just returned home from a car trip to the county fair
with my family. My father, my mother, my sisters

and brothers. We'd just gotten home after driving for
about two hours, and it had just gotten dark, but
none of us had spoken for the whole trip. Are you
listening? It was the same as though we'd all been
asleep, and we drove in the driveway, and my father
stopped the car. But instead of any of us getting out
right away like we usually did we all just sat in the
car staring ahead and not speaking for a very long
time. I was the first to get out and start walking toward the cement steps that led to the porch and I
could hear my family behind me. My father, my
mother, my sisters and brothers. And I could hear
all four doors of the car slam one after the other
like gunshots from a rifle. And I could hear their
feet following me up the stairs to the porch right behind me. Very silent. I was leading them sort of and
I was only about ten years old. I got to the top of
the stairs and I was standing on the porch. I was
the first one there and I turned to see them and they
all looked right at me. All staggered because of the
steps, and all their eyes staring right at me. I saw
them like that just for a second, and then do you
know what I did, little boy? I spit on the very top
step just before my father stepped down. And just
as he stepped on that little spot of spit that had nothing dirtier in it than cotton candy and caramel apple,
my whole family burst into noise like you never ever
heard. And my father took off his belt that he'd just
bought at the county fair. A black leather belt with
a silver buckle and a picture of Trigger engraved on
the front. And my father took one more step to the
top of the porch with the belt hanging down from his
right hand and the buckle clinking on the cement.
Then he swung his arm around slowly behind his
back so that the belt dragged through the air following his wrist and came back so fast that all I could
hear was a crack as it hit my ankles and knees and I
fell. Then they were silent again and waited there on
the steps until my father put the belt back through the

loops and buckled the buckle and hitched his jeans up over his hips. Then they all went into the house in a line. My father first, my mother second, my sisters and brothers third. And I stayed there in a ball, all rolled up, with my knees next to my chin and my hands rubbing my ankles. And I felt very good that they'd left me there by myself.

The Star-Spangled Girl (1966)

by NEIL SIMON

"She is the prototype of the All-American girl. If she had a few freckles on her nose it would be perfect. Her compact, solid form and freshly scrubbed face tell us that this is a purely physical creature. What she can't do with an intellectual problem, she more than makes up for with her strong back-stroke or her straight back astride a horse. The Arkansas drawl doesn't add to her image as an intellect either. And best of all, she smells good."

Thus Neil Simon introduces Sophie Rauschmeyer. She is one of the three characters in the play; the other two are men. One of them, Norman Cornell, has just said, "A beautiful, gorgeous blonde will move into the empty apartment next door and I'll fall madly in love," and in walks Sophie. Norman immediately sets out to woo her. Because she's Southern, he thinks he must be extraordinarily romantic and win her with big gestures. He neglects his work and goes all out. After three days of his attentions, Sophie feels she must do something; she can't take any more but is trying to control her exasperation and be polite, in keeping with her upbringing.

Accents can be a trap because they often lead the actor to jump to a stereotype when a stereotype is not wanted. Sophie is Southern and written to sound that way. But unless a Southern accent is natural to you, work first on developing the character, and let the accent come later.

SOPHIE (*To Andy*): Excuse me. (*To Norman*) Mr. Cornell, ah have tried to be neighborly, ah have tried to be friendly and ah have tried to be cordial . . . Ah don't know what it is that you're tryin' to be . . . That first night ah was appreciative that you carried mah trunk up the stairs . . . The fact that it slipped and fell five flights and smashed to pieces was not your fault . . . Ah didn't even mind that personal message you painted on the stairs. Ah thought it was crazy but sorta sweet . . . However, things have now gone too far . . . Ah cannot accept gifts from a man ah hardly know . . . Especially canned goods . . . And ah read your little note. Ah can guess the gist of it even though I don't speak Italian. This has got to stop, Mr. Cornell . . . Ah can do very well without you leavin' little chocolate almond Hershey bars in mah mailbox . . . They melted yesterday, and now ah got three gooey letters from home with nuts in 'em . . . And ah can do without you sneakin' into mah room after ah go to work and paintin' mah balcony without tellin' me about it. Ah stepped out there yesterday and mah slippers are still glued to the floor . . . And ah can do without you tying big bottles of Eau de Cologne to mah cat's tail. The poor thing kept swishin' it yesterday and nearly beat herself to death . . . And most of all, ah can certainly do without you watchin' me get on the bus every day through that high-powered telescope. You got me so nervous the other day ah got on the wrong bus. In short, Mr. Cornell, and I don't want to have to say this again, *leave me ay-lone!*

FROM Mercy Street (1969)

by ANNE SEXTON

Anne Sexton once wrote to me: "Writing is a solitary act. But at The American Place, I have found a community. One is not alone here. The work itself changes and becomes more vital as each day progresses. I have a feeling I never had before—that I have a family for my art. This is to be cherished beyond all things. Not alone. Together!" She found in the theatre the community she longed for, but is not available in poetry.

This intense confessional poet, re-searching her life for clues, wrote one play, *Mercy Street*, which was first produced at the American Place Theatre. The play is a ritual, a search for peace and forgiveness, an attempt to lay the past to rest. It begins and ends in the Church where Daisy is a communicant. Coming out of a childhood of traumatizing incidents, tormented by guilt and conflict, she is drawn irresistibly toward death and blood. Now she rummages through the debris of her life in short flashbacks, soliloquies and realistic scenes, trying to find relief at the center of experience. She challenges her analyst, flirts with her alcoholic father, entreats her unloving mother, embarrasses her beloved, mad aunt—all in her search for purification, for the Christ within her.

In this soliloquy, Daisy wrestles with her terror and her guilt. The actress must personalize the lifetime of anguish that motivates this text. Beware of playing just the language and the generalized emotion. Study each section, each line; explore its levels of meaning; understand it, then let it find its own life. The language will flow because Anne Sexton was a poet.

This speech also appears as the poem "Consorting with Angels" in the collection *Live or Die.*

DAISY: Things of this world. Will they do it for me? Fire and desire, they will kill. Twelve years of being mentally ill. I'm not ill, I'm diseased. It's not my mind that's diseased, it's my soul. Surely, Doctor Alex would say, surely things are better with your family? Yes, he's right . . . and yet . . . and yet? If it is better, then why am I shrinking this way? While women dream of their manicures and permanents, I lie down at night with my head on the pillow and hear rats eating under the lawns, breeding in the cesspools and the sewers. I'm tired of trying to be a woman, tired of the spoons and the pots, tired of my mouth and my breasts, tired of the cosmetics and the silk dresses. I'm even tired of my father with his white bone . . . I'm tired of the gender of things. Last night I had a dream and when I woke up I said, "You are the answer. You will outlive my husband and my father" . . . In that dream there was a city made of chains where Joan was put to death in man's clothes and the nature of the angels went unexplained, no two made in the same species. One had an ear in its hand! One was chewing a star and recording its orbit! They were all obeying themselves, performing God's functions. A people apart. "You are the answer," I said to them and then I entered, lying down on the gates of their city. Then

chains were fastened around me and I lost my gender, my womanhood. Adam was on the left of me
and Eve was on the right of me . . . both thoroughly
inconsistent with the world of reason. We wove our
arms together and rode under a kind of sun. I was
not a woman anymore! Not one thing or the other.
O daughters of Jerusalem, the king has brought me
into his chamber . . . I am black and I am beautiful.
I've been opened and undressed. I have no arms or
legs. I'm all one skin like a fish. I'm no more a woman . . . than . . . than Christ was a man. Oh Daisy,
a dream is not a vision of God. I don't have any
prayers, any real prayers. All I have is a need, a
dream. Oh Jesus, look down from your tree of nails,
your never-moving tree of nails, and tell me. Take
me out of my body and give me back my soul. I
didn't say I was a saint. You've come back! You're
moving! You're breathing! You're calling my name!
Your fingers are thin as pencils and your mouth,
Christ, open like the sore of a fish where it's been
hooked . . . Your hands . . . Oh my God, your hands
. . . Your hands with great holes in them and the
blood is all sticky and brown and red . . . and
. . . Oh Christ, I'm calling to you because of the fire,
because of everyone that day of the fire . . . I
watched the house burn—red, red . . . someone was
whipping a horse on the lawn, but I didn't move . . .
watched them burn down inside it. They were
burned up like roast pigs on a spit. I let it happen!!!
Oh Christ, will no one forgive me for it? Can I undo
a fire, Christ, with a wound? Christ, busy with your
own dying, don't leave me behind. Wait for me. Wait
for me and forgive me. Blood, like a handful of
drinking water! Thank you. Christ!

House Party (1973)

by ED BULLINS

Ed Bullins is recognized as one of our major contemporary playwrights, working primarily in the rich soil of his life experience and that of the Black people in their struggle to become whole and identified.

In *House Party* (A Soulful Happening with Music), which was first produced at the American Place Theatre, Bullins is experimenting with a new form: a collage of poems, prose, songs, dances, moments and attitudes —all in the environment of the ghetto. The final synthesis is a portrait of urban Black people, their hopes, their defeats, the awful ironies of their lives, their joy, their laments.

These monologues explain themselves. They are meant to be spoken directly to the audience, not seeking propaganda effect, but revealing the truth and contradictions of these people's lives. The humanity and soul should shine through.

HARLEM MOTHER: My boy, Jimmie's away for the summer, you know. Just put him on the plane. . . . Went to Texas . . . visitin' his cousins. . . . My . . . my . . . took him less time to get there than it took me to get back home. . . . I am back from the airport on the subway. . . . Yeah . . . he called me soon as he got there. My phone was ringin' as I was climbin' the stairs. We live on the fifth floor . . . just

around the corner on 137th. . . . He said he liked
it. Just think of that . . . and he just got there. Probably wanted me to feel good and not to worry. . . .
Hmmm . . . I'm really tired. Been standin' all day
in the food line. . . . Yes, the food lines are back.
Just like before when I was a little girl and they had
the WPA. . . . But this time they give out food
stamps . . . and you go around to the school and
they give you food out of the basement. Lots of people were waitin' . . . for hours. It was terrible. The
heat was so bad . . . and people was gettin' mad
cause other people was tryin' to get in front of them
and they had been there since morning. And we
waited and waited. . . . And they ran out of food. . . .
It was terrible. They knew how many food stamps
they had given out . . . so they knew how much
food they needed. But they ran out. And the
people were mad. Most said that they wasn't comin'
back to stand in the line. I don't blame them. I ain't
gon' go back until nex' month. People talk about
stealin' before they come back there and stand in
the line all day in the heat and then don't get nothin'.
I was scared for a minute. Thought there'd be some
real trouble. I remember the riots, you know. . . .
All of them since I was a girl here in Harlem. I know
how it is. When the riots come there ain't no food
at all. The police and Army won't let nothin' in 'cept
whiskey and wine. Yeah, that's right. That's where
most of the money is at in Harlem. In the bars and
liquor stores on every corner. Nex' is the churches
. . . but they don't count as much anymore. Powell
lost befo' he died . . . and he had his big ole church
behind him . . . but it don't count for nothin' no
more. I don't even make Jimmie go, like my mother
made me and my sisters and brothers go. Don't
count fo' nothin' like it usta. . . . But I don't mind
his comin' round here to the theater like he always
does. Nawh . . . I ain't been in yet . . . but my boy
comes . . . and he likes it. . . . Said he'd be back

in time to see what you do nex'. . . . You know
. . . when anything happens they really protect the
liquor. . . . You know . . . if people here in Harlem
could stay away from liquor this would be a different
place. Now wouldn't it? Wouldn't it? . . . You know
it would. And now they talk so much about dope. . . .
I don't even know what that stuff is but I know
it's worse than that ole wine and I usta think that
was the worse. . . . Lawd . . . I'm glad I could send
my boy, Jimmie, away this summer.

Comanche Cafe (1976)

by WILLIAM HAUPTMAN

Comanche Cafe, a prologue to *Domino Courts,* was first performed at the American Place Theatre. These early plays of William Hauptman demonstrate this young playwright's genuine promise.

Set in the dustbowl of Oklahoma in the 1930s, the play presents an arid and empty wasteland, peopled by characters whose lives are also voids, lacking fertile roots or substance. Even their dreams are reruns of movies and radio shows.

Ronnie, a young waitress, has been spending a dull Sunday morning peeling potatoes with an older waitress at the Comanche Cafe. In the following monologue, she finally reveals her hopes and dreams of escape. The actress should give full vent to her excitement, her exhilaration, and let her youthful enthusiasm spontaneously overflow. However, the audience should sense that there is something askew about her exaggerated visions.

RONNIE: I'll never be like you.

(*Pause*)

There's a whole mysterious country out there, Mattie, and I'm going to see it all. As soon as I can, I'm leaving. I'm going to see Chicago and New York—the big cities up North where everybody stays

285

up all night long drinking black coffee. Life's more serious up there. I've heard those all-night programs where people phone in and talk about their problems. They've got a lot of serious problems up there, that's all I've got to say. I want to see Grand Central Station, the crossroads of America, and the tallest buildings in the world. Skywriting floating on the clouds above the buildings all day long. See Tin Pan Alley and Times Square and newsboys everywhere you look and gangsters and baseball players. People talk in newspaper headlines. Everyplace is going out of business, and everybody can be bought. Or I might go to California, where the sun's always hot and you can see the movie stars walk into the drugstore and buy aspirin just like normal people. I might go there—I might—there's orange groves and private eyes, and they say it never rains. Or I might go down South, where people burn crosses on the lawns and hide their idiot sons in the attic. To Florida, where the hotels look like big white wedding cakes, and millionaires drive down the boulevards with the top down, smoking cigars. Moonlight and palm trees and waterspouts! Things I never saw before! Or I might even go to Georgia, where nobody ever goes. To the mountains, where it's always raining cats and dogs, and the hillbillies play their fiddles and drink moonshine. They marry down there when they're eleven years old. You don't know what you might do down there! The rain pours down, and there's a house I heard about where there's no more law of gravity and water runs uphill. Wonderful things! Wonderful things all over America! And I'm going to see them all. Just let me go anyplace but here—in Oklahoma.

Kennedy's Children (1975)

by *ROBERT PATRICK*

Robert Patrick came to New York City from
Kilgore, Texas in 1961 and since then has
had many plays produced off and off-off
Broadway. *Kennedy's Children* was produced
in London before being brought to Broadway.

The setting throughout is a bar on the
Lower East Side in New York. The following
notes are Robert Patrick's:

"The theme of the play is the death of
the idea of heroes as guides for our lives.
The form of the play is fragmentation, separation of people from one another. I think the
sad thing about Kennedy's children is that
they have so very much to offer one another
and are held away from one another by fear
and disaster. . . .

"At no time do the characters relate to
one another, not even at their moments of
greatest duress. Nor do they deliver their
monologues directly to the audience. They
are thinking to themselves, relishing phrases,
suffering pain, reliving happy moments."

WANDA: For me, it was the most important day of my
life. I measure everything as happening before it or
after it. I remember every detail, every instant, every
little bit of information as it came in. I was at my
desk. It was lunchtime. The executive had gone out.
I was in a hurry to finish page 44 of the May-June

issue of "Salon Hair Styles." Not that I wrote it
or edited it or anything. I just pasted the captions to
the photos before they sent it out to the press. I had
to be very neat because they used this cheap repro-
duction process and any little mistake showed up in
the finished magazine. One time I smeared some glue
and when we got the covers for the January-Febru-
ary issue, the model on the cover looked like she
had a runny nose. But, anyway, I was pasting up
these photos, and the Fashions Editor kept interrupt-
ing me to show me her real Chanel suit from Paris,
and I had to pretend to be interested, because she
drank something terrible—I didn't drink in those
days—and she was lifting up her skirt to show me
how the hemline was kept in place with little chains
sewn into the hem—and all I was really thinking
about was my raspberry yogurt in the cooler section
of the water fountain—and I had just had this horrible affair with this fellow who worked in the stock-
room, and he hadn't shown up for four days—I was
feeling really awful. And I remember it was a gray,
gray day here in New York, and then, all of a sudden, all of a sudden Mr. Kanowsky, the Advertising
Sales Manager, came bursting in! He was a little
cross-eyed and always looked crazy. Anyway, he
came bursting in, red-faced and excited, and he said,
"Quick! Turn on the radio! The President's been shot
in Dallas!" Mr. Kanowsky said he'd been standing
in line down at the White Rose bar on the corner,
and it had suddenly come over the TV, this awful
first report. Well, none of us believed it, I mean,
none of us could conceive it. We just sat looking
at him and I guess we thought he was drunk or having palpitations—he was awful fat—and he said,
"Did you hear me? Turn the radio on!" So Carrie,
the Accounts Payable Lady, said, "Now quiet down,
Mr. Kanowsky, I'll turn the radio on." And he got
a little frantic and insulted, and said terrible things,
and the Fashions Editor said a couple of unpleasant

things to him, and they were squabbling right across
me, and then Carrie's radio started up and the news-
caster was saying—oh, I want to get this just right—
". . . reported that three Negroes were seen running
from the overpass and two rifles have been confis-
cated in the immediate area, . . ." and how the President was going to be all right because they got him
right to the hospital and the Dallas Police were
throwing a cordon around the entire area. And then
suddenly we couldn't hear anymore because outside
it seemed that every auto horn in the city had started
blowing, and there was even a crash like somebody
had driven right off the street onto the sidewalk, and
the phones in the office started ringing—every one
of them, instantly, all at once, began to ring. We all
stayed at the office for the whole rest of the day,
right into evening with nobody working except Carrie, who didn't have any relatives. The minute you'd
hang a phone up it would ring again, and everybody
who called was listening to a different station and
getting a different version, and people from other
offices would pop in and tell us what they'd just
heard, and one man, a middle-aged respectable man
who ran the yachting magazine in the next office,
came in bawling, just crying like a baby, crying, "Oh
my God, it's a Communist plot—it's the end of the
world." And the news kept coming in and you'd get
one picture of the whole situation straight in your
mind, and then all of a sudden there would be this
new piece of information and it would all change, and
somebody would break down crying and they
couldn't find the Vice-President—they thought all
the politicians were going to be assassinated, and I
don't know what all . . . and then, at last, very quickly afterwards, not an hour, I think, although it
seemed so much longer, they said the President was
out of danger and everything was okay, and then the
bells started ringing, every church bell in New York
started ringing and we knew that he was dead. I was

the first to say it. I was washing Lena, the Accounts Receivable girl's face, because she was crying and had smudged ink all over her face and so I was right by her phone when it rang, and I picked it up and it was my mother saying, "Wanda, come home, he's going to be all right, they just said so," and the Fashions Editor fell out of her office with a big drunken smile on her face and a bottle in one hand to say, "JFK's going to pull through," and *that's* when the bells started ringing and none of them were Catholic, so they didn't know what it meant, and they were all smiling like fools and I said, "He's dead, the President is dead, God rest his soul."

Hold Me! (1977)

by JULES FEIFFER

Feiffer's cartoons are readily adaptable as acting monologues, sketches, and short scenes. The trap with this material is the tendency to treat the characters as living cartoons. Feel them as real people, with their Feiffer pain and confusion, struggling to deal with the problems of living in an anxious age.

I TALK TOO MUCH

WOMAN: I talk too much. I'm quite bright, so it's interesting, but nevertheless, I talk too much. You see, already I'm saying more than I should. Men hate it for a woman to blurt out, "I'm bright." They think she's really saying, "I'm brighter than you are." As a matter of fact, that is what I'm saying. I'm brighter than even the brightest men I know. That's why it's a mistake to talk too much. Men fall behind and feel challenged and grow hostile. So when I'm very attracted to a man I make it a point to talk more slowly than I would to one of my woman friends. And because I guide him along gently from insight to insight he ends up being terribly impressed with his own brilliance. And with mine for being able to keep up with him. And he tells me I'm the first woman he's ever met who's as interesting as one of his boy friends. That's love.

FRANK'S BUSINESS TRIP

SHE: By the time Frank told me he was leaving on a business trip for a month I had lost all feeling for him. Each dinner when he'd come I'd try to rekindle the flame, but all I could think of as he gobbled up my chicken was: "All I am is a servant to you, Frank." So when he announced he had to go away I was delighted. While Frank was away I could find myself again! I could make plans! The first week Frank was away I went out seven times. The telephone never stopped ringing. I had a marvelous time! The second week Frank was away I got tired of the same old faces, same old lines. I remembered what drove me to marry Frank in the first place. The third week Frank was away I felt closer to him than I had in years. I stayed home, read Jane Austen and slept on Frank's side of the bed. The fourth week Frank was away I fell madly in love with him. I hated myself for my withdrawal, for my failure of him. The fifth week Frank came home. The minute he walked in and said, "I'm back, darling!" I withdrew. I can hardly wait for his next business trip so I can love Frank again.

Fefu and Her Friends (1978)

by MARIA IRENE FORNES

Maria Irene Fornes is one of the best-known of the writers who developed in the "experimental" theatre of the 1960s. *Fefu and Her Friends,* produced at the American Place Theatre, is generally considered her finest work.

The setting is Fefu's spacious country home in the 1930s, and the event is a reunion of women friends. The play reveals their interior lives as well as the multileveled relationships among them. The dialogue and speeches are not motivated by plot, but rather spring from the interactions of the characters, as feelings and thoughts which have been locked up are released.

The reunion has crystallized Paula's awareness of her feelings about relations between economic classes. Her speech should be delivered in a simple, direct way, with no large theatrical gestures or effects. She is trying to present her feelings rationally and calmly and not show the resentment that she has felt for years. However, the hurt will and should come through despite her attempts to hold it back. The actress should first prepare the inner life, then try to keep it covered.

PAULA: I had been so deprived in my childhood that

I believed the rich were all happy. During the summer you spent your vacations in Europe or the Orient. I went to work and I resented that. But then I realized that many lives are ruined by poverty and many lives are ruined by wealth. I was always able to manage. And I think I enjoyed myself as much when I went to Revere Beach on my day off as you did when you visited the Taj Mahal. Then, when I stopped feeling envy, I started noticing the waste. I began feeling contempt for those who, having everything a person can ask for, make such a mess of it. I resented them because they were not better than the poor. If you have all you need you should be generous. If you can afford to go to school your mind should be better. If you didn't have to fight for your place on earth you should be nobler. But I saw them cheating and grabbing like the kids in the slums, or wasting away with self-indulgence. And I saw them be plain stupid. If there is a reason why some are rich while others starve it must be so they put everything they have at the service of others. They should take the responsibility of everything that happens in the world. They are the only ones who can influence things. The poor don't have the power to change things. I think we should teach the poor and let the rich take care of themselves. I'm sorry, I know that's what we're doing. That's what Emma has been doing. I'm sorry . . . I guess I feel it's not enough. (*Sobs*) I'll wash my face. I'll be right back. (*She starts to go*) I think highly of all of you. (*She goes*) part 5

Monologues
for Men

---

by ARTHUR MILLER

(See previous notes on this play, p. 135.)
   In this monologue Chris is trying to explain his difficulty in proposing marriage to Ann, the young woman who was to have married his brother who was killed in the war. His guilt is compounded because he has been working for his father, a manufacturer who prospered selling to the military. These inner conflicts must be deeply felt by the actor, together with the weight of Chris's combat experiences, which he now wants to share with Ann.

CHRIS: It's all mixed up with so many other things. . . . You remember, overseas, I was in command of a company? . . . Well, I lost them. . . . Just about all. . . . It takes a little time to toss that off. Because they weren't just men. For instance, one time it'd been raining several days and this kid came to me, and gave me his last pair of dry socks. Put them in my pocket. That's only a little thing . . . but . . . that's the kind of guys I had. They didn't die; they killed themselves for each other. I mean that exactly; a little more selfish and they'd've been here today. And I got an idea—watching them go down. Everything was being destroyed, see, but it seemed to me that one new thing was made. A kind of . . . responsibility. Man for man. You understand me?— To show that, to bring that on to the earth again like some kind of a monument and everyone would feel it standing there, behind him, and it would make a difference to him. (*Pause*) And then I came home and it was incredible. I . . . there was no meaning in it here; the whole thing to them was a kind of a—bus accident. I went to work with Dad, and that rat race again. I felt . . . what you said . . . ashamed somehow. Because nobody was changed at all. It seemed to make suckers out of a lot of guys. I felt wrong to be alive, to open the bankbook, to drive the new car, to see the new refrigerator. I mean you can take those things out of a war, but when you drive that car you've got to know that it came out of the love a man can have for a man, you've got to be a little better because of that. Otherwise what you have is really loot, and there's blood on it. I didn't want to take any of it. And I guess that included you.

by EDWARD ALBEE

(See previous notes on this play, p. 213.)
    Jerry, almost at the end of his own history, designing his own suicide-murder, confronts Peter, an older man with a proper family, a proper job, a proper life, in Central Park. Crazed by the need to tell his tale, he reaches all out to this stranger on the park bench. The speeches—stark, charged, poised in a perfect dramatic beat—come out of his agitation and bitterness.

JERRY: You're a very sweet man, and you're possessed of a truly enviable innocence. But good old Mom and good old Pop are dead . . . you know? . . . I'm broken up about it, too . . . I mean really. BUT. That particular vaudeville act is playing the cloud circuit now, so I don't see how I can look at them, all neat and framed. Besides, or, rather, to be pointed about it, good old Mom walked out on good old Pop when I was ten-and-a-half years old; she embarked on an adulterous turn of our southern states . . . a journey of a year's duration . . . and her most constant companion . . . among others, among many others . . . was a Mr. Barleycorn. At least, that's what good old Pop told me after he went down . . . came back . . . brought her body north. We'd received the news between Christmas and New Year's, you see, that good old Mom had parted with the ghost in some dump in Alabama. And, without the ghost . . . she was less welcome. I mean, what was she? A stiff . . . a northern stiff. At any rate, good old Pop celebrated the New Year for an even two weeks and then slapped into the front of a somewhat moving city omnibus, which sort of cleaned things out family-wise. Well no; then there was Mom's sister, who was given neither to sin nor the consolations of the bottle. I moved in on her, and my memory of her is slight excepting I remember still that she did all things dourly: sleeping, eating, working, praying. She dropped dead on the stairs to her apartment, my apartment then, too, on the afternoon of my high school graduation. A terribly middle-European joke, if you ask me.

FROM Who's Got His Own (1966)

by RONALD MILNER

Writer of novels, short stories, essays, and numerous plays, Detroit-born and reared, Ron Milner and the American Place Theatre first brought this play to the New York stage. It subsequently became the premiere production of the New Lafayette Theatre in Harlem. As an early play in the burgeoning Black theatre movement of the late 1960s, it had a penetrating effect on the consciousness of both Black and white audiences.

It is a vivid work about a Black family at the moment of the father's death. After an absence of four years, Tim, Jr. has returned home to be present at his father's funeral, but he "can't find any tears for a father I've cursed all my life." Nothing will prevent him from speaking the truth at last.

As Milner describes Tim, Jr., he is "youthful looking, yet maturity shows in his bearing, his expression. There is a tense, smoldering, smirking quality about him. The flavor of both college classrooms and coffee-jazz houses, of intimacy with both the best of Western civilization's culture and the sharply mundane wisdom to be had on slum streets, is sensed in his gestures, postures, heard in his tone, and the modes of his speech."

For this monologue, the actor must pre-

pare his rage, he must know Tim, Jr.'s hatred
born of bruises and body blows, of embarrassment and guilt, of cruelty and violence to
himself and his mother.

TIM: Mama, when I left this house, four years ago,
I had all he ever gave me: bruises and welts, Mama,
bruises and welts—bruises so deep that people can
just touch me with their eyes, and my soul aches,
Mama, my soul aches—That's what he gave me, Mama, bruises and welts on my back and soul, my back
and soul, Mama. (*Mother and Tim communicate
deeply with eyes; he turns away. There is a long
pause, as Tim moves upstage. Mutters*) Strong
enough, yeh. I remember one day I was out playing
on the street, and the streetcar passed, and I looked
up and saw him sitting in the back—I just forgot
everything, and started running for that car stop. I
was on the other side of the street, about to cross
over, when the streetcar pulled away and I saw him
—standing there in his dirty work clothes. I remember thinking that he didn't look as tall as he had
seemed when he left that morning. He lit a cigarette,
and I remember it was a warm summer day, but
he hunched over that cigarette as though we were
in the middle of a blizzard, as if he were afraid that
the wind would snatch it out of his hands—it was
like he was stealing something in broad daylight!—
And then he looked right at me, across the street,
right at me. But I could see that his eyes were so
tired, so beat, they couldn't even look that far. He
didn't see me; didn't recognize me—I watched him
start up the block; his head kinda' down; the cigarette smoking; his shoulders sagging like that lunch
pail weighed four hundred pounds. I don't think I
ever wanted anything as bad as I wanted to carry
that lunch pail. But even as young as I was, I knew
that it wouldn't be right for him to know that I had
seen him like that: with his eyes and his shoulders

like that. So I started running across to the alley.
Down the alley—all wild inside with some weird,
crazy-jumping joy. I wanted to get home before he
did; tell you and Clara he was coming, get everything
ready—hmmmmmm—But I fell down, and scarred
my hands, and my chin, and my knees, I think. And
—and—I was so excited, so all jumbled-up with
this—this—anxiety, that I just sat there and cried
for a while, trembling all over—sort of laughing and
crying at the same time, you know. I just stayed
there in that alley like that for a while, until it eased
off, until I came down a little—Then I got up and
started again, trying to beat him, trying to get there
first. But the minute I hit the back steps I knew I
was too late. I could hear him up there, hollering,
shouting, banging things around! I knew what it was
like before I opened that back door and saw you
all huddled at the table, and heard Clara crying up
front somewhere, and saw him waving that damn
lunch pail around thundering about nothing like he
was some damn god or something!

FROM House Party (1973)

by ED BULLINS

(See previous notes on this play, p. 282.)

BLACK WRITER: You see, man . . . I got this dream, man. You know I've had it for a long time, man. Yeah . . . that's to be a writer . . . yeah, a writer, man. And I've lived this dream, man . . . lived it for the past couple years. As soon as I got out of the service and got home I started in writing this novel. I didn't know what a job it would be at first, but I got hung up in it, you see. At first I would just write so much . . . and then show it to my girl, or my mother and dad. And then I found myself working more and more on it. Man, I didn't even see my friends much, cause I was workin' on this novel. I still got some checks from the service and I took a few night courses in English and writing so that they would send me more checks, so I didn't have to work right away. And my girl thought I was crazy. Yeah, she did. And I'd tell her about my dream. Tell her all about it. Tell her how I was gonna finish my novel. Then begin another I had in my head. And get them published in hardback and be a real author. And show everybody. Show my family who was thinkin' I was crazy like my girl thought I was. Show all my old partners who had put me down for bein' strange. I'd show them. But, man, the more I wrote . . . the more I had to write . . . and the more I did write. I wrote and wrote . . . then my girl didn't call anymore . . . and when

I had time to call her she didn't answer her phone. And my mother stopped speaking to me. And my ole man just turned his back on me when I walked through the room. . . . So I went out and got a job at the post office. . . . I drive a Mustang now . . . with only thirty more payments on it to go. And I locked up the room where I used to write. Didn't touch anything in there. Just locked it up with all my notes, papers and books in there . . . maybe it'll become the nursery . . . now that I'm married to my girl; and my mother is smiling . . . but I drink myself into a stupor each night with my dad as we sit in front of the TV . . . I guess I'm happy, man . . . cause I don't dream at all . . . no more.

FROM **Nourish the Beast** (1973)
by STEVE TESICH

Steve Tesich's third play, a wacky, realistic
comedy first produced at the American Place
Theatre, further defines family life in America. This time the extended family lives in
Queens, where Mother-of-us-all, Goya, nur-
tures two wayward children—one an orphan,
Bruno the other, a hip flower-child fallen
from grace, Goya's blood daughter, Sylvia.
Goya picks up strays and turns them out
again when they can risk the mad, mad
world. Bruno is such a stray, now about 25,
vulnerable, sympathetic, serious to the point
of hilarity. He is totally honest but has difficulty expressing himself freely. We do not
laugh at him; we laugh because of his serious involvement in what he is saying.

This scene occurs just after Sylvia has
returned home from her wanderings. Bruno
is very attracted to her and now feels he
must reveal that they are not related by
blood. He has kept it to himself all this time
but cannot stand "phoniness." He tells his
story straight and unaffectedly.

BRUNO: . . . I don't know how old I was when they
put me in the orphanage . . . not very . . . and the
first time I heard the word "orphan" I thought it was
this guy's name. Billy Orphan. Then I found out
that I was an orphan too, and I figured that Billy and

I were related. Then I found out that we were all orphans . . . and I figured . . . hell . . . somebody must be lying . . . we can't all be relatives. . . . So we were all orphans but I still didn't know what the word meant except that we talked about everything in terms of that one word . . . the outside world was a non-orphanage . . . those that got placed were de-orphanated . . . those that came back were re-orphanated. For a long time I thought only boys were orphans . . . so when I grew up I wanted to be a girl. Then I found out that there were female orphans too . . . we called them orphenes. But I still didn't know what the word meant. So I asked one of the guards one day . . . what's an orphan? He said it was somebody that nobody liked. But these other orphans liked me . . . Billy liked me . . . so I asked him if that made me an non-orphan. He said no . . . He said being liked by another orphan didn't count. . . . So I started thinking that nothing that happened in the orphanage counted. The only things that mattered happened on the outside. For the whole time that I was there some police athletic league kept promising to take us to a ball game. We went to bed every night hoping that tomorrow was the big day when we'd go to a ball game. Hell, we didn't know what a ball game was . . . properly speaking . . . but it was on the outside so we assumed it was something incredible . . . something unheard of . . . and finally the big day came and this man took us all to a ball game. . . . The Yankees won. . . . That was it. The Yankees won . . . And all of us orphans sat there scratching our ass thinking . . . You mean this is it . . . this is the real thing . . . That's why I still go to ball games . . . I figure one of these days I'm going to see it the way I thought it would be . . . you know . . . the ball game of the century . . . the ball game of all time . . . And you know what? . . . when I go there I see some of those orphans I once knew . . . Billy's there every time . . . They're all grown up and

everything but still looking orphany as hell . . .
still waiting for the ball game . . . you see don't
you . . . you see how we were tricked into thinking
that the outside world was so exciting and full of won-
ders . . . not that we thought it was all good . . .
but we did think it was full of extremes . . . that's
it . . . extremes . . . the most beautiful and the ugliest
things were on the outside . . . nothing in between
. . . the orphanage was in between . . . and that's
why I became a cop. . . . I thought that by being a
cop I'd be able to find those extremes . . . and sometimes I think I'm close . . . Sometimes I'd be walking
my beat and suddenly I hear this screaming . . . I
mean screaming so painful your heart wants to commit suicide . . . and I think to myself . . . Hot dog!
This is it! This is the saddest goddamned thing that
ever happened in the world! And I rush to the house
. . . I rush upstairs and what do I find . . . This
old lady's screaming because her parakeet ate something foul and was vomiting all over the cage. . . .
that damned parakeet was barfing like a truck driver . . . the old lady screaming her head off . . . for
some reason she turned a fan on it . . . there it was
. . . birdbarf all over the wallpaper . . .

The Year of the Dragon (1974)

by FRANK CHIN

Over one hundred years after the first Chinese immigration to this country, the American Place Theatre produced the first plays written by a Chinese-American, Frank Chin's *Chickencoop Chinaman* and *The Year of the Dragon*. A poet, philosopher, and activist, Chin dramatizes problems common to ethnic minorities in America: the disintegrating family feuding with its misunderstood artist-prodigal son, the struggle for identity and good self-image, and the effect of this struggle on family life and relationships.

This monologue occurs in a final confrontation between 40-year-old Fred Eng and his father, 60-year-old Wing Eng, the honorary Mayor of Chinatown. In the old-world pattern, the father is the absolute authority. He has refused to let Fred and his younger brother leave the San Francisco ghetto, a closed society where the most they can expect is a repetition of father's life and work. Fred is currently a tour guide for Chinatown tourists, towards whom he is resentful and belligerent. His own ambivalence and insecurity, his father's dominance and impending death have shut Fred and his ambition behind self-destructive walls of bitterness and anger. His stored-up anguish and sense of loss must be surging through him as he

tries, one last time, to make his father understand him.

FRED: Then this bald white guy came in and sat at
the counter . . . And he was in my class in high
school. And I don't want to talk to him. But he sees
me and comes creeping down the counter at me . . .
I hid my napkins and got involved with my noo-
dles . . . ha . . . ha . . . "Didn't I go to high school
with you?" he says. . . . "Yeah, yeah," I say and he
tells me he's married, Pa, got kids, hates it, drives
a truck for the *Examiner* and hates that and asks
if I'm Chinese or Japanese . . . Ha. "Yeah, yeah,"
I say and want him to go away, and he asks whatever
happened to the Chinese guy, Fred whatshisname,
who was all kinds of student body officer and goin'
to bust New York . . . ? "Couldn't tellya, bud," I
said. "Didn't he graduate with us?" . . . "Couldn't
tellya, bud," I said. Heh! Then the bastard sat down
next to me and he sighed, Pa. I looked straight ahead
and there he was in the mirror behind the pies. People from the class before us were in the news all
the time, he said, people after us were, you know
. . . he looked at me over the lemon meringue and
I was over the pound cake . . . And he said . . .
"I wonder if anybody from our class will ever make
it? . . . And I wanted to say, "Me . . ." I wanted
to but I didn't. "Couldn't tellya, bud," I said. Ha.
Ha. Ha. I remember that guy 'cus I was gonna surprise him. After you died. I was gonna go. Make
it so big you'd only be remembered to have been
my father. Nobody was gonna think of you without
me.

FROM **Action** (1974)

by SAM SHEPARD

Action is a statement about the 1970s: about
standing still or holding on in a world that
produces catastrophes; about people in
search of a place to stop, curl up, hide away
from pain, experience, knowing, fright or
possibility. Moments come and go in their
lives without being recorded or remembered.
Ritual meals are eaten and forgotten as the
last forkful is consumed. If you are an op-
timist as I am, you think that the people will
prevail, that existence itself is positive. If you
are a pessimist, you will assume that their
inaction is a kind of death.

This speech does not relate to the
"plot" of the play, since there is no "plot" in
the conventional sense. It rather pours out of
the character who is part of the collective un-
conscious of the play and of us all. It iden-
tifies our sense of displacement—of living
in emptiness and terror, the terror of inaction
and the terror that results in action. The
speech should flow without attempts to break
it up with realistic details, such as pausing
to remember or illustrative gestures.

SHOOTER: One night there was some moths. A bunch
of moths. In the distance they could see a candle.
Just one candle in a window of a big house. The
moths were tormented by this candle. They longed

to be with this candle but none of them understood it or knew what it was. The leader of the moths sent one of them off to the house to bring back some information about this light. The moth returned and reported what he had seen, but the leader told him that he hadn't understood anything about the candle. So another moth went to the house. He touched the flame with the tip of his wings but the heat drove him off. When he came back and reported, the leader still wasn't satisfied. So he sent a third moth out. This moth approached the house and saw the candle flickering inside the window. He became filled with love for this candle. He crashed against the glass and finally found a way inside. He threw himself on the flame. With his forelegs he took hold of the flame and united himself joyously with her. He embraced her completely, and his whole body became red as fire. The leader of the moths, who was watching from far off with the other moths, saw that the flame and the moth appeared to be one. He turned to the other moths and said: "He's learned what he wanted to know, but he's the only one who understands it."

Hold Me! (1977)

by JULES FEIFFER

(See previous notes on this play, p. 291.)

I USED TO READ THEM ADS . . .

MAN: I used to read them ads—know what I mean? "Even your best friend won't tell you" ads—and it used to bother me because if you're a right guy— nice to your mother and everything—what kind of girl is it who'd throw you over because of the wrong toothpaste you used—or what kind of phoney friend is it who'd spend his time not drinking with you but smelling you? And then it would bother me how these people in the ads would become popular over- night by changing brand names. I mean they didn't change their insides—they weren't better people. But suddenly they'd switch brands and become pride of the regiment. Well this used to bother me because, frankly, people never have taken to me. Like at the job, the only desk during breaks where you can't hear a steady buzz-buzz of conversation is mine. No- body ever comes over to me! I always got to go over to them. All my life. When I was a kid and three of us would walk down the street? I'd never once be in the middle. I'd always be on the gutter side. I never got invited to join up with any clubs. I went through the entire army without once being asked to play cards. And I admit sometimes I used to wake up in the middle of the night dripping sweat—and going on and off in my head like a big neon sign was: "Bad breath, bad breath, bad breath." I got married and my wife treated me like a janitor. The only thing she could say nice for me was that I'm good with my hands. When the other wives boasted about their husbands' talents she'd call me in to fix the sink. So at parties I'd do my famous "fixing the sink bit" and the rest of the time we were acquaintances. And more and more in the back of my head it went: "Change your soap. Change your toothpaste." But—I don't know—I always felt that I'm me for better or worse. I'm me! Then my kids who my wife says are at a sensitive age began to make cracks. So I finally gave in. I changed my brand of toothpaste, my brand of hair oil, my soap, and my suit style. And son of a gun, the ads were right! My wife glowed at me. The kids loved me. Suddenly everybody was my buddy for the first time in my life! Three weeks of it was all I could take. Then I went back to the old ways. If they prefer that brand over me the hell with them.

BREAD CRUMBS

MAN: So I'm going out with this girl for the first time and we're going to the movies and, as usual, I'm throwing out my bread crumbs. And she asks me what is it that I'm doing and I tell her that I'm throwing out bread crumbs so I can find my way home because I have this bad sense of direction. So she laughs like it's a big joke and I say I don't see why my personal troubles should make such a big joke. And she said "Look—don't worry—I'll take you home!" So I got mad. I said "Look—we each have our own way of finding ourselves. Who is to say yours is better than mine?" And she said "You can't make a whole life's philosophy out of bread crumbs." So right out on the street we had a fight. And I got so mad I walked away and I completely forgot to follow my bread crumbs. And an amazing thing happened—I had no trouble getting home. It seems to make my whole past life invalid.

MORE SOCKS

MAN: I go to the laundromat to do a wash. Included in the wash are 8 pairs of socks. Out of the wash come 6 pairs of socks plus 1 gray sock and 1 blue sock. A week later I go to the laundromat to do a wash. Included in the wash are 6 pairs of socks. Out the wash comes 4 pairs of socks plus 1 black sock and 1 green sock. A week later I go to the laundromat to do a wash. Included in the wash are 4 pairs of socks. Out of the wash come 2 pairs of socks. The other socks never show up. The next day I go to the laundromat. As an experiment I put in nothing but my last 2 pairs of socks. Out of the wash comes a body stocking. In the body stocking I find a note. The note says: "Quit trifling with the laws of nature and bring the machine more socks."

"JOEY WANTS TO SCREAM"

MAN: It started when I was a little kid and I was playing ball and I was in a tight spot—so inside my head I began announcing my way through the ball game: "O.K. The count is three and two. Joey steps out of the box. Digs a toe into the dirt. O.K.—He's back in now. He checks the runners. He's into the windup. And here's the pitch—" From that point on, inside my head I announced my way through everything! School for instance: "The old secondhand is ticking away, three minutes to go in the history exam. Joey can't seem to come up with an answer to Question 5. He looks out the window. He picks at a nail. He looks over at the other kids—and wait a minute—is he? Yes, he is! He picks up his pen!" And even after I got out of school: "The supervisor is looking over Joey's shoulder. Joey pretends to be busy. The supervisor has found a mistake. Joey can't seem to listen. The supervisor asks Joey if he understands. Joey says he does. Joey stares out the window. The supervisor moves on—" I even announced my way through my marriage: "Joey has nothing to say. Joey's wife has nothing to say. Joey's father-in-law says, 'Isn't it time you were making serious plans, Joey?' Joey digs a toe into the carpet and stares out the window. Joey's little boy says, 'Fix it, Daddy.' " And so it goes. From early morning to late at night. Even when I'm in bed: "Joey pounds his pillow. He closes one eye. He closes the other. He feels sleep coming. It's coming—Joey's wide awake. Joey sneaks downstairs and makes himself a drink—'Joey wants to scream.' "

Index of Plays

Index of Playwrights

Bantam Classics bring you the world's greatest literature—books that have stood the test of time—at specially low prices. These beautifully designed books will be proud additions to your bookshelf. You'll want all these time-tested classics for your own reading pleasure.

Titles by Charles Dickens:

☐	21123	THE PICKWICK PAPERS	$4.95
☐	21223	BLEAK HOUSE	$3.95
☐	21265	NICHOLAS NICKLEBY	$4.95
☐	21234	GREAT EXPECTATIONS	$2.75
☐	21176	A TALE OF TWO CITIES	$2.25
☐	21016	HARD TIMES	$1.95
☐	21102	OLIVER TWIST	$2.50
☐	21126	A CHRISTMAS CAROL & OTHER VICTORIAN TALES	$2.95

Titles by Thomas Hardy:

☐	21191	JUDE THE OBSCURE	$2.95
☐	21024	THE MAYOR OF CASTERBRIDGE	$1.95
☐	21269	THE RETURN OF THE NATIVE	$2.25
☐	21168	TESS OF THE D'URBERVILLES	$2.95
☐	21331	FAR FROM THE MADDING CROWD	$3.50

Titles by Henry James:

☐	21153	THE BOSTONIANS	$2.95
☐	21127	PORTRAIT OF A LADY	$3.50
☐	21059	THE TURN OF THE SCREW	$1.95

Look for them at your bookstore or use this handy coupon:

- -

Bantam Books, Dept. CL3, 414 East Golf Road, Des Plaines, IL 60016

Please send me the books I have checked above. I am enclosing $_____ (please add $2.00 to cover postage and handling). Send check or money order—no cash or C.O.D.s please.

Mr/Ms _____

Address _____

City/State _____ Zip _____

CL3—5/88

Please allow four to six weeks for delivery. This offer expires 11/88. Price and availability subject to change without notice.

BANTAM
SHOP·AT·HOME
C·A·T·A·L·O·G

Special Offer
Buy a Bantam Book
for only 50¢.

Now you can have Bantam's catalog filled with hundreds of titles plus take advantage of our unique and exciting bonus book offer. A special offer which gives you the opportunity to purchase a Bantam book for only 50¢. Here's how!

By ordering any five books at the regular price per order, you can also choose any other single book listed (up to a $5.95 value) for just 50¢. Some restrictions do apply, but for further details why not send for Bantam's catalog of titles today!

Just send us your name and address and we will send you a catalog!

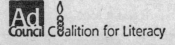
LWA